365876

His/pol

7²⁹

THE VIRGIN DIPLOMATS

THE *VIRGIN* DIPLOMATS

ELMER BENDINER

Alfred A. Knopf · *NEW YORK, 1976*

THIS IS A BORZOI BOOK
PUBLISHED BY ALFRED A. KNOPF, INC.

Library of Congress Cataloging in Publication Data
Bendiner, Elmer.
The virgin diplomats.
Bibliography: p.
Includes index.
1. United States—Foreign relations—Revolution,
1775-1783. I. Title.
E249.B46   1976   973.3'2'0922   76-13686
ISBN 0-394-48977-2

Manufactured in the United States of America
First Edition

To Esther, Jessica, Winnie, and Paul

CONTENTS

THE VIRGIN DIPLOMATS

I

THE ARTS, DEVIOUS
AND OTHERWISE, WHICH AMERICAN
AGENTS WORKED UPON THE BRITISH
TO REPEAL THE STAMP ACT

"AMERICANS ARE THE SONS, not the bastards, of England."

This acknowledgment of paternity in the year 1766 by the elder Pitt may have reassured Americans of their legitimacy, but it also emphasized their status as children. The British liked to think of themselves as loving parents, and, in fact, their discipline in America was mild, for Britain had not yet mastered the imperial manner.

It had been only three years since the British were declared the unquestioned victors of the Seven Years' War, that global conflict among the European states for hegemony over the colonies of the world. (The struggle was termed the French and Indian Wars by those who found it hard to look beyond the American sector.) Although victorious, England had been left with a depleted treasury and a postwar depression, but great glories had been won in distant parts and these, it was hoped, could be translated into glittering profits. The French had been driven out of Pondicherry and Quebec; England was supreme in India and North America; and its diplomats in the courts of Europe now took the preeminent place of power and prestige hitherto reserved for the French.

Having paid in blood and taxes for England's new empire, the traders and planters of North America expected the kind of gratitude that could be reckoned in their ledger books. Ten years before 1776, a rupture of the commercial and sentimental family ties with the old country seemed unthinkable. All that was wanted was a formula by which love of king and country could be harmonized with sound business growth.

For half a century it had been common practice for Parliament to levy tariffs and taxes upon the American colonies by way of regulating trade. When these were not too onerous they were complied with; otherwise Americans smuggled with impunity while the Mother Country indulgently winked an eye. Such a policy was found to be not only agreeable but the least expensive. It was estimated that it would have cost the British government £8,000 to collect £2,000 in customs duties from the ingenious and refractory colonists.

To keep Parliament complacent, to ease the manifold frictions of the transatlantic trade, to see that cash and credit flowed in orderly channels without undue legislative obstruction, eighteen agents of the separate American colonies were on hand in London. Though they were primarily business lobbyists, they practiced the techniques of diplomacy. The skills they developed in argument, charm, bargaining, bribery, and press relations would ultimately be used to bring to the camp of republican rebels the wealth and might of emperors.

In the decade before independence, most of these agents considered themselves Englishmen. Some, indeed, had never been to America but, as British lawyers or Members of Parliament, took the pay of one or another colony as a sideline, seeing therein no conflict of interest. Other agents might call themselves Pennsylvanians, Virginians, New Englanders, Bostonians, or New Yorkers. Many, even the most reputable, openly cultivated their own business interests while operating in their official capacities. The individual was regarded as the agent of divinity, profiting his country and the world while he profited himself.

Ordinarily, in the absence of some overriding crisis, the eighteen American agents did not form a cohesive lobby. They were divided by personal ambitions and competition for the 2.5 percent commission an agent earned for each slice of the parliamentary budget that went to his colony. The colonies themselves were often at odds with each other over boundaries, grants, or speculative land schemes, and frequently embroiled their agents in controversy. To make matters still more awkward, a colonial assembly might fire one agent and hire another, usually instructing him to check his predecessor's account books for fraud. (The agents were natural targets of suspicion for their employers, who tended to blame the mishaps of politics or the stock market on personal skulduggery.) The agents thus made up a diplomatic corps steeped in rancor. That they ever managed to work together for a common objective may be explained first by the difficulties in transatlantic transmission of instructions, which often came too late to be a hindrance; and second by the acumen and vision of some of the agents themselves.

They did much of their work in coffeehouses, where they met with merchants, planned strategies, read the newspapers, received their mail, ate their mutton, and sipped their tea or coffee. (They dined copiously, if not well, and mistakenly considered the gout, which was common among them, an occupational ailment.) These early American "embassies" clustered close together in London's City district, heart of the mercantile empire and capital of the trade that was the lifeblood of the colonies. The coffeehouse proprietors hung out their shingles like flags. Right across the road from the Royal Exchange on Threadneedle Street stood the New England, and down a few yards from there was the New York. The Pennsylvania was close by in Birchin Lane. If the agents wanted neutral territory on which to confer they met at Lloyd's of London (which grew to its subsequent glories quite naturally, for vast schemes were hatched over its bare wooden tables and beneath its dim lights). In Westminster, Parliament itself had its adjuncts in Waghorn's and the Parliament Coffee House.

If the strategies of colonial agentry in London were brewed in coffeehouses, they were carried out in the offices of the bureaucracy that prefigured the awesome British Civil Service of later years. The agents' technique called for the liberal expenditure of "vails," those perquisites of the underpaid clerks, the tips too small to rank as bribes, which could ease the presentation of a project or, if a generous agent so desired it, consign a petition to a pigeonhole. (Thus, for example, New York once neatly tied up New Jersey's plea for a boundary revision.)

A knowledgeable agent dripped money as he made his daily rounds; a trifle for a messenger or doorman; something more substantial for a clerk; grander and more secretive offerings of gratitude-in-advance to members of the Board of Trade. And there were clerks and doormen and messengers to be wooed at every stage of the complex processing of a petition or a claim or an argument or a law passed by a colonial assembly needing approval. The stops along the way might include the office of Secretary of State, the Privy Council, the Board of Trade, one of the Crown counsels (whose opinion might be withheld for years unless prodded by a donation). Even if the ways were suitably greased there might be the delays caused by incompetence: a letter missing from the dossier, a mistake by the copyist, the untimely intervention of a Christmas holiday or a long weekend. In short, England in the 1760s presented the American agent with the obstacle course of a modern state in embryo.

A higher diplomacy involved more complex operations—the appearance of the agent at the proper receptions, where a word could be dropped in milord's ear; visits to country houses; discreet attendance at Court functions; careful cultivation of MPs; a willingness to visit the taverns where one might meet and influence the merchants or the radicals; and assiduous letter writing to the free-swinging newspapers of the time.

There were certain standard and indispensable channels in those years. For example, no efficient agent could do his work without cultivating John Pownall, secretary to the Board of Trade, who not only drafted the proclamations and policy papers of that august body but also was known to have the ear of Lord Halifax, Secretary of State for the Southern Department, which then included the American colonies. For other paths to power, each agent might develop his own. A strategically placed doorkeeper might prove an invaluable eavesdropper if properly sweetened, or a Treasury Lord might be accessible if approached with due charm. John Cleveland, Secretary of the Admiralty, was considered a splendid pipeline.

By and large the members of this fledgling American diplomatic corps were miserably paid. Jasper Mauduit, who served with his brother Israel in the Massachusetts agency, once had to send off an indignant letter to Boston: "What have I done? or wherein have I been deficient in my duty to the Province, to deserve so publick an affront, as the Voting me a Salary of a hundred per year?"

Of course, the agents' commission on grants helped their personal finances considerably, and the job offered unparalleled opportunities to pursue one's private interests. Dennys de Berdt, for example, one of the representatives of the Massachusetts Bay Colony, acknowledged in 1766 that he had close to £50,000 invested in America and had been dickering with the Board of Trade for some Canadian land grants for one of his private clients. His most distinguished asset, however, was his connection with Lord Dartmouth, First Lord of Trade. Few colonial assemblies would forgo that door to official favor merely because the man who held the key derived from his position a few favors for himself. Indeed de Berdt found little trouble in persuading his employers in Boston to raise his salary from £200 to £300 a year. Actually, like many other agents, de Berdt exaggerated the importance of his connections. His colleagues complained that his information seemed to be skimmed from tedious coffeehouse talk. It was said that he interpreted "every squeeze by the hand and come tomorrow" at a lord's levee as a mark of favor, pregnant with diplomatic possibilities. It is difficult to say whether this characterization was genuine or born of the backbiting atmosphere.

The dean of American agents was Benjamin Franklin, a sixty-year-old man in plain brown coat and breeches, peering through spectacles at the dawning Age of Enlightenment. To Europeans he seemed the quintessence of New World virtues, which were in fact eighteenth-century European virtues decked out in a wilderness setting whose very novelty carried intimations of a beguiling innocence.

Franklin embodied the salon set's favorite belief in the perfectability of man, a process much encouraged by the highly moral aphorisms of his *Poor Richard's Almanack*, which he had published every year for a quarter of a century to the delight of Americans and Europeans alike. Franklin was a man who could use words in an age that gloried in verbal legerdemain. And he had come up from obscure beginnings on a remote frontier, a fact that bolstered the pride and hopes of the burgeoning middle class and titillated the fashionable democratic sensibilities of enlightened aristocrats.

Franklin also made the customary obeisance to philosophy, the cult of the time, having institutionalized the pleasant conversations of a group of Philadelphia intellectuals into the American Philosophical Society. Moreover, this self-tutored printer-journalist-businessman had, by an unflagging inquisitiveness, scored a scientific coup. He had discovered the electrical nature of lightning, thereby winning the rapturous admiration of the romantic amateurs of science as a homespun Prometheus. He had described a technique for verifying his conjecture, and French scientists had followed it to the letter with world-resounding results. His subsequent demonstration of the phenomenon by means of a kite added color to the story. He had then proceeded to apply his findings to practical ends and invented the lightning rod.

Similarly Franklin had joined the effort to shape religion to an agreeable eighteenth-century form—a comfortable deism requiring little sacrifice, no priesthood, and no unbridled ecstasies, encouraging only the most solid virtues of prudence and propriety. As a creed it was as cozy, as warm, as practical, and as rational as the open stove he invented to warm the houses of Philadelphia. He was, above all, for comfort in body and soul—a hater of extremes whether they ran to saintliness or sin. Although a kind-natured man, he viewed the elimination of the Indians from settlers' lands by any available means as a part of that inevitable progress which was in itself an overriding compulsion. He hoped for a society of the middle ground—what he called the "happy mediocrity."

He was, in short, the ultimate reasonable bourgeois, whose moderate virtues and moderate vices, whose wit and urbanity won him the acclaim of intellectuals, the ready ear of British merchants, and the unrestrained envy of his colleagues in the corps of American agents.

He had come to England originally in 1757 as the agent for Pennsylvania, returning home in 1762 to engage in a series of acrimonious quarrels with the Penn family and to contend with some niggling detractors who objected to his expense accounts. In 1764 he came back to England to lobby for his colony once again. His absence from America apparently did not interfere with his job as postmaster for all the colonies in North America, a post that helped to supplement his agent's income.

Franklin's position as postmaster also did much to exacerbate the lively suspicions of envious patriots. Not only was Franklin in the King's pay as postmaster, but his illegitimate son, William, was the royally appointed—and royalist-minded—governor of New Jersey. William's royalist taint was more damaging than his illegitimacy, for such irregularities were not uncommon in the mid-eighteenth century on either side of the Atlantic. Benjamin Franklin himself never married his common-law wife, Deborah, and his illegitimate son William (who was not Deborah's son) presented him with an illegitimate grandson.

Franklin's politics in 1766 were moderate enough to irritate the firebrands further. He saw the young King George III as a generous, virtuous monarch. The King did not reciprocate his high regard, however, preferring gardening, music, and old-fashioned theology to philosophy, science, the amorphous new deism, and the rational tradesman's morality exemplified by Franklin.

The King also took an unpleasant view of Franklin's taste for real-estate speculation, an interest shared by most American and British politicians, irrespective of their politics. To Franklin as to his colleagues, whether British or American, it was prudent and practical to turn the wilderness to good account, privately as well as publicly.

Franklin and his son, William, had long been speculating in real estate. They had bought up the restitution claims of fur traders driven out by Indian uprisings and formed the Suff'ring Traders Company. When that failed, they joined with others to seek a royal charter for a new colony that would encompass a vast tract of wilderness between the Illinois and Mississippi rivers. They dreamed up exotic names for the inland empire —Pittsylvania and Indiana were candidates before they settled finally on Vandalia, believing this would help elicit royal favor, because Queen Charlotte was supposed by some genealogists to be descended from the chiefs of the ancient tribe of Vandals.

However, that delicate reference to Her Majesty's forebears did not help at Court. The King took a dim view of the westward push—whether by the Mississippi and Ohio companies or by any other. In a royal memorandum on the situation in 1766, George emphasized that it was "absolutely necessary to prevent the Traffick of wandering Traders, who by cheating and misusing the Natives frequently bring on National quarrels. The country to the Westward of Our frontier quite to the Mississippi was intended to be a Desert for the Indians to hunt in and inhabit."

He was unmoved by tales of Indian raids on colonists in the wilderness because he thought they ought not to be there, and he vehemently opposed the use of British troops to help them: "If we had no Forts, Garrisons or Settlements in the Indian Country it is probable that we should never be in a State of National hostility with those people. Should any of our colonies by misconduct get themselves into War with the Indians, let them get themselves out of it, as they always us'd to do when they were not so strong: Or else let them beg for Military assistance, acknowledge their want of it, and be thankful for it and pay its expence."

It must be said that George's Indian policy was not wholly based on humanitarian grounds or even on budget considerations. He made it clear that the only economic development in America that interested him was American commerce with England. That would have to be seaborne. There seemed little point, therefore, in penetrating into areas beyond the reach of British ships. A small but profitable sideline might be built up by trade with the Indians whenever they chose to come to the colonists' settlements, but for the rest, he proposed, let them keep their wilderness.

Disingenuously and in vain, the American agents pleaded that the Indians were so incensed at not being permitted to bargain away their territory that they might "go on the warpath." But though ministries vacillated, the King and Parliament stood firm against the land speculators, except for those politicians who were to get their cuts of Indian property.

In his earlier apprenticeship at the trade of agent, Franklin had committed the tactical mistake of approaching the sources of power through the front door, receiving the beguiling but unavailing courtesies which led men like de Berdt to rosy expectations. By now, however, Franklin had learned from veteran agents the way to the back stairs. By means of charm and a judicious dispensing of gratuities he gained access to the files of the Board of Trade; here he could seek out precedents. He was also familiar with the diplomatic profits to be derived from passing time in the proper places: a Welsh rarebit in the company of influential merchants at St. Paul's Coffee House could be useful; a pint at the Dog

Tavern or at the George and Vulture would keep him au courant. Thursday nights were given over to the Honest Whigs Club in St. Paul's Churchyard, where, regardless of the political advantage, he could dip into the literary stream of British liberalism.

He led the life of a London gentleman of modest means, somewhat embellished by his own eccentricities. He boarded at the widow Stevenson's on Craven Street, attended not only by the widow and her daughter Polly, who adored him filially, but by two menservants brought with him from America. He scandalized the Stevensons and all his friends by his addiction to fresh air and exercise. So obsessive was this folly that he insisted on leaving his bedroom windows open at night despite the baleful humors of the night air. He would rise early in the morning and sit stark naked in his chilly room for half an hour or so. (He called this ritual his tonic bath.) Then he would pop back to bed for a couple of hours' sleep and start the day at a more gentlemanly hour. A passionate athleticism drove him to regular workouts of forty swings with a pair of dumbbells and frequent swims in the Thames. On a dare he once swam from Chelsea to Blackfriars Bridge.

His connections, ranging up and down the social scale from strategically placed doormen to Members of Parliament, included newspaper publishers, Lords of Trade, and the savants of the Royal Society, which he used as his London club. Among his friends he counted Sir Francis Dashwood, who then presided over some remarkable hijinks at a former abbey. It was extensively reported—and unconvincingly denied—that Sir Francis' circle, variously named the Monks of Medmenham Abbey and the Hell-Fire Club, playfully practiced a form of diabolism replete with black masses and night-long orgies involving anonymous ladies of high rank.

Another celebrated agent was Richard Jackson, known as "the omniscient" because of the wide range of data at his fingertips—from animal husbandry in the English Midlands and farming in New England, to British and American constitutional law. Jackson was an expert in hedging his bets, accepting posts in the British government under Grenville while retaining the confidence of his American employers. He wrote Franklin in 1764: "I have really little interest with Ministers of any kind though I keep a Post [secretary to the Chancellor of the Exchequer] that gives me Access to them, perhaps it may be of Service. . . ."

During the Seven Years' War, Franklin and Jackson had worked closely together advising the British on their military campaigns in America and on their approach to the colonists. Afterward Franklin leaned on Jackson's legal expertise as a barrister, MP, and counsel to the Board of Trade. The faint aura of double-agentry that hung over "the omniscient" did not alienate Franklin as it might have a more doctrinaire patriot. Jackson represented Connecticut at the time and, thanks in part to Franklin's recommendations, he was to add other colonies to his list of clients.

Another MP with lofty connections was Charles Garth, a patient and conscientious man who made no bones about opposing his influential patrons to lobby for the interests of South Carolina and the unity of the American colonies. It was he who rallied the merchants of England to back a bill granting a subsidy on hemp and to oppose the Mutiny Bill, which would have billeted British troops in American homes.

The most significant American agent of all—aside from Franklin—was the Bostonian Barlow Trecothick, a man in his mid-forties with twenty years of English political and mercantile life behind him. He was acting then as an independent broker for Massachusetts and as a representative of New Hampshire as well.

The task of the American agents was to orchestrate—for their own purposes—the merchants, the country gentry, the aristocracy, the bureaucracy, the press, the radicals, the Whigs of all stripes, the Tories, Parliament, and the King. If the King had been an absolute tyrant the job would have been simpler, requiring only the proper approach to a single source of power.

George III, however, had been bred to be a constitutional monarch, to be "the first among equals," and to revere the British Constitution, which existed intangibly but ineradicably in the minds and moods of Englishmen. His grandfather George II had learned that his courtiers' bows were mere ceremonial courtesies. When the Lord Chancellor, Lord Hardwicke, told the second George: "Your ministers, Sir, are only your instruments of Government," the King smiled and said: "Ministers are the Kings in this country."

Lord Hardwicke's son subsequently wrote that while the "Ministers are accountable for every act of the King's Government to the people . . . whatever the King does should seem to [be] . . . the result of his own wisdom and deliberate choice. This gives a grace to Government in the eyes of the People, and here is the dignity of the Monarchy."

The King had not yet achieved the graceful position of exalted cipher accorded to subsequent British monarchs. George III could still exert a political influence and, from a preferred position, play the parliamentary game of patronage and bribery. The royal effort at corruption, however, was a tribute to England's burgeoning and unformulated democracy, an implicit acknowledgment that the bribe had become mightier than the sword.

Then there were the weavers, smiths, shipbuilders, steel makers; and the merchants who placed the orders, developed the markets, determined their investments, and oiled the machinery of the Age of Reason. One out of every three Englishmen lived in the world of trade or was dependent on it.

To the merchants of England, America was a source of iron for British steel mills, timber for ship masts, beaver for hats, whalebone for corset stays, flour, tobacco, and furs. Even more important were the 3,000,000 colonial customers for British wares. The Indians, to the merchant's eye, were not fierce enemies on the frontier, but potential buyers of the manufactured goods of England, which, it was hoped, would one day civilize them into even more profitable consumers. For the English, civilization rode on trade winds.

"The rising tradesman swells into the gentry," wrote Daniel Defoe in 1726. ". . . The word tradesman in England does not sound so harsh, as it does in other countries; and to say a gentleman-tradesman is not . . . nonsense."

Merchants flocked to the Herald's Office to seek some familial tie that would qualify them for a coat of arms to adorn their coaches and their silverware. The first Lord Craven, whose father had dealt in wholesale groceries, once defended himself against the charge of being a nouveau noble by declaring: "I am William Lord Craven, my father was Lord Mayor of London, and my grandfather was the Lord knows who. . . ."

These gentlemen-traders and merchant-adventurers, as they sometimes romantically termed themselves, were brothers in spirit, and often in blood, of the tradesmen of the colonies. They felt a commercial bond closer than brotherhood to the Americans, but their geographical position imposed a difference. They saw ahead endless vistas of trade with America, and for such a prospect they extended generous and long-term credit. Many of them were unable to collect the debts owed by the colonists and some took land as payment, thus acquiring a stake in the fortunes of America. But that stake could be assured only if they held a monopoly of the North American trade. The Anglo-American relationship must be that of mother and daughter, in which authority and love are intertwined. The instrument of authority, if not of love, was Parliament rather than the King.

The American agents, seeking to manipulate the elements of English politics, had to work in a distracting time. The year 1765 began with a royal crisis. In January, George III was being bled, cupped, and fed asses' milk to relieve a strange malady. He had suffered a similar attack three years earlier. Like the first bout, this one had begun with a cough and had gone on to provoke a mental confusion and produce urine the color of wine. The ailment was not actually diagnosed until two hundred years later, when it was identified as porphyria acuta, a metabolic abnormality that can have devastating, although intermittent, effects on the nervous system.

When he rallied toward the end of winter the King set his ministers to thinking about a Regency Act that would provide for an interregnum, should he succumb while the Prince of Wales was yet an infant. That question stirred up all the touchy factionalism that simmered chronically in palace and Parliament. How could the regency be kept out of the hands of that elegant Scot Lord Bute, whom Parliament had striven to exorcise from the King's affections? Parliament was mortally afraid of the ambitions of the King's favorites in general and particularly Lord Bute, who had been George's boyhood tutor and idol. And if the King's mother, the Princess Dowager, were to succeed as Regent, would she not open the back door to Bute, who, it was said with probable accuracy, had used a similar route to her bed when both were younger? The bickering was fierce and ended with a compromise that merely postponed the decision on an eventual regency.

Then in the spring the weavers came out of Spitalfields to bring the threat of bloody revolution to the heart of London. It was all part of the price of empire. The businessmen of England had rejoiced in Lord Clive's heroic conquest of India, but the King, viewing the victory with the eyes of a country squire, called it "rapine" and thought it deplorable that Clive had "opened the door to the fortunes we see daily made in that country." And while the "nabobs were shaking the pagoda tree," as the coffeehouse talk put it, the government had to do something about the Indian economy, particularly the silk trade. But silk from India and elsewhere was coming into England and threatening to ruin the silk weavers of Spitalfields. When the House of Lords, prodded by the Duke of Bedford, rejected a bill that would have given tariff protection to the British weaving industry, some eight thousand weavers stormed into the capital. They attacked the Duke of Bedford's house, broke the windows, and came close to burning it down. They took possession of two inner courts of the Palace of Westminster and forced the noble lords to enter their own house by the back door. There the peers engaged in a debate which was termed contemptuously *"une guerre de pôts de chambre"* by the King's uncle, the Duke of Cumberland. Cumberland managed to be a political fire-eater although he was excessively fat, asthmatic, and suffered from an ailing heart and poor eyesight.

Actually the weavers' discontent went beyond the price of silk, and their rancor engulfed not only the House of Lords but the prerogatives of the gentry. When they overturned and sacked a carriage they told the looted occupant that no one needed more than £1,000 a year to be a gentleman. The King was troubled, but the tough, if decrepit, Cumberland sent him a note: "I don't imagine these reports ought to break a moment of Your Majesty's rest. I wish to God you had no more formidable enemies than these poor wretches." The tone was reassuringly royal, and when a cavalry charge broke up the weavers' riots at Bedford House, the King mistook the ensuing truce for lasting peace.

In all his troubles the King relied on the support of that most stolid sector of English political life, the country gentry, characterized by a dependable lack of imagination and a passion for meticulous gardening. Thomas Whately, MP and Secretary of the Treasury, for example, was best known as the author of *Observations on Modern Gardening*. In politics, as in the gardens of England, "he could not leave things alone," as the historian Lewis Namier has suggested. It was he who had drafted the legislation which was then provoking a storm far more troublesome to the King's ease than the weavers of Spitalfields. The bill was the Stamp Act. It had been born in the discontent of the country gentry over the burdens of taxation that came with the Seven Years' War.

To appease the taxpayers George Grenville, the King's First Minister, had cast about for economies and fresh sources of revenue. He began by cutting the breakfast rations of the palace chambermaids. (Parliament had already pinched a penny or two by denying His Majesty the luxury of a private secretary, thus forcing him to write his letters himself, with all the royal imperfections of grammar.) Grenville then looked overseas and resolved to weed the American smugglers from the imperial gardens. He also proposed an abrupt break with past policy by levying a tax on the Americans, not for the sake of trade, for which ample precedent was available, but to raise revenue.

It seemed a modest proposal—requiring the transplanted Englishmen to do no more than what was demanded of those who stayed at home— to purchase stamps with which to validate their wills, diplomas, deeds, and other documents, and to adorn their decks of playing cards, newspapers, almanacs, and such amenities. Admittedly the burden would not be onerous but it ran up against one great obstacle—the notion that had grown up in America that the King, not Parliament, merited the whole-hearted allegiance of the colonies. The legislative prerogative of Parliament was particularly offensive, it was felt, when it sought to tax the colonists.

The problem for the agents was that even their natural allies regarded such concepts as heresy. The American position troubled the gentry because it left them to carry the tax burden. The belittling of Parliament disturbed the radicals, ideologically sympathetic to the colonists, because they shuddered at any sign of recrudescence of royal power. (That issue had been settled for all time, it was hoped, when James II crossed the Channel.)

The Stamp Act, which passed the Commons on February 27, 1765, and the Lords ten days later, was designed to raise about £60,000 a year. That sum, added to other tariffs, might be hoped to defray about a third of the £300,000 Britain was then spending annually on the military establishment in North America. The American agents lobbied against the bill strenuously, but after it was passed they took a more relaxed attitude. Franklin expressed a philosophical resignation. In a letter to a fellow Pennsylvanian dated July 1765, he wrote:

"Depend upon it, my good neighbor, I took every step in my power to prevent the passing of the Stamp Act. . . . But the tide was too strong against us. The nation was provoked by American claims of independence, and all parties joined in resolving by this act to settle the point. We might as well have hindered the sun's setting. That we could not do. But since it is down, my friend, and it may be long before it rises again, let us make as good a night of it as we can. We may still light candles."

Actually Franklin seemed to be preparing his own candle when he indicated to Grenville his readiness to serve as a distributor of the hated stamps or to recommend other Americans for the job. When public opinion in America proved less philosophical, Franklin quickly abandoned the idea, though he continued to deplore the violence of Bostonian resistance. This encouraged his detractors afterward to suggest, without any discernible evidence, that Franklin had actually worked for enactment of the Stamp Act.

None of the agents was prepared for the reaction in the colonies: the furious manifestos and petitions, some of them so hot the agents dared not touch them for fear of exacerbating British feeling. The sheer passion of the American response did wonders, however, to galvanize the agents and stimulate their ingenuity. They were moved to action by an American boycott—the nonimportation agreements—which was playing havoc with the British economy. The boycott gave the Americans the semblance of power which distinguishes diplomacy from wheedling. The problem for these embryo diplomats was how to use the power of the boycott, which was hitting hardest at their likeliest allies, the merchants of England.

By the end of 1765 Americans had canceled orders amounting to £700,000. Ships stood idle at the piers. The workers at the steel mills of Birmingham were unemployed and were rioting for food. American products, to which the English taste had grown accustomed, were becoming scarce and exorbitantly priced because shipowners could not afford to carry American goods to England and go back empty. The American market had suddenly dried up. Merchants saw little hope of collecting the often staggering debts owed by American traders, who, even in good times, were not the best of risks. To bring together American debtors and British creditors in common cause against Parliament was the immediate job of the American lobby.

The regency imbroglio and the weavers' riots had soured the King on Grenville and Bedford; by midsummer both were out. (George thereafter consistently misspelled Grenville's name out of pique.) The King was forced to take as his First Minister Lord Rockingham, a moderate pro-American and no partisan of Grenville's penny-pinching policies.

In June the first reports of American reaction appeared in the *St. James's Chronicle*, which said New Yorkers had termed the Stamp Act "the Folly of England and the Ruin of America." By October the Stamp Act riots in America had become the biggest story in the London press and the issue was being fought out in the letters pages. Lord Sandwich's chaplain, the Reverend James Scott, wrote furiously for retention of the act and brought upon his head the fury of the pro-Americans, who identified him with his sponsor's well-known lechery and denounced him as, among other things, "a most scurrilous, profligate priest."

Having only the shakiest support in Parliament, less among the squires, and no great affection from the King, Rockingham was dependent on the merchants. This, then, was the moneyed wedge to be used by the American agents to pry apart the Stamp Act. Barlow Trecothick conferred with Rockingham in November and used his aides to help draft a letter to merchants in thirty key towns of England. At the same time he organized a committee for repeal among London businessmen.

Parliament was due to open debate on the Stamp Act on January 14, 1766. All through the previous November and December, American agents had drummed up petitions from merchants who were persuaded that it was the bungling Stamp Act and not the colonists' boycott that was responsible for idle ships and idle men and for the dissolution of the mercantile dream of American riches. From Lloyd's Coffee House came strategies which culminated in torrents of letters to Members of Parliament, demanding repeal as an economic necessity, ignoring the constitutional issue of Parliament's rights. The Americans were now coordinating their efforts in a massive diplomatic offensive that even included an alliance with the West Indian agents.

Benjamin Franklin worked ceaselessly. He saw Lord Dartmouth, who presided over the Board of Trade, and who ventured to suggest a face-saving suspension of the stamp tax, which later could be quietly interred, thus avoiding a head-on clash with Parliament. Franklin gently turned aside all halfway measures, knowing that nothing less than outright repeal would satisfy his constituents. When one MP asked Franklin to come up with some alteration that would make the act acceptable to the Americans, without imposing the humiliations of a complete turnabout, he replied: "I must confess I have thought of one amendment; if you will make it, the Act may remain, and yet the Americans will be quieted. It is a very small amendment, too; 'tis only the change of a single word."

"Ay," said the MP, "what is that?"

"It is in that clause where it is said 'that from and after the first day of November, one thousand seven hundred and sixty-five there shall be paid, etc.' The amendment I would propose is, for *one* read *two*, and then all the rest of the Act may stand as it does. I believe it will give no one in America any uneasiness."

The MP so relished the "amendment" that he tried to persuade Franklin to offer it again when the latter was called formally to the bar of the House of Commons to testify. Franklin decided it was too frivolous and confined himself to factual answers to questions of Members seeking a way out from under the avalanche of protests stirred by the lobbyists. Franklin stood for four hours before the bar of the Commons. Trecothick, weathering a similar inquiry, educated the House of Lords. Their argument was basically economic, depicting the dire consequences of the act to America and Britain. It was an approach that appealed to the merchants and hence to Rockingham.

The parliamentary debate went on in day and night sessions, some lasting until three in the morning. Worn out, the agents continued to coordinate tactics and strategy on the floor and in the lobbies. The Rockingham ministry gave the repeal movement full support behind closed doors, always seeking a way to preserve the shadow even if it had to sacrifice the substance of the act. The fire-eating Cumberland had died from his numerous ailments, prompting the "omniscient" Jackson to observe that if he had lived a few months longer, "instead of a repeal of the Act there would have been a number of regiments in America before this."

Witnesses had to be carefully rehearsed before testifying against the act, waverers patiently persuaded, and a publicity campaign mounted to flood the newspapers with letters and articles. Franklin wrote many of these under a variety of pseudonyms, each with its own particular appeal: "A New England man," "A Londoner," "A Friend to the Poor," "A Traveller," "Homespun," "A Well Wisher to the King and all his Dominions."

Franklin fought with logic, passion, and, most effectively perhaps, an earthy humor. When someone suggested that, if the Stamp Act were repealed, at least the Americans should repay Parliament the expenses incurred in printing the stamps, Franklin's answer made the rounds of coffeehouses and salons. He told the story of an out-of-temper French workman who was heating iron rods on the Pont-Neuf in Paris and offered to shove one of them up the rear end of an inquisitive onlooker. When the offended citizen declined the offer, the workman said, "The least you can do, then, is pay for my coals."

To the King, William Pitt the elder, war hero and pro-American, was another gadfly of outrageous impertinence. He had spurned a ministry, preferring to badger the government from the opposition. George needed Pitt in his administration as he needed the American colonies in his empire but could scarcely bring himself to tolerate either. He read the daily reports from Lieutenant General Conway: "Sir, I did not come from the House last night till past eleven, which I thought too late to trouble your Majesty. . . . Mr. Pitt had said some impudent things which I thought indisposed the House much to the petition [from the American Stamp Act Congress]; particularly that he thought the original compact with the Americans was broke by the Stamp Act. . . . Sir, Mr. Pitt came down and spoke; Mr. Greenville [*sic*] who answered him, was much enraged to see him walk out of the House while he was speaking."

George III, tired of the controversy, noted in a memo on February 10: "Lord Rockingham this day came and complained to me as if he was accused of having wrong stated my opinion on the Stamp Act; I told him I had on Friday given him permission to say I preferred repealing to enforcing the Stamp Act; but that modification I had even thought both more consistent with the honor of this country and all the Americans would with any degree of justice hope for."

Britain's honor was served by a Declaratory Act, enunciating Parliament's prerogative to tax the colonies. Once the theory was upheld the practice of it could be forgone. The act was repealed, to the great satisfaction of most if not all concerned. Even the lack of representation in a Parliament that reserved the right to tax was viewed by some Americans as not an unmixed liability. For did it not provide an argument against future taxation? Franklin, who still hoped for parliamentary participation by Americans in a united empire, reflected sadly that in times past the colonies might have felt honored by the right to send their own MPs to Westminster, but "the time has now come when they are indifferent about it, and will probably not ask it, though they might accept it if offered them."

A delegation of one hundred merchants representing their colleagues in the major ports of Britain haunted the lobbies of the Commons throughout the debates in February and March, all eager to see their country capitulate to the demands of the Americans. Whenever Members of the House came out, the merchants were on hand to hiss George Grenville, that hapless balancer of budgets, and cheer the champions of repeal. The unnerved Grenville, now out of favor with King and Commons, violated the proprieties by seizing one demonstrator and shaking him. The American lobbyists, though not the only factor in the turnabout, had reason to congratulate one another as much as their customary rivalries would permit.

On March 3, when the repeal bill passed a key committee in the Commons, King George himself received the news delightedly. In his euphoria he thought he was hearing the last of the American drama, though it was in fact only the closing chords of the overture. He wrote to his First Minister, Lord Rockingham: "I am glad the American affair has ended this day without any great altercation."

On March 4, 1766, twenty men, booted and spurred, waited outside Parliament for word that the bill had passed the House. When the vote was tallied (250–122 in favor of repeal) the couriers galloped off to Sheffield, Birmingham, and Leeds to spread the cheery news. In Bristol, a key port in the American trade, the churches set their bells to ringing to announce the victory. In the harbor, ships ran the colors up their masts. From the windows of the American Coffee House, British merchants beamed delightedly and flung coins into the street. At night bonfires and torchlight processions turned the port into a carnival.

The bill was rushed through the House of Lords in record time between March 5 and March 17, and on March 18 George gave it the royal assent. In York two hundred men rode out along the highway to greet Lord Rockingham and bring him triumphant into the city to the clanging music of the church bells. London, the chief focus of radical pro-American sentiment, organized a procession of triumph to the House of Lords with fifty coaches in the line of march. Crowds gathered in St. James's Park to cheer the King. At the Half-Moon Tavern in Cheapside the parliamentary heroes of the fight for repeal were dined and toasted. And at the King's Arms the hundred merchants wound up their vigil with an address of thanks to His Majesty.

Franklin and the other agents rejoiced in the church bells' paean of praise for the triumph of British practicality that would once more set the ships to sailing. The London *Chronicle* was moved to Biblical parody in summing up the general jubilation—which always excluded the Scots, who were considered diehard anti-Americans: "And behold the music in the steeples, and on the cleavers, and on the parchments were heard throughout every street and every alley and court . . . and the instruments of the fiddle were also heard; but the bagpipe was not heard all the day long."

The British merchants lost no time in claiming credit for the victory, which prompted an acidulous answer in the *Gentleman's Magazine* from "A British American" who warned his fellow colonists that the businessmen of England had "acted upon mere commercial principles of expedience and not from those more rational ones of humanity and justice. . . ." Whatever the motivations of the merchants and their claims to be the champions of the hour, most of the American agents were prepared to take the cash and let the credit go.

It was the first victory of those prototypical American diplomats, the colonial agents. With consummate skill, unburdened by excessively ideological considerations, they had built alliances by a blithe acceptance of strange bedfellows. In so doing they had constructed a pattern of diplomacy soundly based on expediency that was to last America for centuries.

II

IN WHICH THE BROTHERS LEE
BEGIN A FATEFUL FEUD,
AND BENJAMIN FRANKLIN SUFFERS
A DIRE HUMILIATION

Toward the end of 1766, in the euphoric boom that followed repeal of the Stamp Act, the brothers Arthur and William Lee arrived in London. The Lees of Virginia were one of the great clans of landed gentry who dominated the politics of patriotism in America. Arthur and William Lee inherited from them an unbounded faith in their own chaste virtues and a profound mistrust of all those who were not Lees.

Embodied in less resourceful and ambitious men such an obsession might have been merely tiresome. If the two Lees had remained in America throughout the Revolution they might have worn out their energies in the brawling factionalism of the Continental Congress. On the stage of Europe, however, they were in a position to blow their suspicions into international scandals, disrupt diplomacy, alter the course of war and peace, and present to the world for the first time the American spectacle of patriotic inquisitors in full cry after putative traitors and sinners. The hunt came naturally to the Lees, and their quarry was at hand—Benjamin Franklin.

Arthur Lee, the elder and dominant of the two brothers, was twenty-six years old when he came to London in the winter of 1766, certain that he possessed the talents and experience to deal with the Old World in the name of the New. Few Americans of that era could have been as well schooled or as well traveled. He had been to Europe before. He had studied at Eton and later at Edinburgh, where he had taken his doctorate in medicine and botany. On holidays he had gone on jaunts to Holland and Germany. And he could speak German fluently, a rare accomplishment for an American.

Arthur Lee had practiced "physic" for a year in Williamsburg but found a provincial doctor's life too confining. His elder brothers Richard Henry Lee and Francis Lightfoot Lee were already active in Virginia's politics of resistance. Indeed they dominated it, and Richard Henry had begun to irritate the best families of Virginia by putting public interests above their land claims.

Arthur, unable to grow in the shadow of any man, even another Lee of Virginia, decided that the field of foreign affairs would be his particular arena. He put aside his interest in the therapy of human and plant life and went to London to study at one of the Inns of Court. In the atmosphere of the Temple he hoped to master British constitutional and international law. While he studied law and digressed only modestly into business, he practiced politics and built bridges to influential pro-Americans in London.

As Arthur was overshadowed by his brothers in Virginia, so William was outclassed by Arthur, but he accepted his fate with far more resignation. He let Arthur have the field of patriotic policy making and confined his ambitions to the commercial sphere, although distinctions between the political and the commercial tended to be blurred. In any case, William took his opinions of politics and people directly from Arthur and accepted his brother's most fanciful suspicions as if they had been divinely revealed.

They both joined the tight factional circle of agent Dennys de Berdt on Artillery Row. From this vantage point they could fire salvos at any Americans who seemed seduced by the parks, the elegant neoclassic mansions on the squares, the circuses, theatricals, brothels, and rowdy gin-soaked slums of wicked, luxurious London.

While William rose in the de Berdt tobacco trade, Arthur took readily to the de Berdt clique among American agents. De Berdt's highly critical view of Franklin, for example, was readily accepted by Arthur Lee. Franklin offended by his very eminence, and showed no readiness to toss the torch to young and eager hands. No other agent could hope to rise in the shade of that lofty American, whose wit was circulated in salons, coffeehouses, and the Royal Society, whose manners—at once avuncular and flirtatious—charmed ladies half his age, who enjoyed a reputation as a writer, political philosopher, and scientist (though Arthur Lee outclassed him in academic honors). Moreover, Franklin's gentlemanly life style seemed scandalous to the austere rectilinear republican Arthur Lee. Thus envy took on the brighter hues of patriotic vigilance.

There was also an ingredient of business rivalry in the burgeoning feud between the Lees and Franklin. Lee represented the Mississippi Company, a group of southern speculators seeking the colonization and exploitation rights over more than two million acres in what was then called the Northwest but is now part of Pennsylvania and Ohio.

It was not remarkable that patriots, on the eve of revolution, should concern themselves with seeking to turn a dollar in wilderness real estate. (From Washington on down, the American leaders speculated in land.) And it was not hard to see a sociopolitical value in such profit seeking, for how else was the land to be settled unless adventurous speculators were prepared to buy and sell it? What was peculiar to the Lees was their ability to identify their deals with the national interest and damn their competitors as outrageous moneygrubbers.

When the Lees' company collided with Franklin's Vandalia venture, Lee clothed the business conflict in moral outrage and thus began the first of what would be a long series of diatribes against Franklin and his associates. "Take my word for it," he wrote, "there are not a set of greater knaves under the sun. As their Scheme originated in a most villainous fraud, it has been carried on in expence [and] corruption."

When Arthur Lee in his early years in London sought a toehold in the corps of colonial agents, the British scene was undergoing mercurial changes, marked by abrupt entrances and exits of political heroes, wits, and buffoons. It was also a time when tumultuous crowds clamorously intruded into the affairs of state in London as in Boston. The elder Pitt had at last succumbed to royal blandishments and accepted a peerage as the first Earl of Chatham, a distinction which sorely dismayed his radical London supporters. They ceremonially burned copies of the speech he had made for repeal of the Stamp Act. And at least one tavern keeper, who hitherto had proudly exhibited Pitt's portrait on his swinging sign, turned the shingle upside down, leaving the Great Commoner standing on his head.

Unperturbed by such turnabouts, Arthur Lee cultivated Chatham as he did the pro-American Earl of Shelburne. But these old-timers were giving ground before the new, tempestuous phenomenon of John Wilkes and the Wilkesites. Here was no polished statesman to be courted at a levee, but a madcap, riding a tide born of the hungers and desperation of plain men in a revolutionary age. Arthur Lee set about trying to swim in those stormy waters and to salvage from them something of use to America.

The lean and homely but nonetheless charming Wilkes had the greatest difficulty in bridling his wit before it plunged into scurrility. For a time at least he had been a regular at Sir Francis Dashwood's Hell-Fire Club. In the grounds of Medmenham Abbey, ingeniously landscaped into a series of phallic jokes, Wilkes had sought both pleasure and political advancement.

His sponsor at the Hell-Fire Club was the son of the Archbishop of Canterbury, Thomas Potter. That well-connected rake also introduced Wilkes to Earl Temple, the brother-in-law of Pitt. Temple, an admirer of Wilkes's wit, and in need of a literary mouthpiece, was thenceforth to be his vehicle to glory. As Temple's protégé, Wilkes rose to be sheriff of Buckinghamshire and later a publisher of a waspish newssheet, the *North Briton*. His politics were naturally those of his sponsor and in the 1760s Wilkes delighted in tormenting the King's favorite, Lord Bute, and his Scottish coterie.

In No. 45 of the *North Briton*, Wilkes adroitly lambasted the King's speech to Parliament. Exonerating the King from any complicity in composing his own address, Wilkes blamed the politicians around the throne for what he called "the most abandoned instance of ministerial effrontery ever attempted to be imposed on mankind." When the minister rashly attempted legal action, Wilkes found himself a hero of the battle for a free press and for civil rights. Thus he became a patriot and soon convinced himself that the heroic mantle sat well on his bony frame.

He wore it becomingly even under charges of printing pornography (a somewhat witless parody of Pope, called "Essay on Woman"). Through a series of court trials and parliamentary upheavals, Wilkes had the constant acclaim of the London crowds. "Wilkes and Liberty" was shouted in the streets and chalked on walls even while he took his pleasure in France and Italy to avoid the hounding of the law.

In 1768, back in England again though still under an edict of outlawry, Wilkes stood for Parliament in Middlesex. When he won, the people of England who had fashioned him into their own particular hero brought all England close to revolution. For a day and a half the crowds commanded the streets, forcing passing nobility to step from their coaches and drink a toast to "Wilkes and Liberty." They chalked the number 45 on buildings and, when they caught the Austrian ambassador, they inscribed it on the soles of his boots. The rampaging unemployed donned blue cockades in the flamboyant Wilkes manner. When the royal forces proved powerless Wilkes gallantly undertook to wave his wand and still the mobs. His committees enforced an uneasy peace while he went off triumphantly to take the waters at Bath.

When he returned to carry his legal appeal against the decree of outlawry, the government was so intimidated by his presence that Wilkes had to summon the sheriff himself and ask to be taken to jail. Reluctantly the sheriff complied, but the crowds unhitched the horses from the sheriff's coach and pulled it to prison as if escorting a conqueror to his palace. By now Wilkes, whether he liked it or not, was the living symbol of popular revolt, identified with the cause of striking seamen, with the age-old complaints of the weavers, with every cause for reform or revolution afoot in England.

As Wilkes pursued his career (he was elected to Parliament three times before that body would give him his seat) his reputation spread across the Atlantic. At first he was indifferent to the claims of Americans, but he grew more ardent as money and cargoes of tobacco arrived from Virginia and South Carolina to aid his cause. One Bostonian wrote to him: "Be of good courage. I hope you will have the satisfaction to see Britain saved as well as France conquered in America." And one of the Sons of Liberty wrote: "The fate of Wilkes and America must stand or fall together."

The specter of revolution by unmannerly people, whether in Boston, New York, or London, appalled many of the American agents. During the Wilkesite riots in 1768, Franklin wrote in horror: "Even this capital, the residence of the King, is now a daily scene of lawless riot and confusion. Mobs patrolling the streets at noonday, some knocking all down that will not roar for Wilkes and Liberty; courts of justice afraid to give judgement against him; coal heavers and porters pulling down the houses of coal merchants that refuse to give them more wages; sawyers destroying sawmills; sailors unrigging all the outward bound ships and suffering none to sail 'til merchants agree to raise their pay; watermen destroying private boats and threatening bridges; soldiers firing on the mob and killing men, women and children; which seems only to have produced a universal sullenness that looks like a great black cloud coming on, ready to burst in a general tempest. What the event will be God only knows. But some punishment seems preparing for a people who are ungratefully confusing the best constitution and the best king any nation was ever blessed with, intent on nothing but luxury, licentiousness, power, places, pensions and plunder."

Though by temperament Arthur Lee was no more suited to street riots than was Franklin, he viewed the rise of Wilkes somewhat differently. A quiet Wilkesite from the start, he is generally credited with having inserted the American cause into Wilkes's catchall campaign for popular liberties. Working at first without the handicaps of official accreditation (though hankering after them with a desperate hunger), Lee could enter the hurly-burly of British politics as a private person, answerable primarily to his own conscience. And no aspiring politician in those years could ignore the reality of Wilkes's strength, particularly but not exclusively in London. Lee saw Wilkes as a vehicle for pro-American hopes and for his own ambitions, the two inextricably intertwined.

In 1769 Lee took a hand in organizing the Supporters of the Bill of Rights. (The Bill of Rights in those days referred to the Constitution of 1689, won in the Glorious Revolution, which had supplanted the autocratic Stuarts with the more tractable William and Mary.) The group, which met in London taverns, included a number of MPs, a lord, a few baronets, a rector, and a number of merchants. Although "Wilkes and Liberty" offered the organization its primary slogan, the membership required that any candidate for Parliament seeking its support must pledge himself to work for the American colonists' representation in Parliament as a precondition to their taxation.

The Supporters of the Bill of Rights was not the only or the most radical of the clubs that stoked the rebel fires of London. The Society for Free and Candid Inquiry, operating out of the Robin Hood Tavern on Butchers Row, had been cultivating ardent spirits since 1613. Members met in an upstairs room around a punch bowl, for which each pitched in a couple of pennies. For that modest sum one could hear Burke rehearse his more glittering oratory and chat with Colonel Isaac Barré, an MP who very early on joined the cause of British parliamentary reform with that of the Sons of Liberty in Boston. (Wilkes and Barré ended up indissolubly linked in Pennsylvania, where patriots named a new settlement Wilkes-Barre.)

The group that met in the Robin Hood Tavern was broader in its membership than the more statesmanlike, legalistic, and middle-class Supporters of the Bill of Rights. Around the punch bowl were not only the usual handful of barristers and merchants that might be met in any number of political pubs, but tailors and cabinetmakers as well. Protestant clergymen mingled with an occasional Catholic priest and the gathering even boasted a Jew as a duly elected member. At one time its president was a baker.

The Society for Free and Candid Inquiry was as convivial as any local pub. The president, in jovial mock despair, was reported to have warned on one occasion: "If you bawl out for porter at this end of the room, for ale at that, for lemonade in one corner, for a mixture of all in another, will not the world say that we come here not in search of truth, but of drink? Our glory will pass away; our rival the King's Arms Tavern will reign in our stead, and be the only nursery for orators and patriots."

London radicalism indeed had a cheery air about it in those days. The difficulty from the American point of view was that though the English radicals might be in earnest about the liberties of Americans, they, too, saw them as children. Their disagreement with the King and the Tories frequently sounded like a debate on child rearing. The recently ennobled but still liberal Earl of Chatham declared: "I love the Americans because they love liberty . . . but they must be subordinate. In all laws relating to trade and navigation especially, this is the mother country, they are the children; they must obey and we prescribe."

Arthur Lee put up with the condescension and went the road of the radical clubs and Wilkes. He attempted to follow the example of that most daring, devastating, and still unidentified polemicist who wrote under the name of Junius. (Lee used the pseudonym Junius Americanus, but never attained the elegance of his model.) It was the original Junius, for example, who in one sweeping paragraph put down both Wilkes and George III. In an open letter to the King, which appeared in the *Publick Advertiser* of December 19, 1769—and was quickly reprinted by other papers—Junius wrote: "Sir, it is the misfortune of your life . . . that you should never have been acquainted with the language of truth, until you heard it in the complaints of your people." He held up the Stuarts as dire precedents: "The Prince who imitates their conduct should be warned by their example; and while he plumes himself upon the security of his title to the crown, should remember that as it was acquired by one revolution, it may be lost by another." He urged a pardon for Wilkes, declaring: "It is only the tempest that lifts him from his place."

The resulting prosecution of every publisher who ran the open letter became a cause célèbre for the British press and freedom. Franklin meddled little with the radicalism that was Lee's province. He continued to play a cool diplomacy in a heated time. The Townshend Acts were far more oppressive than the Stamp Act and stirred a flurry of nonimportation agreements in America, but this time the old allies of America—the British merchants—were less excited because they were more prosperous. They signed a few petitions, they gave lip service to the American cause, but by now they were selling the goods of England to Russia, and the undependable American trade was no longer so important. One after another the colonies went their separate ways, breaking the boycott or weakening it until little was left of the resistance except the refusal to import tea.

Lee's flair for radicalism and rhetoric, combined with an inflexible disposition, kept him from the charmed circle of the Great Men of England. Franklin took it as his mission to deal precisely with those men because they held the power. For Franklin, moderate even in revolution, this was a more congenial—and a more realistic—style of diplomacy. In turn, the influential, respectable leaders sought him out.

At a social gathering early in 1769 a dignitary (identified by Franklin only as a "noble lord") asked him if he had a plan to solve the American question. "My answer was," he recalled later: " 'Tis easy to propose a plan; mine may be expressed in a few words: repeal the laws, renounce the right, recall the troops, refund the money, and return to the old method of requisition." The noble lord thought the alliteration attractive and the plan acceptable except for the demand that Parliament forgo the right to tax. "I do not insist upon that," said Franklin. "If continuing the claim pleases you, continue it as long as you please, providing you never attempt to execute it: we shall consider it in the same light with the claim of the Spanish Monarch to the title of King of Jerusalem." Unlike many of his colleagues at home, Franklin saw little point in rallying against abstract formulations without practical effect.

Franklin operated at levels out of Lee's reach, which roused the latter's suspicions. Not only did Franklin cling to his job as royal postmaster but, even as the revolutionary temper of Americans rose, he continued to tolerate his son's fiercely anti-revolutionary, loyalist attitudes. Though Franklin was as unwavering as Lee in his defense of American interests, his philosophical approach often seemed to put him above transitory partisanship. He wrote to his son, the royal governor of New Jersey, on October 6, 1773: "If you can promote the prosperity of the people and leave them happier than you found them, whatever your political principles are, your memory will be honored."

Perhaps even more irritating to Lee was Franklin's continuing pursuit of the Vandalia scheme. That proposition ran into heavy opposition in 1770 when Lord Hillsborough became Secretary of State for the American Department. Franklin called on the secretary in Hanover Square to present his credentials as the newly delegated agent for Massachusetts, which he now served along with Pennsylvania, Georgia, and New Jersey. According to Franklin, His Lordship received him with "something between a smile and a sneer," regarded him "with a mixture of anger and contempt," and refused to acknowledge any accreditation not approved by the governor of the colony, a wholly new requirement for agents. When the fuming Lord Hillsborough handed back the accreditation unread, Franklin responded elegantly: "I beg your Lordship's pardon for taking up so much of your time. It is, I believe, of no great importance whether the appointment is acknowledged or not, for I have not the least conception that an agent can at present be of any use to any of the Colonies. I shall therefore give your Lordship no further trouble."

Arthur Lee had just acquired at long last an appointment to an American agency. It was not the Virginia agency, which he had coveted and for which he had brought into play the power and prestige of the Lee name —all in vain. It was, ironically, Pennsylvania that gave Lee his official accreditation. Philadelphia, an ocean away from the infighting of the agency men in London, had decided to reward Lee for his strenuous journalistic efforts as Junius Americanus by appointing him an assistant to the man he most cordially hated, Benjamin Franklin.

Lee collaborated with Franklin as well as his feelings would allow, but he apparently felt no compunction about writing to Samuel Adams that Franklin was "not the dupe but the instrument of Lord Hillsborough's treachery." Lee was never one to allow plain facts to interfere with the conduct of a vendetta.

In any case, Franklin won that round with Hillsborough by moving in mysterious ways to ease him from office, thereby helping Vandalia and America. In a letter to his son, Franklin hinted at the part he played in Hillsborough's downfall:

"Seeing that he [Hillsborough] made a point of defeating our scheme [Vandalia], they [the English politicians] made another of supporting it, on purpose to mortify him, which they knew his pride could not bear. . . . The King too is tired of him and his administration, which had weakend [*sic*] the affection and respect of the colonies for a Royal government; of which (I may say it to you) I had used proper means from time to time that His Majesty should have due and convincing proofs."

The retirement of Lord Hillsborough from the American Department paved the way for the appointment of Lord Dartmouth, who seemed far more sympathetic both to the American colonies and to Franklin personally, although Arthur Lee had grave doubts about him. "In fact," Lee wrote of him, "he was a religious overmuch, and even addicted to methodism. Such a disposition argued a weak mind, or hypocritical heart."

The Vandalia scheme, however, continued to be frustrated, in part at least by the skillfully pressed competing claims of Lee's group. Seeking to hedge his bets, Franklin had taken a tip from his fellow agent and speculator Richard Jackson and had bought 20,000 acres of Nova Scotia wilderness. He found, however, few willing settlers.

Franklin could handle reverses in business or politics with far better grace than Lee, who thought that every misfortune was a personal affront. Where Lee seethed righteously at aristocratic snubs, Franklin relished them. While staying with his friend Lord Despencer (formerly Sir Francis Dashwood of the Hell-Fire Club) Franklin would occasionally encounter the loftiest dignitaries of the realm, even the redoubtable Prime Minister Lord North. "He seemed studiously to avoid speaking to me," Franklin wrote to his son. "I ought to be ashamed to say that on such occasions I feel myself to be as proud as anybody. His lady was more gracious. She came and sat down by me on the sofa and condescended to enter into a conversation with me agreeably enough, as if to make some amends. Their son and daughter were with them. They stayed all night so that we dined, supped and breakfasted together without exchanging three sentences."

In 1773 all of Franklin's meetings with the King's ministers were likely to be accidental and pointless. The doors of the Great Men were beginning to close against him. And the radicals were growing cooler to Lee. The Townshend Acts had been repealed—except for the tax on tea—and the feeling of even pro-American Englishmen was that this should satisfy those "umbrageous" Americans, as Chatham had called them. Indeed, the militants were finding a cool reception even in Boston.

When Lord North put through his Tea Act in the spring of that year, he therefore expected no resistance. Under the act's provisions the East India Company could ship tea directly to America, paying the Townshend tax but no further customs duties. This, he reasoned, would please almost everybody. The company would dispose of its large surplus and the Indian colony would reap some of the benefits; the Americans would be able to buy their tea at prices considerably less than those they were paying to smugglers from the West Indies. Parliament would be happy in preserving its prerogative to tax and the nation would be saved the expense, bother, and humiliation of trying vainly to combat the American addiction to smuggling—an activity viewed by the colonists as in the interests of patriotic policy and shrewd business. Again the two happily coincided. John Adams is reported to have stopped at an inn at Falmouth, Massachusetts, and asked the barmaid: "Madam, is it lawful for a weary traveler to refresh himself with a dish of tea, provided it has been honestly smuggled, or paid no duties?"

Lord North and most of the English had never rightly understood that the Americans were not objecting to taxation because it was onerous. (The Stamp Tax was singularly trivial and the Tea Act actually promised lower prices.) It was Parliament's prerogative to tax at all that was in question. Even that consideration might not have stirred the American tea drinkers if it had not been for the tactlessness of the governor of

Massachusetts, and Benjamin Franklin's adroit use of some stolen letters.

Governor Thomas Hutchinson, Massachusetts born and bred, was not unpopular as royal governors went in those days, even in Boston. At the time of the Boston "massacre" he calmed the fevered city by calling for a legal trial, not a mob trial, of the offending British officers, even though the evidence of "provocation" by the American crowd was so abundant that John Adams himself undertook to defend the British commander. Hutchinson's popularity was serving to dilute the ardor of the patriots. But perhaps he mistook the lull in revolutionary opposition for permanent tranquillity and so presumed to lecture the General Court of the province on the overriding authority of Parliament.

That lecture did not go down well in Boston, and it was followed by far worse. Benjamin Franklin in London had come into possession of letters written by Hutchinson and his brother-in-law and lieutenant governor, Andrew Oliver. The letters had been addressed to Thomas Whately, the man who had drafted the hated Stamp Act, and who served as Undersecretary of the Treasury until his death in 1772. They were accompanied by warnings to keep them from the eyes and hands of American agents.

There were nine letters in all. Six of them could be read as recommending harsh measures for Americans. They denounced "the licentiousness of such as call themselves the Sons of Liberty." This characterization by Hutchinson, harsh and lopsided as it was, had a certain personal justification: his house had been sacked and gutted by outraged patriots in 1765 and Oliver had been burned in effigy. The letters went on to argue, however, that it was not practical for a colony three thousand miles from the motherland to "enjoy all the liberties of the parent state." Hutchinson advised that "what are called English liberties" ought to be abridged in the colonies for the colonies' own good.

Three other letters to Whately revealed Hutchinson's more moderate side. Americans as a whole were loyal to England, he insisted, and warned that military force must always be controlled by civil power and used only as a last resort.

The letters had ended up in the files of the Colonial Office and might have remained buried there forever if John Pownall had not kept them in mind. John was a Member of Parliament. His brother Thomas Pownall, formerly of the Board of Trade, was now an undersecretary for colonies. By comparison with Thomas, John was a violent radical, though Americans considered him moderate. He had long disliked Hutchinson and served as correspondent for the Boston patriots. Samuel Adams labeled him "a doubtful friend," but John Pownall had cryptically warned in June 1770: "Judge not of the tree by the coloring of the blossoms; wait the bearing time and judge by the fruits."

The fruits ripened in 1773, and Benjamin Franklin was on hand to gather them. John Pownall and Franklin saw eye to eye in those days. Both thought war an unmitigated horror; both had an abiding affection for England and hoped that America would yet save her from her own folly, and live with her in the mutual esteem of good trading partners.

Hutchinson's letters could be made to serve these purposes. The blame for the misunderstanding could be fastened upon Hutchinson and a few "mischievous men" who had poisoned the minds of Parliament and King. England could disown them and by so doing dissolve the impasse. Franklin therefore sent copies of the letters to half a dozen Massachusetts leaders, keeping their source mysterious and emphasizing that they were to be treated as confidential, on no account to be published.

He must have known that fastening a tag of confidentiality on the letters would only facilitate their dissemination and stimulate an appetite for them. That June 1773, the letters were read to the Massachusetts Assembly in closed session, and at once rumors of an impending news sensation seeped out from behind the locked doors. John Adams was all for abiding by the secrecy provision, though he referred to Hutchinson as a "vile serpent . . . bred of our bone," who was envenoming his own people. Within two weeks of their hearing before the Assembly, the letters were published in pamphlet form, described on the title page as "the fatal source of the confusion and bloodshed in which this province especially has been involved and which threatened total destruction to the liberties of all America." The result was a petition from the Massachusetts Assembly demanding the removal from office of both Hutchinson and Oliver.

Thus the temperature of Bostonians was high and mounting when the *Dartmouth*, carrying one hundred and fourteen chests of Indian tea, dropped anchor in Boston Harbor. Leaflets reported the arrival of that "worst of plagues, the detested tea" carrying Parliament's tax on it. The subsequent tossing of the tea into the harbor by colonists in war bonnets horrified Englishmen of property as an attack upon the very foundations of civilization.

The British answer was to close the port of Boston—which provoked the other colonies to overcome their natural rivalry and go to her aid. General Thomas Gage, fresh from America, married to an American and therefore hailed as an American authority, advised the King that the colonists "will be lions while we are lambs but if we take the resolute part, they will be very meek." Other repressive measures followed. Both

North and the King confided to each other that conciliation must come but only after a show of authority. George and Parliament remained quite willing to forgo any further taxes and write off all hopes of deriving revenue from the American colonists—if only they would acknowledge Parliament's right to levy taxes.

The British seemed forever impaled upon that somewhat abstract point, and floundered. Whatever they did seemed to exacerbate the situation. Parliament passed a liberal law granting religious and civil rights to the Catholic province of Quebec, which had been won from the French. To American patriots this was an added outrage. On the one hand, it favored a hotbed of Papism in the New World and, on the other, seemed to foreclose the possibility of expansion into the Northwest. The stock of Vandalia, in which even George Washington and Patrick Henry held shares, thereupon plummeted in value to the vanishing point and dreams of fortunes in the wilderness flickered out.

England was now doubly outraged—by the destruction of tea in Boston and the theft of the Hutchinson letters in London. In Court and coffeehouse the question ran: Who had stolen government secrets and how could the leaks be plugged?

Franklin would say only that his accomplice was "a gentleman of character and distinction."

Accusations spread from target to target until one accuser and his accused fought an inconclusive duel in Hyde Park. To prevent a rematch which seemed inevitable, Franklin declared he would accept full responsibility for the affair.

Thus was the stage set—in January 1774—for Franklin's presentation of the petition of the people of Massachusetts for removal of their high officials, Hutchinson and Oliver, already impeached by the legislature. Franklin had no doubt that in the existing climate of opinion the petition would be rejected, but he hoped that it might be received and disposed of in a routine manner without argument or public hearing. Instead, however, he was summoned to appear at the "Cockpit"—the Privy Council chamber.

Franklin sent a messenger to Lee's chambers at the Temple but Lee was off on a holiday at Bath. Standing alone at the preliminary hearing, Franklin encountered his erstwhile fellow agent Israel Mauduit, now representing Hutchinson and Oliver, and the Solicitor General, Alexander Wedderburn. After an opening skirmish in which Mauduit said he would need legal counsel to oppose so formidable a spokesman as Franklin, the hearing was adjourned to January 29, 1774.

By that time Franklin had found a lawyer, and Lee had come back to

London. Together they appeared at the Cockpit and the result was a humiliating shambles for Franklin. The Privy Council seemed to have arranged not so much a hearing as an auto-da-fé. Wedderburn heaped what Franklin later described as "invective ribaldry" on the hapless diplomat's head. With few exceptions, Franklin noted, the lords of the Council "seemed to enjoy highly the entertainment and frequently burst out in loud applause." Franklin's lawyer was utterly ineffective. "Being very ill," Franklin later recalled, "and much incommoded by standing so long, his voice was so feeble as to be scarce audible. What little I heard was very well said, but appeared to have little effect."

The petition was rejected vehemently, and on the following day Franklin was notified that he had been fired from his job as postmaster general. On top of that he faced a private lawsuit in connection with the letters.

The humiliation of Franklin in the Cockpit won him considerable sympathy in the London press, which opened its columns to him. Writing under his various pseudonyms, he reported the scene at length and emphasized that publication of the letters might be considered an outstanding service. They revealed, he said, how the misunderstandings between America and the Mother Country had been caused by official misinformation and hence paved the way to reconciliation if the government were of a mind to take that path.

In any case, it seemed clear to Franklin that his usefulness in London had come finally to an end. He was sixty-eight years old. At home he was being accorded the scant sympathy that is the lot of failed heroes. Georgia and New Jersey dismissed him from their service and he asked to be relieved of the Massachusetts agency as well. The rumor mill spread the story that he was dickering to regain his postmaster's job by offering to desert America and the American cause. In answer he wrote to his sister that the postal service "have done me honour by turning me out, and I will take care they shall not disgrace me by putting me in again."

He feared that the vengeance of the Privy Council would fall upon his son and cost him the governorship. "Perhaps they may expect that your resentment of their treatment of me may induce you to resign, and save them the shame of depriving you when they ought to promote," he wrote his son. Franklin advised young William not to resign. (Actually the governor had shown no inclination to sacrifice himself for his father's honor.) Ever mindful of the realities, the elder Franklin wrote: "Let them take your place if they want it, though in truth I think it is scarce worth your keeping since it has not afforded you sufficient to prevent your running every year behindhand with me. [The governor of New Jersey had had to borrow regularly from the rebel statesman.] But one may make something of an injury, nothing of a resignation."

Early in 1774 Benjamin Franklin was prepared to yield his post to the man who had so long waited to step into his shoes, Arthur Lee. But at that crucial moment, when Franklin felt he was only a liability to the cause, his successor had gone on holiday to Italy. This did not seem altogether fortuitous. The man who persuaded Lee to travel so inopportunely and who actually gave him £300 to guarantee his absence was Paul Wentworth of New Hampshire, who saw the troubled waters as a prime fishing ground.

Wentworth had begun his career by agreeing to represent homesteaders (in what is now Vermont) who wanted parliamentary confirmation of their rights against the designs of New York land speculators. In his constituents' name he won official accreditation as a New Hampshire agent and then did little to protect their interests. Throughout the crises of 1774 he sided with Governor Hutchinson and won a welcome at government ministries by supporting the view of Americans as a riotous, disloyal mob. He openly belittled the petitions of the Continental Congress and where he was involved in the strategy of his fellow agents he frequently leaked their plans to the press. His predilection for playing the game of British ministries was based not only on an emotional abhorrence of revolutionary manners but on his position as the proprietor of large estates in New Hampshire. This gave him a very solid stake in the status quo. He hoped to adorn that stake with the title of baronet; to that end he backed Hutchinson and the Tories.

Wentworth lived quite comfortably in London in those days, not on his agent's salary so much as on commissions from stock jobbing. The £300 he gave Lee for his holiday might thus have come easily from his own pocket. But why Lee, who radiated suspicions and who bristled at the slightest whiff of impurity in a patriot, would have taken Wentworth's advice—and his money—is difficult to understand.

Franklin therefore lingered at a post in which he felt useless, awaiting Lee. He busied himself at scientific assemblies and at chess. He wrote in self-defense to the newspapers and saw his close friends, but he felt cut off. He gave up his attendance at levees. When at last Lee did return, in the spring of 1774, he undertook most of the responsibilities that had been Franklin's. It was Lee who thereafter transacted much of the routine business of the colonies, rallied whatever was left of the American agencies, and tried, without conspicuous success, to stir the merchants to their old pro-American stance.

The backstairs diplomacy, however, continued to lie outside Lee's competence. He had never been adept at delivering an idea in the shape of a *bon mot* at a dinner party and he was not regarded seriously by the powerful men who used to take Franklin into their confidence. As the drift toward war continued, statesmen of all stripes still found their way to Franklin's door. Few came in person, either because they had been present at his humiliation in the Cockpit and feared Franklin's resentment, or else because they did not want to risk the censure and odium of their colleagues by publicly wooing a man in disgrace. But in one way or another those who sought to deal with America in order to avert the impending catastrophe had no one else with whom to carry on the necessary dialogue. Lee, they felt, was far too rigid and played the game by rules they did not comprehend.

It was Lord Chatham who finally made a public demonstration of his friendship with Franklin, a friendship which had never been close in smoother times but which ripened oddly in adversity. When Chatham planned to speak in the Lords to demand the withdrawal of troops from Boston, he brought Franklin with him, the two of them limping badly from their recurrent gout. "I am sure," Chatham told him, "your being present at this day's debate will be of more service to America than mine." When they neared the door of the chamber near the throne, a guard reminded Chatham that "none were to be carried in at the door, but the eldest sons or brothers of peers."

Chatham then escorted Franklin to another door near which a group of lords had gathered. They gawked and whispered as Chatham called out: "This is Dr. Franklin whom I would have admitted into the House." So Franklin again attended the House where he had once lobbied on familiar terms. It was a season of anticlimaxes, however, and Franklin watched the House of Lords reject the motion of his friend.

Still more official was the Howe gambit. The affair began at the Royal Society one evening early in November 1774 when a fellow member approached Franklin to say that a lady—a sister of Lord Howe, as he later found out—fancied she could beat Franklin at chess and would like to try. Franklin agreed, then thought it all too awkward, and put it off. On November 30, shortly after Parliament had opened, his fellow member of the Royal Society reminded him, fixed a date for the following Friday, and picked him up for the chess match in Miss Howe's drawing room on Grafton Street. Franklin played a few games with the lady, whom he found "of very sensible conversation and pleasing behavior." He willingly agreed to a return engagement. The second session was as amiable as the first and Franklin was delighted to find a woman who not only could play a good game of chess but could discuss mathematical problems with keen interest. The lady then deftly turned the conversation from mathematics to politics and asked Franklin what should be done in the dispute between the Mother Country and the colonies. "They should kiss and be friends," said Franklin gaily.

"I have often said," she went on, "that I wished government would employ you to settle the dispute for 'em; I am sure nobody could do it so well. Do not you think that the thing is practicable?"

"Undoubtedly, madam," Franklin replied, "if the parties are disposed to reconciliation; for the two countries have really no clashing interests to differ about. 'Tis rather a matter of punctilio which two or three reasonable people might settle in half an hour. I thank you for the good opinion you are pleased to express of me; but the ministers will never think of employing me in that good work; they choose rather to abuse me."

"Ay," the lady sighed, "they have behaved shamefully to you. And indeed some of them are now ashamed of it themselves."

Franklin thought it was no more than a pleasant chat with a sympathetic lady, unaware that he was being sounded out by some of the most influential peace party politicians in England.

He left Miss Howe's chessboard to meet two friends who had lately been cultivating him. They seemed even farther removed from politics than the charming Miss Howe, for both were Quakers and seemingly more interested in Franklin's science than in his politics. Nevertheless, David Barclay and Dr. John Fothergill talked politics with driving urgency. There was no time to wait for the Continental Congress to formulate plans and send them across the Atlantic, to let them be torn apart in debate and returned again. They asked Franklin to draw up his own plan, which they could show to a few reasonable men in the ministries. Franklin hesitated to launch a peace offensive on his own and he had no notion that it could go very far with the backing of two unknown Quakers, but he agreed to try.

He drew up seventeen points. So that his enemies might not charge him with committing the colonies to a pact, a plan, or even a proposal, he entitled his memorandum with careful modesty: "Hints for Conversation upon the Subject of Terms That Might Probably Produce a Durable Union Between Britain and the Colonies." And he appended no signature to it.

In general the "hints" called for a lifting of all the oppressive taxation, including the tea tariff, but, on the other hand, required the colonies to pay for the tea that was dumped in Boston Harbor. (Barclay and Fothergill insisted that any formula that omitted that recompense would be impossible.) The memorandum also suggested that Britain agree to billet no troops in any colony without consent of its legislators, and to disclaim any right of internal taxation in the colonies.

Barclay and Fothergill promptly brought the "hints" to the men who had devised their mission, Lords Dartmouth and Hyde. The Barclay-Fothergill channel of diplomacy now began to carry a growing traffic: A letter offering the opinion, ostensibly Mr. Barclay's, that it would be tactful to postpone a petition from the merchants while "our superiors" contemplate the "hints"; or a report, transmitted at a dinner table, that Lord Hyde finds the "hints" too hard.

Such delicate diplomacy in a city of eavesdroppers, spies, voracious journalists, and politicized dinners—not to mention chess games—could scarcely be expected to remain secret. And Franklin was obliged to deny publicly, with regrets, that he and Lord North had already settled the whole Anglo-American conflict.

On the evening of Christmas Day 1774, Franklin was again playing chess with the engaging Miss Howe when she told him that her brother Lord Howe happened to be in the neighborhood and had expressed a desire to meet him. The Howes had been intimately connected with America. One brother had died at Lake George during the Seven Years' War. Another had fought at Quebec and Louisburg and was now a general. Sir William, who had arranged the approach over his sister's chessboard, was a Member of Parliament and a rear admiral. He assured Franklin that at least some of the high ministerial officials wanted to come to terms with the colonies; he, too, asked for a negotiating plan from Franklin, and arranged to meet with him again at Miss Howe's chessboard to prevent a new flurry of rumors.

By now the British diplomatic offensive was in full swing and Franklin was spending his weekends and his evenings at "confidential" dinners in town or at country houses, assuring one lord or another that the first step toward disengagement must be to take the troops out of Boston because Americans could not negotiate "while the bayonet was at their breasts."

On one occasion in Miss Howe's drawing room, the admiral assured Franklin with "emphatic certainty" that Lords North and Dartmouth were actively seeking a way out short of war. He then sounded out Franklin on the advisability of sending a high-level commission to America to confer with the colonial leaders on the scene. Miss Howe suggested that she would rather see her brother the admiral go to America as negotiator than have her other brother go there as a general. Admiral Howe smiled agreeably and then pulled from his pocket the seventeen "hints." It was useless for Franklin to deny his authorship. The admiral found them disappointingly tough and asked whether Franklin would be good enough to reconsider. The admiral was quite certain that Franklin would not be moved by selfish motives, but he thought it best to say that if Franklin could be instrumental in formulating acceptable terms he might "with reason expect any reward in the power of government to bestow."

Franklin later described this delicately phrased offer as "what the French call spitting in the soup." He said that he would try to formulate new proposals but that he would not promise that these would be more agreeable than the first batch of "hints." Indeed the new terms were courteously phrased but no softer. Actually Franklin could not, even if he wanted to, go much beyond the petition from the Continental Congress which was already before Parliament. The dance of the lords around Franklin was motivated by the belief that the Americans would not leave so eminent a representative in London without power to negotiate. Actually Franklin had very little power left. Even the petitions of Congress had been sent with instructions to a list of five American agents, and heading that list was neither Franklin nor Lee but Wentworth.

Every protestation from Franklin that he was in fact powerless to concede more was taken as a diplomatic maneuver. Howe asked Franklin to join him on a mission to America to help persuade the colonists to a peaceful settlement and, as a mere preliminary token of esteem, offered to pay the full back salary owed to Franklin as agent, "which I understand they have stopped for some time past." Franklin said he would accompany the admiral only if the terms were such that he could recommend them to his countrymen and if people would cease offering him bribes, which, if he accepted them, would forever destroy any influence he had in America. That did not stop the offers.

Lord Hyde upped the ante and promised that if Franklin would scale down the toughest points he would be "honored and rewarded, perhaps, beyond my expectation," as Franklin later reported. Franklin said he was not empowered to make any commitment but he would pledge his entire fortune to pay for the tea that had been dumped in Boston Harbor if that would appease Britain's honor.

Time was running out, and the lords grew weary of the effort to wring concessions from Franklin. Only Lord Chatham held to Franklin as to a life raft. On Sunday, January 29, 1775, he dropped the secretive technique of visits incognito and messages carried by couriers. He was driven to the Stevenson house on Craven Street, where Franklin still lived, and let the coachman wait outside for two hours in plain view of those coming out of church. It set the London gossip mill to working, but it seemed too late to worry over appearances. Chatham was to make another speech at the Lords and wanted Franklin's views on the state of affairs in America. He was convinced that the ministry was grossly misinformed. He left a copy of his proposals with Franklin and set a date for another talk at his country place near Hayes. "Such a visit from so great a man, on so important a business, flattered not a little my vanity," Franklin later recalled, "and the honor of it gave me the more pleasure as it happened on the very day twelve-month that the ministry had taken so much pains to disgrace me before the Privy Council."

Chatham's plan was a compromise, yielding on some points, but obstinate on others. Franklin turned up at Hayes with a briefcase full of memoranda on the subject. He stayed for four hours with Chatham and never got through half of it. The old debater was "not easily interrupted," Franklin explained, "and I had such pleasure in hearing him that I found little inclination to interrupt him." In any case, Franklin reasoned, the bill, at best, would not pass in its present form and if it was to be considered at all, it could be modified in debate. Franklin was again leaning on the bar at the House of Lords when Chatham eloquently offered his bill. Franklin listened in faint hope as Lord Dartmouth moved to accept the bill for consideration by the House. But Lord Sandwich, the corpulent veteran of the Hell-Fire Club, moved its rejection with contempt. No British peer could have drafted it, Sandwich said. It seemed to be the product of an American. Then, glaring ominously at Franklin, he declared that he "fancied he had in his eye the person who drew it up, one of the bitterest and most mischievous enemies this country had ever known." In the end the tide ran against even considering the bill, and Dartmouth himself recanted the speech he had made in favor of receiving it. The bill died and so did Franklin's hopes for any kind of accommodation.

On March 19, 1775, Franklin wrote a hurried note to Arthur Lee: "I leave instructions with Mrs. Stevenson to deliver you all the Massachusetts papers, when you please to call for them. . . . I shall let you know how I find things in America. I may possibly return again in the Autumn, but you will, if you think fit, continue henceforth the agent for Massachusetts, an office which I cannot again undertake. I wish you all happiness, and am ever yours affectionately . . ."

On the following day Franklin left aboard the packet *Pennsylvania*, bound for Philadelphia.

Arthur Lee now stepped into the post he had long coveted. In a sense the time was ripe for him because it was no longer possible to play the courtly diplomatic game of bribes and threats in England. The ambitions of the colonists had burst the narrow confines of politics-by-payoff.

A Puritan prophet named Henry Marchant, after visiting England, foretold a horrendous doom for the British Empire, in which the body would waste away to nourish a swollen head: "Thus the Head feeding upon the Body, without procuring any supplies to it, will sooner or later become all Head and no Body, when Louis Baboon and his Continental brothers will make a Foot Ball of it for their Cubs."

Nevertheless, if the Franklinesque style was no longer of any avail in England, the alternative seemed to be war and the colonies would need wealthy friends, the likeliest being precisely that "Louis Baboon" in Versailles. Though the North American colonists might be English at heart and republican in their thinking, they would, if need be, climb into bed with the enemy of England and the exponent of absolute monarchy. It was a regrettable but natural consequence of a policy of expediency. And what nation in an age of reason can dare to practice any other?

On December 12, 1775, Franklin in Philadelphia wrote a letter of instructions from the Committee of Secret Correspondence to Arthur Lee: ". . . It would be agreeable to Congress to know the disposition of foreign powers towards us, and we hope this object will engage your attention. We need not hint that great circumspection and impenetrable secrecy are necessary."

In carrying out that assignment Arthur Lee sought the tool for his diplomacy, not at Court or Parliament, but among the errand boys of kings.

III

WHEREIN A PLAYWRIGHT WINS RENOWN BY SAVING A QUEEN FROM A TRANSVESTITE BLACKMAILER, AND OPENS THE WAY TO PARIS FOR THE AMERICANS

THE TOOL CHOSEN by Arthur Lee to pry open the money chests of Louis XVI was a Frenchman who used the name of Ronac. It is difficult, however, to know who was manipulating whom, for Ronac was not one of the usual dealers in cast-off confidential trivia who made their bargains in whispers around the pillars of St. Paul's. He was far more astute and operated with a grander style.

Ronac had derived his pseudonym from an anagram of his actual family name, Caron. The son of a modest watchmaker, he followed the family trade but sought his customers among the ladies of the French Court. With the help of a well-contrived marriage he became, by turns, an "Officer of the King's Pantry," a music master to the three royal princesses, and an honorary royal secretary.

Pierre Augustin Caron wore a sword and with his own hands placed the King's meat upon the table, as his rank in the Royal Pantry required. It was a dignity to which a French commoner might aspire if he had sufficient influence or the cash to pay for it. It was on a par with the post of "Cravat-Tyer-in-Ordinary to His Majesty" or "Captain of the Greyhounds of the Chamber." The sale of these titles brought the Throne a ready revenue at no expense save the ingenuity required to invent them. In an earlier reign Montesquieu had written: "The King of France has no gold mines like the King of Spain, his neighbor, but he has far greater wealth in the vanity of his subjects, which is more inexhaustible than any mine. He has been known to undertake or continue a war without any resources but the titles of honor which he had to sell, and, owing to a miracle of human conceit, his troops were paid, his towns fortified, and his fleet equipped."

For the royal secretaryship, which involved no duties whatsoever, the ex-watchmaker paid 85,000 francs. Among other things the post gave him the rank of a petty noble, and accordingly he could append to his name that of a fictional geographical fief. He thus became "de Beaumarchais." Later, with tongue in cheek, he insisted that his claim to nobility, unlike that of more prestigious families, was absolutely beyond question because he held a receipt for the purchase price.

A parvenu noble with an acerbic wit and an envy-rousing prestige as author of the hit comedy *The Barber of Seville*, Beaumarchais naturally tended to make enemies. After one scandalous clash with powerful forces in Parliament, he was forced to kneel before a judge and hear himself branded as "notorious," a designation which stripped him of his civil status. By way of redeeming himself he undertook a secret mission in the latter days of the reign of Louis XV to save the honor of the King's mistress, Mme du Barry. This was a quixotic gesture, rather like throwing a cape over a puddle. A French journalist named Théveneau de Morande, calling himself "Le Gazetier Cuirassé"—the Journalist in Armor—had been operating a thriving blackmail business out of London for a French market. Only a sizable amount of money could forestall his publication of a biography of the King's favorite, entitled *The Secret Memoirs of a Public Woman*.

Beaumarchais did the job discreetly, paying off the Journalist in Armor and personally supervising the incineration of three thousand copies of du Barry's alleged memoirs in a furnace in a London suburb. He returned to Versailles to claim his reward only to find that he was too late; Louis XV lay dying. The new Louis XVI and his wife, both young and glowing in self-conscious virtue, wanted no part of the old regime and its scandals.

Fortunately for Beaumarchais, another blackmailer in London let it be known that he was about to publish a pamphlet besmirching the new Queen, Marie Antoinette, and Beaumarchais was sent off to do the necessary. He did it—with incredible flourish, according to his own report—pursuing the libeler to Amsterdam, wrestling with him in a Bavarian forest, and landing himself in a Viennese jail for the sake of his Queen.

Although his civil status was not completely clarified, Beaumarchais had earned the personal gratitude of Their Majesties and the respect of the Ministry for Foreign Affairs. He was assigned to shuttle between London and Paris on minor missions to pick up tidbits of information relished by the intelligence forces of Louis XVI. His orbits approached ever nearer those diplomatic circles in which he was to meet Arthur Lee and through him enter into American history.

The key to Beaumarchais's ascent into diplomatic importance was the affair of the Chevalier d'Eon, a knight of such compelling mystery that for four years London gamblers had been giving odds on whether he was a man or woman. Elegant, delicately built, with a voice that verged on the soprano, the Chevalier was known to be a formidable duelist, to have an enviable battle record as a Captain of Dragoons, and to hold the Cross of St. Louis, one of France's most distinguished decorations. On the other hand, d'Eon had appeared at the Court of Empress Elizabeth of Russia in woman's clothes, calling herself Mlle Lia de Beaumont. Ostensibly she had been sent there as a *lectrice*—a reader—for the Empress but actually as the secret and personal representative of Louis XV, who was anxious to have a channel of communication untapped by his own ministers, those of the Empress, or the agents of his mistress. (The Empress herself was addicted to transvestite masquerades which allowed her to dress as a man and thus exhibit the universally acclaimed shapeliness of her legs.)

In 1763 when the Duc de Nivernais arrived in London to secure George's ratification of the treaty ending the Seven Years' War, d'Eon, in male dress, was in his retinue. The duke was himself a charming ambiguity. He versified prettily, and devoted himself to organizing quadrilles. The hearty British press referred to him as "the political sylph" and sneered: "The French sent the preliminaries of a man to sign the preliminaries of peace." Nivernais dispatched the Chevalier d'Eon to bring the ratification papers to Louis XV, who embraced the courier, spoke of him fondly as "my little d'Eon," and awarded him the Cross of St. Louis.

The Chevalier served as secretary of the French legation in London and for some eight months as minister plenipotentiary. Then he—or she —quarreled scandalously with the ambassador and was ostensibly recalled. Actually d'Eon was retained in London on a handsome salary as the King's private eyes and ears. At some point in this turbulent career the Chevalier was entrusted with the secret contingency plans drawn up by Louis XV for an invasion of England. Now, in 1775, having fallen on hard times with the death of the old Louis and the accession of the new, the Chevalier was reduced to hinting that the secret papers might have to be revealed to the English unless an adequate pension and annuity were agreed to. The negotiations dragged on unproductively, though not without amusing moments: one negotiator proposed marriage with the Chevalier, assuming that he was a woman.

Past forty, out of favor and running out of time, the Chevalier contrived an introduction to Beaumarchais, who had a record of dealing generously with blackmailers of the Court of France. D'Eon later disclaimed such calculations. "We met," he—or she—said, "owing no doubt to a natural curiosity on the part of extraordinary animals to see one another." Stirring Beaumarchais's chivalry, the Chevalier told him that she was indeed a woman and in dire distress. Beaumarchais dashed off a letter to his King: "When it is thought that this creature, so much persecuted, is of a sex to which everything is forgiven, the heart becomes moved with pity."

Beaumarchais thereupon entered into lengthy negotiations with the ambiguous Chevalier and became convinced that she was in love with him. He complained humorously that never had he imagined that his devotion to King and country would oblige him to court a Captain of Dragoons. The two "extraordinary animals" met for chats at various places, occasionally at parties thrown by the Lord Mayor of London, John Wilkes, who had been elevated to respectability by the victorious radicals of the town. As the negotiations continued favorably the stock of Beaumarchais rose to dizzying heights at Versailles. Most significantly he had a direct line now to the Foreign Minister of France, the Count de Vergennes, who showered unaccustomed praise upon the once disgraced courtier-playwright. "You are enlightened and prudent," Vergennes wrote. "You know what men are, and I am not uneasy about your arriving at a good result with M. d'Eon, if it is possible to do so. If the enterprise fails in your hands, it must be taken for granted that it can never succeed, and we must make up our minds for whatever may be the result."

Beaumarchais succeeded brilliantly, according to his own report to Vergennes. "I assured this young lady," he wrote, "that if she was good, modest, silent, and behaved herself well, I would give a good account of her to the King's minister, even to His Majesty himself. . . ." He reinforced his assurances with regular cash remittances to d'Eon, which, he specified, were to be regarded only as "gratuities not as payments," the fruits of "the special generosity of the King." It was by this "secret proceeding," he went on, "that I still hoped to govern and rule this impetuous and cunning creature."

He returned in triumph to Versailles bearing the chest containing the highly compromising correspondence between the "cunning creature" and Louis XV. For d'Eon there was money and for Beaumarchais there was the lifting of the black cloud of disgrace, certified in a handsome document which declared that His Majesty had been much pleased with his zeal, intelligence, and skill.

Beaumarchais, still chivalrously solicitous about the future of the charming Chevalière, sought to clarify all the conditions of her return to France, principally the one requiring that she thenceforth live the politically untroublesome life of a lady. Through Vergennes he sent a questionnaire to the King, which was answered in His Majesty's hand.

"Does the King grant to Mademoiselle d'Eon permission to wear the Cross of St. Louis on her woman's clothes?"

The King: "In the provinces only."

"Does His Majesty approve of the gratuity of two thousand crowns which I have given to this young lady on her assuming woman's clothes?"

The King: "Yes."

"Does His Majesty in this case leave her man's clothes at her entire disposition?"

The King: "She must sell them."

The Chevalière sailed for home, but when she arrived in Paris she was still wearing the dashing uniform of a dragoon. She was reminded of her agreement, however, and reluctantly changed into a gown which seemed to become this chameleon quite as well. Later, in coiffe, petticoat, and skirts of high fashion, she returned to London. She seemed to settle all outstanding bets by writing accounts of how she had survived the lack of privacy in barracks life without losing her virginity. It was thus a shock to gamblers and a distinct embarrassment to her suitors to read the report of a post-mortem examination in 1810, abundantly attested by witnesses. She was, declared the doctor, every inch a man. The stakes, however, were high enough, some skeptics thought, to have influenced the final verdict. And so the doubt remains.

In any case, it was clear that France was entering the Age of Enlightenment with a flair that was remarkably un-English. Though bribery was rife in both countries, French corruption was not geared to the tradesman. France's philosophers dealt in abstractions and her politicians in pride and prestige even more than in business. They had tried their hands at commercial empires, and admitted their inadequacy when they lost the Seven Years' War. Now French statesmen yearned to regain their vanished glories as the cultural and political leaders of Europe. For that victory it was necessary to humiliate England. And Beaumarchais was about to present the means, for he had met Arthur Lee on the Wilkesite fringes of London society.

Although Arthur Lee, in his voluminous and self-congratulatory correspondence, maintained that the King of France had dispatched Beaumarchais as his personal envoy especially to open talks with Lee in London, the facts seem to belie that grandiose claim. Actually, Beaumarchais had been reveling in the heady Americanism of Wilkes's friends and hangers-on months before he met Lee, while he was still negotiating the d'Eon affair.

From the Americans at Wilkes's, Beaumarchais derived a somewhat exaggerated impression of the colonists' unity, will to independence, and military power. He also had another source which fed him an equally overdrawn picture of England on the brink of revolution and chaos. This was Lord Rochford, Lord North's Foreign Minister in that autumn of 1775. Beaumarchais had known Rochford a decade earlier in Spain when the lord served as the British ambassador there. The two used to sing duets together and Beaumarchais was not one to let such a useful intimacy cool. Indeed the Count de Vergennes, Louis's Foreign Minister, thought Rochford very useful because, as he noted, "it cannot be difficult to make him say more than he intends." Beaumarchais took careful note when Rochford sighed and said: "I am much afraid, sir, that the winter will not pass without some heads being brought down, either among the King's party or the opposition."

Beaumarchais added to that foreboding a quote from Wilkes in a bravura mood: "The King of England has long done me the honor of hating me. For my part I have always rendered him the justice of despising him. The time has come for deciding which of us has formed the best opinion of the other, and on which side the wind will cause heads to fall."

All this talk of heads rolling in England inspired Beaumarchais to address a highly confidential report to his King in September 1775, in which he passed on these ominous opinions, and added his own: "All sensible persons, then, are convinced in England, that the English colonies are lost to the mother country, and that is also my opinion. . . . The open war which is taking place in America is less fatal to England than the intestine war which must yet break out in London. . . . The least check which the royal army receives in America, by increasing the audacity of the people and the opposition, may decide the affair at London at a moment when it is least expected; and if the King finds himself forced to yield, I say it with a shudder, I do not think his crown more secure on his head than the heads of his ministers upon their shoulders."

Though Beaumarchais was usually inclined to be ironic rather than effusive about royalty, he took care in this memorandum to assure his monarch of the virtues of absolutism: "This unhappy English nation, with its frantic liberty, may inspire the man who reflects with true compassion. It has never tasted the sweetness of living peaceably under a good and virtuous king. They despise us, and treat us as slaves because we obey voluntarily; but if the reign of a weak or bad prince has sometimes caused a momentary evil to France, the licentious rage, which the English call liberty, has never left an instant of happiness and true repose to this indomitable nation."

It is clear that Beaumarchais had graduated from the role of bag man in blackmail adventures to that of a respected observer. He could even afford to voice his impatience when Vergennes was slow to act upon his information: "All this ought to have been discussed in the council, and this morning I hear nothing from you about it. The most fatal things to all affairs are uncertainty and loss of time. Must I wait for your answer, or am I to start without having one? Did I do well or ill in sounding minds whose dispositions are becoming so important to us? Shall I for the future take no advantage of confidential communications, and shall I repel instead of welcoming the overtures which must have an influence on the final determination? Finally, am I a useful agent to my country, or only a deaf and dumb traveler? . . . I shall wait for your answer to this letter to start."

Vergennes responded promptly and courteously, encouraging Beaumarchais to cultivate those partisans of "frantic liberty" who yielded such welcome news of England's discomfiture. The idea of sabotaging the British Empire in America was scarcely an original one. Vergennes's predecessor the Duc de Choiseul had sent observers to America in 1764, but these agents had been uniformly discouraging. The colonists, it seemed, were not only without even the shadow of military resources but lacked any will to revolt, bogged down in a sentimental loyalty to the Mother Country. Choiseul himself thought that in some distant future Americans would throw off their allegiance, but the outbreak would not come in his time, he feared.

In 1767 Choiseul had assigned a member of the French legation in London to sound out Franklin, who noted that a M. Durand was "extremely curious to inform himself in the affairs of America, pretends to have a great esteem for me . . . has desired to have all my political writings, invited me to dine with him, was very inquisitive, treated me with great civility . . ." The report must have been as dismal as those of the French agents in America, for Franklin, in that year when American independence still seemed to him either an impossibility or an abomination, commented: "that intriguing nation [France] would like very well to meddle on occasion and blow up the coals between Britain and her colonies, but I hope we shall give them no opportunity."

Since then, however, the rampages of the Sons of Liberty in Boston, of Wilkes and the weavers in London, and the blunders of successive ministries had wrought great changes. Moreover, noting the facility with which George III was buying up boroughs to stack the House of Commons in his favor, Vergennes's envoy to England calculated that French money could buy as much as British money in the flea market of British politics. He went shopping and in 1774 reported triumphantly to Vergennes: "You will learn with interest that you will have in the House of Commons a member who will belong to you. His vote will not help us much; but the copies of even the most secret papers, and the clear and exact report which he can daily furnish us, will contribute essentially to the King's [i.e., Louis's] service."

Vergennes, who had entered the diplomatic corps through the familiar gate of family connections, had nevertheless been well schooled in half a dozen ambassadorial posts, and was properly cautious. He sought to double-check the information that came from so romantically imaginative a source as Beaumarchais.

He sent a confidential agent, Achard de Bonvouloir, on a mission to Philadelphia in October 1775. Vergennes's instructions, transmitted through the ambassador in London, stipulated that nothing concerning the mission be put in writing, that Bonvouloir was to report in detail on events in America and "to indicate to the Americans that France is a friendly nation which admires the grandeur and nobility of their endeavors and one which would be happy to see them avail themselves of her ports." Canada, Vergennes warned, would be a "sticky point" with the Americans and they must be told that France has no further ambitions in that part of the world. He also suggested that Bonvouloir assure the Americans "that we are far from hostile to their independence . . . that we have no interest in doing them any harm," and that "if happy circumstances grant them their liberty, they would find in our ports the facilities which would bear witness to the respect which they inspire among us."

Americans were then pondering the temptations and pitfalls of the outside world, wondering whether the lure of the American trade could open the doors of palaces and chancelleries to those who had rebelled against their own sovereign.

"Suppose then we assume an intrepid Countenance, and send Ambassadors at once to foreign Courts, what Nation shall We court?" asked

John Adams. "Shall We go to the Court of France, or the Court of Spain, to the States General of the United Provinces? to the Court of Lisbon, to the Court of Prussia or Russia or Turkey or Denmark, or where, to any, one, more, or all of these? If we should, is there a Probability, that our Ambassadors would be received, or so much as heard or seen by any Man or Woman in Power at any of these Courts. He might possibly, if well skill'd in intrigue, his Pockets well filled with Money and his Person Robust and elegant enough, get introduced to some of the Misses and Courtezans in Keeping of the statesmen in France, but would not that be all?"

Adams imagined—with considerable accuracy, as it turned out—the suspicions with which the rulers of Europe would view any pledge the Americans might make to win a treaty of alliance or commerce. "What Security could they have that we should keep it? Would they not reason thus: These People intend to make Use of us to establish Independency, but the Moment they have done it Britain will make Peace with them, and leave us in the Lurch. . . . Would not Spain reason in the same manner, and say further our Dominions in South America will be soon a Prey to these enterprising and warlike Americans, the Moment they are an independent State? Would not our Proposals and Agents be treated with Contempt? and if our Proposals were made and rejected, would not this sink the Spirits of our own People, Elevate our Enemies and disgrace Us in Europe?"

Far better, Adams thought, to run the new country like a general store, tell the world it is open for business and let the customers come. He acknowledged that this would require guaranteeing full protection for those vessels that might drop anchor in American harbors. "We may build Row Gallies, flatt bottomed Boats, floating Batteries, Whale Boats, Vesseaux de Frize, nay, Ships of War. . . . To talk of coping Suddenly with G.B. at sea would be Quixotism indeed, but the only question with me is, can We defend our Harbours and Rivers? If We can We can trade."

Franklin, who only a little earlier had expressed the hope that America would serve to confound the enemies—particularly the French enemies —of his gracious sovereign George III, now foresaw the probable necessity of foreign aid in the coming conflict. In July 1775 he wrote to his friend Joseph Priestley in London: "We have not yet applied to any foreign power for assistance, nor offered our commerce for their friendship. Perhaps we never may; yet it is natural to think of it, if we are pressed." The debate on foreign trade raged intermittently in Congress throughout the winter and spring of 1775.

Americans could allow themselves to detest Parliament and even the

King himself; they could conceive of the awkward necessity of independence; but they could not easily root out an English distrust of foreigners. And of all continental Europeans the French were most foreign. France was not only absolutist but Catholic, and the burgeoning revolutionary sentiment in America was so staunchly Protestant that even George III was suspected of Popish behavior. Frequently when crowds burned Lord North or the King in effigy they burned the Pope for good measure. Little was known in America of the stirrings inside France, of the philosophical dreams of a pastoral rebirth of humankind rendered incorruptible by a wilderness simplicity. And still less was known of the darker French miseries that would one day erupt and frighten even the most passionate American rebel.

The men concerned with the odious necessity of considering foreign assistance were, above all, practical revolutionaries who saw no sense in rejecting aid, even from Papists and princes. They were formed by the Continental Congress into the "Secret Committee for Corresponding with our friends in Great Britain, Ireland and other parts of the world." (The very title of the committee suggested the priorities.) The membership of the committee would change from time to time, but it included the least provincial of the American rebels—Franklin, Jefferson, John Jay, John Dickinson, and Benjamin Harrison. These were the men whom Achard de Bonvouloir would have to seek out in order to take the temperature of the rebels and confer upon them the secret blessings of Louis of France.

The committee functioned underground, and the approach of this first ambassador to the United States had to be devious. He made contact with a French bookseller in Philadelphia who numbered Franklin among his customers. Franklin met the French envoy among the bookshelves, and subsequently brought him to the very heart of the American conspiracy, the committee itself. Bonvouloir and Vergennes wanted to know above all whether the rebels would content themselves with rioting for reforms or would push toward a break with the Mother Country. The committee took great pains to persuade the emissary that the fateful decision had been made: the colonies would shortly declare their independence and fight for it. Achard de Bonvouloir, convinced, slipped out of Philadelphia to bring to Paris the cheerful news that the English—who had defeated France twelve years before, whose navies had swept the French fleet off the seas and diminished the luster of French diplomacy in Europe—would soon be in trouble. And England's trouble would be France's opportunity. To that end American rebels and French royalists might work together. At the moment, however, the partnership must be secret, known only to a multitude of spies, double agents, and eavesdroppers.

After Bonvouloir left Philadelphia it occurred to the Secret Committee members that perhaps they had been talking to an impostor, perhaps an agent not of Louis but of George. It was then that they dispatched instructions to Lee to sound out, with the greatest circumspection, of course, the attitude of foreign powers, for which purpose they appropriated £200. Lee did not go near the French ambassador in London, for this was not the eighteenth-century way. Secret diplomacy was to be pursued unofficially at soirees, not at levees. Beaumarchais was the most conspiratorial unofficial Frenchman in London. Lee found him enjoying the wit, gossip, and secret diplomacy of John Wilkes.

It is quite possible that the two had met earlier, for both were accustomed to using the Lord Mayor's Mansion House as a fishing ground for gossip and contacts which, properly seasoned with references to secret and high-placed informants, might enhance their respective diplomatic reputations.

His meetings with Arthur Lee gave Beaumarchais a fresh source for his reports on the state of America, which, like his earlier theatrical efforts—*The Barber of Seville,* for example—lent itself to operatic treatment. In a memorandum written early in 1776 and marked "for the King alone," Beaumarchais quoted—and very likely rewrote—Arthur Lee. He depicted Lee as desperate after failing to get guns and ammunition, demanding to know: "For the last time, is France absolutely decided to refuse us all assistance, and to become the victim of England and the fable of Europe through this incredible apathy? Obliged to give a positive answer, I wait for reply in order to give my own." Beaumarchais reported that Lee, speaking for Congress, was offering France "all the advantages, by which we have, for more than a century, enriched England, besides guaranteeing her possessions [in the Caribbean] according to the forces at our disposal."

As reported by Beaumarchais, the rebels' proposition was couched in peculiarly mercantile terms, rather like the hard pitch of a storekeeper offering a special customer the chance to buy up the bargains before they go on public sale. Lee suggested that the colonies would shortly "make a public proclamation by which they will offer to all the nations in the world, in order to obtain their assistance, the conditions I now offer to you in secret."

Along with the tempting inducement to be in on the ground floor of a growing enterprise was a threat: the Americans would send their first prizes of war into French ports. If France accepted them, she would be forced into war with England; if she refused them, the Americans would make peace with the Mother Country and in reprisal would join in seizing all the French possessions in the Caribbean.

The entire offer was capped with the ancient ploy of the marketplace, declaring—quite falsely, as it turned out—that the prospect's competitor, Spain, was already buying the deal.

Beaumarchais, writing in his own name, argued that the sugar islands so dearly cherished by Louis would be taken by the English if they won, or by the Americans if they won without French connivance; or by both if they were reconciled. The only way to save them, Beaumarchais argued, was to give aid to the Americans in secret. This would render unnecessary a French break with England and make the American Revolution inevitable.

"You will only preserve the peace you desire, Sire, by preventing it at all price from being made between England and America, and in preventing one from completely triumphing over the other." Beaumarchais volunteered to negotiate the whole secret compact, stipulating that, as the price of French aid, America must keep the negotiations secret and must promise never to embarrass the French by sending their war prizes into French ports. He then wrapped the whole matter in a conspiracy to which only King Louis XVI of France and Caron de Beaumarchais would be admitted. It was a daring thing for a man who had only recently purchased the right to wear a sword in his King's pantry, and even then had to suffer for his insolence and talent at the hands of envious courtiers.

"Your Majesty can judge by these papers whether my zeal is not as enlightened as it is ardent and pure; but if my august master, forgetting all the dangers which a word escaping from your mouth might cause to a good servant, who knows and serves but him alone, should allow it to appear that it is from me he receives this secret information, then even the exercise of all his authority would with difficulty preserve me from ruin, so much power have cabals and intrigues, Sire, in the midst of your court to injure and upset the most important enterprises."

Louis did not at once embrace Beaumarchais in this secret and exclusive partnership. He did not fancy the blatant commercialism which seemed to him to taint his code of kinghood. He scorned to take such mean advantage of a rival King. Louis XVI was a young man born too late for chivalry. His Minister of Finance, Anne Robert Jacques Turgot, on the other hand, was a liberal who saw beyond his century. He had the firm notion that independence of the transatlantic colonies, French as well as British, was quite inevitable and their preservation not worth the risk of French lives or French money. Vergennes, however, was decidedly a man of his own time, at home in eighteenth-century cloak-and-dagger. But, wiser than Beaumarchais, he thought it best to subdue the flamboyance and stick strictly to business.

Beaumarchais had wanted direct subsidies from Louis and from that Bourbon monarch's uncle, Charles III of Spain, which would be secretly conveyed to Beaumarchais for transmittal to the Americans. Vergennes suggested instead that a dummy corporation be set up. "The operation," he told Beaumarchais, "must essentially in the eyes of the English government, and even in the eyes of the Americans, have the appearance of an individual speculation, to which the French ministers are strangers. That it may be so in appearance, it must also be so, to a certain point, in reality."

The proposition was that the French government would secretly back a company to be formed by Beaumarchais with an initial subsidy of a million livres. It would persuade Spain to put up an equal sum. The French arsenals would be at Beaumarchais's disposal, but any guns or munitions he took would have to be paid for or replaced. "You shall ask for no money from the Americans, as they have none," Vergennes stipulated. Instead they were to send "products of their soil." Vergennes offered to "help . . . get rid of them [the products] in this country, while you shall grant them on your side every facility possible."

It was hoped that the enterprise would be self-supporting, and Beaumarchais might keep whatever profits there might be along with all the risks—political and commercial. Vergennes held out hope of further subsidies if they became necessary. With that in mind he required a periodic accounting of Beaumarchais's profits and losses.

Thus the first solid foreign support for the cause of the American Revolution came in the form of an ostensibly private commercial venture —Roderigue Hortalez and Company—directed by a playright-adventurer and fostered by the governments of two absolute monarchs. The Spanish ambassador took the added precaution of paying his sovereign's million to the public treasury of France and getting a receipt for it, thus washing his hands and the money—as a later generation would put it. The receipt was turned over to Beaumarchais, who could then pick up the cash from the royal treasury at Paris.

It was shortly after that transaction—in August 1776—that cargoes of Roderigue Hortalez and Company began to arrive in the colonies, which had just declared their independence. The entire affair had redounded to the glory of Arthur Lee, who was not inhibited by any modesty in claiming the credit. Not only did he boast that Vergennes had sent a secret agent—Beaumarchais—expressly to deal with him, Arthur Lee, but he exaggerated the amount of money involved and totally neglected to report the commercial aspects of the deal. The result was that Congress tended to regard the shipments of Hortalez and Company as gifts from the kings of France and Spain, neglecting in subsequent years to ship tobacco and other cargoes that might be sold to pay for the munitions. (Lee described that aspect of the deal as a cover.) This misconception did not trouble the kings of France and Spain, though it drove Beaumarchais to near bankruptcy and forced him into debt to keep the guns sailing in. (Beaumarchais's descendants finally collected a part of the bad debt after a bitter and protracted lawsuit.)

Actually Beaumarchais had little to do with Lee after the preliminary meetings at Wilkes's parties, for he had in Paris another, more congenial American envoy, Silas Deane. In his turn Lee found Deane an odious rival in the nascent diplomatic corps and a target for ferocious diatribes.

There can be no doubt that Lee could find authentic ammunition for his attacks, since Deane was a complex man whose faults and virtues were so intertwined that almost anything he did could delight both his friends and his detractors. His evident ambition was a case in point. The son of a blacksmith in Connecticut, he nonetheless managed to go through Yale, to teach school, and to enter into legal practice. Such drive seemed unexceptionable. That he married a very rich widow and came to be entrusted with the full management of his father-in-law's extensive estates might be attributed to a happy combination of luck and acumen. After his wife died he married Elizabeth Saltonstall, a granddaughter of the former governor of the colony and a member of one of Connecticut's most illustrious and wealthiest families. He came to political notice by lending his voice to the attacks on the Townshend Acts, thereby becoming both patriotic and politically popular. And when he lost ground in local politics he fell back on a safer and potentially more useful constituency. He had become a favorite of the big men of his day: Washington, Franklin, Robert Morris, John Jay.

It was not, then, altogether surprising that Silas Deane, schoolmaster, lawyer, landowner by marriage, and delegate from Connecticut to the Continental Congress, was chosen for a delicate mission to France, "there to transact such Business, commercial and political, as we have committed to his Care, in Behalf and by Authority of the Congress of the thirteen united Colonies." The Committee of Secret Correspondence which appointed him included his friends and sponsors: Franklin, Morris, and Jay.

On receiving the good word, he dashed off a letter to his wife which breathes excitement and ambition suitably couched in patriotic virtue. This was a familiar mixture discernible in most patriots, including the censorious Arthur Lee. "I am about to enter on the great stage of

Europe," Deane wrote, "and the consideration of the importance of quitting myself well weighs me down . . . my enemies thought to triumph over me and bring me down, yet all they did has been turned to the opening of a door for the greatest and most extensive usefulness if I succeed; but if I fail—why then the Cause I am engaged in, and the important part I have undertaken, will justify my adventuring."

In launching young Deane on the stage of Europe, Franklin—in the name of the Committee of Secret Correspondence—briefed him expertly in a letter of instructions.

First there was the matter of Deane's cover: "On your arrival in France you will for some time be engaged in the business of providing goods for the Indian trade. This will give good countenance to your appearing in the character of a merchant, which we wish you continually to retain among the French in general, it being probable that the court of France may not like it should be known publicly that any agent from the Colonies is in that country."

Franklin added that tourism was another serviceable cover for a secret agent: "It is scarce necessary to pretend any other business at Paris than the gratifying of that curiosity, which draws numbers thither yearly, merely to see so famous a city."

Yet how was this tourist-business man to do the political work of an ambassador? Franklin suggested two contacts in Paris who could not only teach the Connecticut lad a good Parisian French but provide an approach to Vergennes at the Foreign Ministry. At his first audience with that minister, Franklin instructed, he was to show his credentials from the Congress, reveal that he had been sent to Europe to shop for arms and supplies and that France had been chosen as "the power whose friendship it would be fittest for us to obtain and cultivate" when the colonies finally broke with England.

Deane was to dangle the hopes of profitable American trade with France in return for a shipment of one hundred cannon plus clothing, arms, and ammunition to equip 25,000 men. Deane was to offer to pay for these supplies "as soon as our navigation can be protected by ourselves or friends"—meaning, no doubt, that France would have to help with convoys if it was to collect. He was then to tell Vergennes that he was prepared to pay in cash for "great quantities of linens and woolens" along with other items for the Indian trade which might go with the arms shipment, all to be convoyed by French warships.

Deane was instructed not to press Vergennes for a quick answer at the first interview but to make apologies for taking up his time and to indi-cate that he would be on call in Paris. At subsequent meetings he was to raise the matter of recognition, should the colonies declare their independence, and of a possible treaty of alliance and/or commerce.

There were other contacts known to be friendly to Americans: Charles William Frederic Dumas in the Netherlands; a former French chargé d'affaires in London, referred to only as Garnier; and, almost as an afterthought, Arthur Lee in London.

Franklin stressed one contact that was to have devastating diplomatic repercussions. "You will endeavor to procure a meeting," he wrote, "with Mr. Bancroft by writing a letter to him, under cover to Mr. Griffiths, at Turnham Green, near London, and desiring him to come over to you in France or Holland, on the score of old acquaintance."

Unknown to Franklin, Dr. Edward Bancroft, to whom he had sent his protégé, was an agent in the pay of the British Secret Service. He was to become one of the most remarkably adept and lucky double agents in the history of Anglo-American shadow play. Franklin knew that Deane had once been Bancroft's tutor and thought this a likely pretext for renewed contact. Thus Bancroft was enabled to weave himself inextricably into the tangled life and ultimately the strange death of Silas Deane.

Edward Bancroft was barely two when his father died in the midst of an epileptic seizure in his pigsty at Westfield, Massachusetts. He was six years old when his widowed mother married the proprietor of the Bunch of Grapes, an inn at Hartford, Connecticut. And he was fourteen when he became the pupil of Silas Deane, newly graduated from Yale. All accounts speak of his kindliness, his affable charm, and his brilliance.

Whether by charm or good fortune is not known, but in any case Bancroft found himself under the protective wing of Paul Wentworth, that New Hampshire landowner who himself ended up in the British Secret Service after a career of double-agentry that never equaled Bancroft's performance either in subtlety or in effectiveness. Thanks to Wentworth's intervention, Bancroft went to work for a doctor in Surinam, where he had an excellent teacher, a remarkable library at his disposal, all expenses paid, and spending money as well. While there he became an accomplished chemist and something of a specialist in the customs of the Guiana Indians, the making of dyes, and the properties of tropical poisons. After a brief return visit to New England he went off to London to study medicine at St. Bartholomew's Hospital. By the time he was twenty-five he was publishing learned monographs on the electrical nature of the shock produced by tropical eels and the chemistry of curare and other poisons. He even offered to supply, to gentlemen of certified character and a willingness to experiment, samples of poisons "capable of perpetrating the most secret and fatal villainy."

Deane wrote to this genial dabbler in poisons as soon as he landed in Bordeaux in June 1776. Bancroft answered promptly, declaring: "Nothing can give me greater pleasure than to renew and improve our old acquaintance." Unfortunately, he pointed out, he was at the moment "burning under the Paroxysm of a quotidian Intermittent," by which pedantic flourish he meant to convey that he was suffering from a low-grade recurrent fever.

When he was somewhat recovered Bancroft wrote again to say he would come to Paris "in all possible haste" to meet Deane. Some suspicious historians have raised their eyebrows at this eagerness to see a tutor who had gone out of his life fifteen years earlier, and wondered whether Bancroft knew that Deane was visiting Paris for some purpose other than sightseeing or gathering materials for the Indian trade. In any case, Bancroft dashed to the rendezvous with singular enthusiasm.

Deane was proceeding more slowly. He stopped in Bordeaux to dispatch gift boxes of claret, capers, and olives to his family and to his hard-pressed patriot friends, John Hancock and Robert Morris. He also loaded his own coach with claret, in order to inaugurate his mission with a suitable glow. He wrote to the friendly Bordeaux wine seller a brief report of that journey: "We drank plentifully on the road, paid duty for two dozen and smuggled in two dozen more, which was brave doings but you know Americans will smuggle."

In Paris, Bancroft and Deane washed away the intervening years in claret and high spirits. Deane unhesitatingly confided his mission to Bancroft. By then it was the end of July 1776, and the colonies had already declared their independence, though Europe was still unaware of it.

Two days after Deane met with Bancroft he had a three-hour audience with Vergennes that was all he could have hoped for. Vergennes put him in touch with Beaumarchais, who could supply him with guns, clothing, and cannon for 25,000 troops. Vergennes urged the strictest secrecy on Deane and suggested that he carry on further dealings in the home of the minister's secretary, Conrade Gérard, because the British ambassador, Lord Stormont, had agents everywhere in all the ministries.

The precautions were wasted; Deane confided all his reports to Bancroft, who transmitted them promptly to Lord Stormont. Bancroft's technique was to write letters, under the transparent pseudonym of Dr. B. Edwards, dealing with such apolitical themes as the nature of true gallantry. He would then write another message in invisible ink between the lines, put the letter into a bottle, seal it, and drop it in front of a particular tree on the south side of the Tuileries on Tuesday mornings before nine-thirty. Lord Stormont's man would retrieve the bottle shortly afterward and drop off any message for Bancroft under a box tree on the terrace.

Thus the head of the British Secret Service, William Eden, knew of Deane's success long before Congress did, and the Foreign Office had a neat copy of Franklin's painstaking instructions to Deane within a few days of his arrival in Paris.

In view of the somewhat airy attitude which Lee and Congress were subsequently to adopt concerning the gun trade, it is worth noting that Beaumarchais was transmitting the terms to Deane in the most explicit, businesslike language. "Nothing but an uninterrupted course of returns on my shipments can enable me to repeat my first efforts, and continue their benefits by employing larger sums," he told Deane. ". . . It is therefore agreed that the first vessels from America, bringing cargoes from your country, are to begin the series of returns for my profit, to enable me to sell the merchandise and thus increase my capital, and the confidence of my friends, that they may be inclined to reinvest money in the scheme."

In London, Arthur Lee found himself shut out of all negotiations with Beaumarchais. He instantly suspected both Deane and Bancroft, but inasmuch as he was chronically and volubly suspicious of everybody from Franklin and Jay on down, he can scarcely be given credit for prescience. (Perhaps the only man he did not suspect was his own secretary, who, in fact, was in the pay of the British Secret Service.) Deane went through the motions of consulting with Lee, as prescribed by his instructions, and in mid-August wrote him: "I am still desirous of knowing if I am to have the pleasure of seeing you here." When three days later he was informed that Lee was on his way to Paris, Deane, in a fit of panic, wrote to Vergennes's secretary: "I could have wished that he had suspended his Visit, as I know not, otherways, how he can serve me, or my affairs now . . . in as favorable a Course as the situation of the times will admit." Deane was worried that Lee, known as an American agent, might damage his disguise as a businessman and tourist. Deane assured Gérard that he would ask Lee to stay out of sight as much as possible. A useless precaution, of course, because by then there was a Deane dossier at Whitehall filled with Bancroft's reports.

Deane had little time for intrigue. He was trying to assure Vergennes that, contrary to the tide of rumors flooding Paris, the colonies were not about to negotiate peace with Britain. So insistent were these reports that for a while Vergennes stopped all arms sales and was persuaded to resume them only by the histrionic appeals of Beaumarchais. "Near proving a mortal stab" was the way the playwright described the crisis. Deane was also broaching the matter of a full-fledged treaty of commerce and offering assurances that as soon as military victory lent substance to the declared independence of the colonies, America would show proper gratitude by extending the greatest privileges to France, not to England.

To back his assertions of American reliability Deane had precious little documentation. He seemed to be set adrift to win what he could from France without a murmur of support from home. Finally he got off an angry outburst to the Secret Committee:

"For Heaven's sake, if you mean to have any connections with this Kingdom, be more assiduous in getting your letters here. I know not where the blame lies, but it must be heavy somewhere, when vessels were suffered to sail from Philadelphia and other ports, quite down to the middle of August, without a single line."

It was late in the year when he received a reassuring letter from Franklin and Morris declaring firmly: "If France will but join us in time there is no danger but America will soon be established an Independent Empire and France drawing from her the principal part of those sources of wealth and power that formerly flowed into Great Britain will immediately become the greatest power in Europe."

Deane had warned the committee that he was surrounded by traitors and spies passing in Paris as Americans or the friends of America. In such a web of iniquity he had, however, one staunch friend. "Dr. Bancroft of London," he wrote, "merits much of the Colonies."

The bickering of American representatives abroad was mercifully hidden from the embattled patriots at home, who had enough trouble in appeasing the conflicting claims and ambitions of the thirteen colonies, each bent on guarding its own sovereignty within the confederacy that was trying to become a nation. (It took, for example, extraordinary diplomacy to persuade Virginia that its charter did not extend to the Pacific Ocean.) From Deane and Lee the patriots at home gleaned, between the lines of acrimony, the news that the French Court, through Roderigue Hortalez and Company, had undertaken to provide the muscle for America's war effort. But the statesmen of America were trying to see past the conflicting reports of their agents to a broader picture of developing foreign relations. It was time to replace guerrilla dickering with a full-fledged embassy.

Deane himself had begun to look beyond the narrow confines of his mission in Paris. He had been approached by agents of the King of Prussia and the Duke of Tuscany for pieces of the American trade. And Holland, he observed, though pursuing its fixed policy "of never quarreling with any one on any occasion whatsoever," might be rendered susceptible to American commercial blandishments.

Franklin was maintaining a brisk correspondence with friends abroad, seizing every opportunity to win additional allies. When Don Gabriel of Bourbon, close to the Spanish throne, sent him a volume of the Roman historian Sallust, Franklin responded in a style quite beyond the reach of either Lee or Deane. "I wish I could send from hence any American literary production worthy of your perusal but as yet the Muses have scarcely visited these remote regions," he wrote. Instead he sent the proceedings of the American Congress along with other documents indicating high hopes for the Revolution's success. He suggested that, whatever the literary merits of the congressional record, Spaniards might find it politically relevant. "Therein," he wrote, "your wise politicians may contemplate the first efforts of a rising state which seems likely soon to act a part of some importance on the stage of human affairs, and furnish materials for a future Sallust. I am very old and scarcely hope to see the event of this great contest; but looking forward I think I see a powerful dominion growing up here, whose interest it will be to form a close and firm alliance with Spain (their territories bordering), and who, being united will be able not only to preserve their own people in peace but to repel the force of all the other powers of Europe."

He wrote also to Dumas in Holland, to his own translator and editor in Paris, Barbeu Dubourg, and to Lee in London, sounding out the possibilities of foreign recognition and aid for the republic that was to be. America's most accomplished diplomat, however, could give only part of his attention to Europe. At the age of seventy, plagued by gout and failing eyesight, he was drafted to join a rugged and futile mission to woo the Catholics of Quebec. Along with Samuel Chase and Charles Carroll of Carrollton, Virginia (the wealthiest and most influential Catholic among the patriots), he traveled by ship up the Hudson to Albany, then by wagon to Lake George, across the lake by flatboat, to board a coach for St. Johns and so to Montreal. The trip was so exhausting that the aged, ailing Franklin wrote a letter of farewell to the world. He found the Catholics of Quebec in an unreceptive mood. A ragged, hungry army of Americans were living off their land, looting what they could to survive the bitter winter, for which they were woefully unequipped, and adding insult to injury by denouncing those they robbed as bloody Papists. The Québecois, not unpredictably, preferred to stay under British rule. Franklin gave some of his own money to feed American soldiers and admitted that "the army must starve, plunder or surrender."

He returned to Philadelphia worn out and ravaged by gout to find that his son, the New Jersey loyalist, had been thrown into jail. Moreover,

Admiral Lord Howe—whom he had last seen at his sister's diplomatic chessboard—was now in America, seeking once again to try the Franklin channel to a negotiated peace, while his brother General Howe was waiting to strike at New York. The frustrations were personal and political.

Franklin wrote the admiral in a mixture of barely restrained rage and elegant irony: "It is impossible we should think of submission to a government that has with the most wanton barbarity and cruelty burnt our defenceless towns in the midst of winter, excited the savages to massacre our farmers and our slaves to murder their masters, and is even now bringing foreign mercenaries to deluge our settlements with blood. . . . Long did I endeavour, with unfeigned and unwearied zeal, to preserve from breaking that fine and noble china vase, the British Empire. . . . Your Lordship may possibly remember the tears of joy that wet my cheek when, at your good sister's in London, you once gave me the expectations that a reconciliation might soon take place. I had the misfortune to find those expectations disappointed, and to be treated as the cause of the mischief I was labouring to prevent. . . . I know your great motive in coming hither was the hope of being instrumental in a reconciliation; and I believe, when you find *that* to be impossible on any terms given you to propose, you will relinquish so odious a command and return to a more honourable private station."

Franklin's tone would seem to make a meeting with the admiral pointless. Nevertheless, a delegation consisting of Franklin, John Adams, and Edward Rutledge was assigned to confer with Lord Howe on Staten Island in order to decisively scotch the peace offensive that was then distracting the American war effort. Perhaps the only significance of that mission was that it provided an occasion for patriot politics to make the strangest of bedfellows. The inn in South Amboy at which the delegation stopped en route was so crowded that Adams and Franklin were obliged to share a bed. As was his lifelong custom, Franklin opened the window wide, which caused the somewhat hypochondriacal Adams to fear he would contract a fatal chill. Franklin, it is said, put Adams to sleep with a lengthy disquisition on the etiology of the common cold. The conference with Howe proved even less stimulating.

It was one thing to thumb your nose at an admiral and quite another to find arms and money for war. Roderigue Hortalez and Company was not producing enough. Though Franklin had long contended that "a virgin state should preserve the virgin character, and not go suitoring for alliances, but wait with decent dignity for the application of others," America was necessarily an impatient virgin.

On September 26, 1776, a commission was designated to go to France to negotiate for money, ships, and supplies in exchange for a promise of trade and the prospect of a humiliated England. Most of the American foreign-policy thinkers worried about the dangers of involving themselves once again in European disputes. They regarded the Seven Years' War as a prime example of American lives lost in a European cause.

Robert Morris, however, was troubled by the morality of entangling Europe in an American problem. Confessing this qualm—a distinct liability in a diplomat—to John Jay, he wrote: "It appears clear to me that we may very soon involve all Europe in a war by managing properly the apparent forwardness of the Court of France; it's a horrid consideration that our own safety should call on us to involve other nations in the calamities of war. Can this be morally right, or have morality and policy nothing to do with each other? Perhaps it may not be good policy to investigate the question at this time."

Morris' conclusion was inevitable. The Americans would not be manipulated, but if they were to be a nation they would have to manipulate others. And a delegation with such a mission would have to include that most flexible and realistic of moral manipulators, Benjamin Franklin. Designated to serve with him were Deane, who was already on the scene, and Jefferson. Jefferson's wife was ailing, as she frequently was, and so her fond husband declined the assignment. (Jefferson's detractors insisted this was an excuse for a premature political retirement for which Jefferson was known to yearn in intermittent spells between bouts of hard work at the Congress.) Lee was chosen to replace him.

The decision to send the commission came a few days before courier Thomas Story brought word of the impending arrival of the first shipment of £200,000 worth of guns and ammunition from Roderigue Hortalez and Company. Franklin and Robert Morris, the only two members of the Committee of Secret Correspondence then on hand in Philadelphia, decided to keep the news secret—even from Congress.

Only a few days before, a Philadelphia businessman had casually asked Morris whether Dr. Franklin was going to Paris as the official ambassador, an appointment designated as a top secret. It was evident that a session of Congress behind closed doors meant only that the results would be publicized with all the speed and inaccuracy of gossip. "We find, by fatal experience," Franklin and Morris wrote, "the Congress consists of too many members to keep secrets . . ."

On October 26, 1776, Franklin went aboard the sloop *Reprisal* (which carried a cargo of indigo so that the expenses of Franklin's voyage need not be a total loss). With him went his two grandsons, the illegitimate

William Temple, aged seventeen, and Benjamin Franklin Bache, seven. It was strange company, perhaps, for an old man who ran a very decided risk of being hanged if a British warship should run the sloop down. But it would have been cruel to send him on a mission of indeterminate length without a touch of the familiar. Moreover, it was the custom in that decorous time for families to sail with admirals and ride with generals to war. Why not ambassadors?

Troubled not only with gout but with boils as well, and finding the chickens and turkeys aboard ship too tough for his teeth, the unhappy Franklin survived the thirty-nine-day voyage mainly on a diet of salt beef. He amused himself by trailing thermometers over the side to gather data on the course of the Gulf Stream. The trip was further enlivened by the capture of two brigantines, one English and the other Irish. Franklin reckoned that if they could dispose of them in France, they would be worth about £4,000.

The *Reprisal* was bound for Nantes, but the Franklin party chose to land at Auray in Brittany, preferring a spell of coach travel to more of the sea. Franklin got off a quick letter to Deane, informing him of his appointment to the committee, suggesting that some confidential means be found to let Arthur Lee know of his membership on the team, and asking Deane to hunt up a place for him to stay. Franklin had the somewhat naïve notion that he would travel incognito because he could not then be sure that the French Court would cheerfully receive any official American ministers.

All thoughts of quietly sneaking into France were shattered when he got to Nantes and faced a crowded calendar of fetes, grand balls, and banquets in his honor. Wearied from the voyage, Franklin fled to a country house for a few days of quiet. Then he and his grandchildren boarded a coach, which jounced along the wintry roads toward Versailles. His spirits seemed to recover, however, for he noted: "On the road yesterday we met six or seven country women in company, on horseback and astride; they were all of fair white and red complexions but one among them was the fairest woman I ever beheld."

On that note began the momentous mission to France in which Franklin, who had thought himself at the end of his days, was to seek America's survival among the intrigues of diplomats, spies, self-seeking businessmen, witty philosophers, scheming politicians, courtiers, flaming revolutionaries, and loves both light and heady.

IV

CABALS AND CONFUSION
AT PASSY, AND HOW THE
ABSOLUTE MONARCH OF FRANCE
IS BROUGHT INTO THE CAMP
OF REPUBLICAN REBELS

"It is singular," wrote Thomas Carlyle, "how long the rotten will hold together, provided you do not handle it roughly."

The rot was plainly visible in pre-revolutionary France. But though occasionally it would well up from the slums or seep in from the country-side, it was in general the kind of decay that might not impress a casual traveler. In 1768 when Benjamin Franklin first visited the country—on a vacation from his chores in London—he admired the grandeur that over-lay the swamp. He found the roads excellent but when the farmers explained that this was so because they had to work on them two months out of every year with no pay at all, he commented: "whether this is truth or whether like Englishmen they grumble, cause or no cause, I have not yet been fully able to inform myself."

The ingenuity of Turgot, Minister of Finance, had failed to reconcile the desires of the overprivileged with the needs of the underprivileged, and he had been forced out. The philosophers of the Enlightenment glowed brilliantly, but no sparks had yet set fires in 1776. The King and Queen had touched the hearts of the starving and the well-fed alike when, still in their teens and faced suddenly with their troubled inheritance, they cried: "O God, guide us, protect us, we are too young to reign." Now, two years later, the Queen had overcome her shyness, her boredom, and her humiliation at failing to produce an heir—possibly due to Louis's six-year impotence. She led the fashion in towering thirty-six-inch hairdos and played at being Queen while Louis, still shy, played at being the liberal monarch. He summoned Parliaments to act in the name of the people. He tried to catch the winds of the Enlightenment. He appointed ministers who might conceivably have made economic sense if left to their own judgment without the obstructions raised by those who enjoyed the status quo. He left the task of scintillating to his Queen while he puttered with his favorite hobby of locksmithing, kept good hours, and offered his impeccable if somewhat dull example of royal virtue, which few in the Court chose to follow.

It was in this disorder of elegance, moral optimism, venality, and widespread hunger that there developed a sweet fiction of a never-never land across the sea. Virtue, it was said, grew like mushrooms in the American wilderness. At grand balls periwigged ladies played at being shepherdesses. An Anglomania swept the fashion marts because, though England was the natural enemy, the English and Americans were known to be democratic, and the liberal aristocrats of France yearned to be enlightened and popular so long as it did not cost too much.

To glimpse the embodiment of rustic democratic virtue, crowds gathered at the Hôtel de Hambourg on the rue de l'Université, where, at two o'clock in the afternoon of December 21, 1776, the myth of American innocence was made manifest in the person of Benjamin Franklin. The French took him for a Quaker and Franklin played the role to the hilt, although at home he had harsh words for that sect, which in general obstructed the military preparations for the Revolution. A newsletter that circulated to the French provinces described Franklin this way: "This Quaker is in the complete costume of his sect. He has handsome features, spectacles always over his eyes, little hair, a fur cap which he wears constantly, no powder but a very clean air, extremely white linen, a brown suit completes his apparel."

"Think how this must appear among the powdered heads of Paris," Franklin wrote in great satisfaction with his costume. (Actually the cap served a purpose beyond public relations. He was suffering from psoriasis, which had invaded his scalp.) He lost little time in seeing Deane and Bancroft and Beaumarchais, but he was most impressed with one of Deane's contacts, a French businessman who had made a killing in the Indian trade and now held the influential post of supervising the Commissary of the French Army. Jacques Donatien Leray de Chaumont had already made available a million livres from his own pocket for Deane's use and had been helpful in facilitating purchases by Hortalez and Company. In short order he set his ceramics factory to turning out a flood of medallions bearing the likeness of the fur-hatted Franklin.

Soon that familiar homespun image appeared on snuffboxes, in miniatures and lockets. Chaumont did a superb job of popularizing America in the features of Benjamin Franklin. The purpose of the campaign was put very neatly by Franklin himself at a dinner party when a Frenchman remarked on "the great and superb spectacle which America offers us today."

"Yes," said Franklin, "but the spectators do not pay."

For those who loved wit, he was witty. For those who admired shrewdness, he was shrewd. And for those intoxicated by Rousseau's view of pastoral innocence, all the evidence to the contrary failed to shake their vision. "Everything in him announces the simplicity and innocence of primitive morals," commented one simple and innocent observer.

This most sophisticated of diplomats, this glorifier of a universal "mediocrity" who relished the wines, wit, and opulence of the most elitist Court in the world, this businessman with the graces of a courtier, this courtier with the canniness of a shopkeeper, was sanctified as a guileless rustic, nature's nobleman. For two centuries thereafter Europeans would see Americans in that Franklinesque glow and Americans would cultivate their pleasant paradoxical image born in the romantic fantasies of Paris in 1776.

From his suite at the Hôtel de Hambourg, Franklin took stock of what Deane had accomplished. The fact was that Deane had neither charmed the Court nor stirred the people of France in America's behalf. The grand design of a diplomacy that could win international support for the Revolution had eluded him, though he had already drafted his own version of a treaty to be proposed to Vergennes and had suggested a variety of schemes for the bedevilment of England. "Troubles are rising in Ireland," he wrote to Jay, "and with a little assistance much work may be cut out for Great Britain, by sending from hence a few priests, a little money and plenty of arms." He also proposed "spiriting up the Caribs in St. Vincent's, and the Negroes in Jamaica, to revolt."

Yet the underground flow of money, arms, clothing, and supplies was proceeding smoothly, at least as far as the French ports. Running the British blockade was another story. Over a million dollars—then a staggering sum—had been spent, and if a small portion of that, in the form of commissions and side deals, had gone into the pockets of Deane, Beaumarchais, Chaumont, and several participating bankers, this was neither to be marveled at nor particularly deplored. Private gain was expected to sharpen a patriot's sense of purpose. And nepotism was taken only as an indication of an admirable sense of family loyalty.

A prime example of this was the enterprise of Robert Morris, who, like Franklin, was a member of the Committee of Secret Correspondence, that embryonic State Department. In the autumn of 1776 Morris and Deane had established a counterpart of Hortalez and Company—though without its governmental subsidies—to trade with the enemy, England. The American Army needed British goods and the profit motive could be safely trusted to cross all national lines. Joining in the international syndicate were Deane, Chaumont, and a number of French and English bankers. This international conspiracy to subvert politics for the sake of trade operated this way: Goods purchased in England would be shipped by way of Dunkirk or Ostend to French ports on the Atlantic. From there they would be transported to America, where they would be used in the fight against England. This system was working well, making money for Morris and his partners and giving the embattled Americans an added flow of supplies. The difficulty lay with the agent at Nantes.

Robert Morris had asked that the new enterprise employ an errant half brother of his, Thomas. Deane and Franklin complied, setting him up to handle affairs at Nantes. Unfortunately Thomas was an alcoholic. Indeed a British agent described him in a confidential report as "the biggest drunkard in Europe." The bookkeeping was a shambles, and whole shiploads went unaccounted for. But then, a business run by a highly imaginative playwright such as Beaumarchais and a confirmed alcoholic such as Thomas Morris could scarcely be expected to produce nicely balanced and authentic ledgers.

Deane and Franklin had to let Thomas Morris go. Robert was depressed by the scandal and exploded when Deane and Franklin sent written reports to Congress on his half brother's derelictions. He thought a decorous and quiet dismissal of Thomas was in order, given the bonds of friendship, comradeship in a cause, and the solidarity of business partners. Franklin chose Jonathan Williams as Thomas' successor. He was a meticulous accountant with a fluency in French, who possessed the additional qualification of being Franklin's grandnephew. Nepotism carried on.

To Arthur Lee in London, the appointment was yet another ominous sign of corruption, all the more suspect because Deane and Franklin had also infringed the commercial prerogatives of William Lee. The move was thus taken as a challenge to the Lees, who could be offended by far less.

Franklin may have had the notion of treading softly in France to avoid embarrassing Vergennes, but, like it or not, he soon found himself holding a kind of royal levee at the Hôtel de Hambourg. To it swarmed the intellectual, commercial, and social luminaries of France. He dined with the glittering Noailles, a family close to the King, and courteously received the Prince de Broglie, who saw himself as a potential benevolent and unifying dictator of America, destined to perform for the American Revolution the services rendered by William of Orange for the English Revolution. Franklin was feted by dukes, duchesses, countesses, and philosophers, and besieged by volunteers to fight in America. The recruits had a distinguished model to follow.

Just as Franklin arrived, Marie Joseph, Marquis de Lafayette, a pale, gawky lad of nineteen, on fire to avenge his father's death in battle with the British, had escaped the vigilance of the Court and of his parents, and commissioned a ship to take him to the American front. He was close to the King, and his enlistment in the cause was to have an important effect in Paris beyond anything he might contribute on the battlefield. Recognizing his significance, Deane promised him the rank of major general.

The British enterprise of scouring Europe for mercenaries had been bitterly denounced by American patriots. This, however, did not deter some Americans from seriously considering doing likewise. Similarly, the notion of stirring up the slaves and the Indians, though regarded as unspeakably vile, was thought by many to be worth imitating on the grounds that fire must be fought with fire.

Hiring Germans was a natural development for George III because Hanover was the source of his dynasty and because he had been turned down everywhere else. Catherine of Russia emphatically and coldly rejected a bid to borrow her troops. Frederick the Great declined to assign his Prussians to the job. The Dutch raised political objections stemming not only from a disposition to neutrality but from something more positive: As one particularly bold Dutch statesman wrote: "In what an odious light must this unnatural civil war appear to all Europe, a war in which even savages . . . refuse to engage; more odious, still, would it appear for a people to take a part therein who were themselves once slaves, bore that name, but at last had spirit to fight themselves free. But above all, it must appear superlatively detestable to me, who think the Americans worthy of every man's esteem and look upon them as a brave people, defending in a becoming, manly and religious manner those rights which, as men, they derive from God, not from the legislature of Great Britain."

King George therefore had to turn to the Landgrave of Hesse-Cassel, who was attracted by the proposition of providing men, of which he had many, for money, of which he had little, to feed his children, legitimate and illegitimate, of which he had many. He is said to have sold the services of 20,000 Hessians for £3 million. Similar deals were made with George's brother-in-law, the Prince of Brunswick-Lüneburg, and the Prince of Hanau.

Franklin was moved to delicious satire by the British purchase of German bodies for the American front. In a letter, ostensibly from the Count de Schaumbergh to the Baron Hohendorf, commanding the Hessians, Franklin pointed out that the British were paying far more for a dead Hessian than for a wounded one or even a live one. (The terms actually provided that "three wounded men shall be reckoned as one killed.")

"I am about to send you some new recruits," wrote Franklin in the name of the Hessian count. "Don't economize them." He recalled gloatingly the battle of Thermopylae, from which not a single Lacedaemonian returned. "How happy should I be could I but say the same of my brave Hessians. It is true that their king, Leonidas, perished with them: but things have changed, and it is no longer the custom for princes of the empire to go and fight in America for a cause with which they have no concern, and besides, to whom should they pay the thirty guineas per man if I did not stay in Europe to receive them? . . . It is true, grown men are becoming scarce there, but I will send you boys. Besides, the scarcer the commodity the higher the price."

In America, Congress was seeking to up the ante by offering fifty acres to any Hessian who would desert. And Deane had been scouting Europe to see if he could buy manpower. He had sent word that Swiss mercenaries were available, "or if you prefer, Germans, which I do not." Indeed, foreign volunteers poured into America throughout the winter and spring of 1777 until John Hancock complained that they were becoming a "prodigious weight upon the service," and Congress decided to accept no more unless they could at least speak English. Some had been motivated by the cause, others by the zeal for adventure or the prospect of a New World fortune in land. In any case, they were soon demanding officers' commissions with commensurate pay and allowances, thereby antagonizing the native talent.

Franklin and Deane grew more choosy as time went on, but both were delighted when an English friend brought around Friedrich Wilhelm Augustin von Steuben, who was then unemployed and eager. He had served as an aide to Frederick the Great on the Prussian General Staff, but Franklin knew that this in itself would not impress the Congress. He therefore dressed up von Steuben's résumé, conferring on him the fictional title of Baron and declaring that he had served in all the campaigns of Frederick the Great and had moreover acted as Quartermaster General.

Thus ennobled and inflated, von Steuben was welcomed by General Washington and went on to toughen the ragged men at Valley Forge with a Prussian discipline which Washington had attempted vainly to apply.

Besieged by candidates for the American Army, Franklin with tongue in cheek drew up a "Model Letter of Recommendation" which he felt he could give to any who asked. It read in part: "The bearer of this, who is going to America, presses me to give him a letter of recommendation, though I know nothing of him, not even his name. This may seem extraordinary, but I assure you it is not uncommon here. Sometimes, indeed, one unknown person brings another equally unknown, to recommend him; and sometimes they recommend one another! As to this gentleman, I must refer you to himself for his character and merits, with which he is certainly better acquainted than I can possibly be . . ."

Within three weeks of his arrival in Paris, Franklin had his first sparring match with the Count de Vergennes, perhaps the most astute diplomat in Europe. Plump, bewigged, polite but cool, the French Foreign Minister faced the ambassador from the infant republic of the wilderness. Deane was present but willingly took a back seat.

Franklin began not with a plea but an offer: a commercial treaty that would transfer from Britain to France the bonanza of the American trade. It was only a week later and by letter that Franklin raised the matter of arms, ships, money, and supplies. Within a week he had a polite turndown on the ships but a fresh loan of two million livres from the French government and another million from the government importing agency. In dispatches, Franklin pretended that the money came from private sympathizers in France, in an effort to keep intact the fragile fig leaf of neutrality so treasured by the French Court.

The British ambassador, Lord Stormont, had by this time picked up all the relevant details from a variety of spies, including the highly efficient Bancroft. Warned of the espionage network that surrounded him, Franklin replied with a disingenuous show of indifference: "When a man's actions are just and honourable, the more they are known the more his reputation is increased and established. If I was sure therefore that my *valet de place* was a spy, as probably he is, I think I should not discharge him for that, if in other respects I liked him."

The cloak-and-dagger aspects of his ambassadorial post were borne in on Franklin very early in his stay. During the summer of 1776 the energetic Deane, who acted on the theory that the holiness of his cause justified the use of any tool he could lay his hands on, met with a Scotsman who combined rancorous hatred for England with pyromania. He proposed to burn down a good part of the British fleet in Britain's own shipyards. Although Deane later spoke of James Aitken's "odd and suspicious look," and his "eyes sparkling and wild," he encouraged him and wrote to Bancroft about the project. Bancroft played along, asking whether the "business was to be done by land or water."

In mid-November, while Franklin was still on the high seas, Aitken crossed the Channel carrying a volume of Ovid, some do-it-yourself pyrotechnical textbooks, and his own plans for the fires he was to set. It is not known what steps Bancroft took to alert his superiors, but in any case Aitken succeeded in burning down some of the installations at Portsmouth, planted bombs in three warships, and set a part of Bristol on fire. Then he panicked and fled to Bancroft's house at No. 4 Downing Street, London. Bancroft, pleading legal niceties which forbade his sheltering a criminal, turned him away and arranged to meet him at a coffeehouse the following day.

John the Painter, as Aitken became known, confessed and implicated Deane, who was of course safe in Paris. The incendiarist completely exonerated Bancroft, possibly as a result of a visit Bancroft made to him in prison. Throughout the crisis—which scared England so badly the government temporarily suspended the much-revered habeas corpus rights—Deane and Bancroft played a game. They wrote to each other using a deliberately transparent code (in which John the Painter was referred to as O), exonerating Bancroft and incriminating Deane. John the Painter was duly hanged after boasting of the sabotage; Bancroft went unscathed and years later some of Deane's more incriminating files had to be bought by Jefferson to avoid embarrassment. Was Bancroft a provocateur, a double agent, or a consistent counteragent of the British Secret Service? It is hard to say, because the game that he and Deane played of writing private correspondence for the eyes of those who would intercept it—though it may not have confused the Secret Service—has mystified historians.

Franklin inherited that messy affair and had to contain its repercussions, but he himself set afoot other projects that exceeded the bounds of drawing-room diplomacy. He ordered sea captains to prey on British shipping in the Channel, always being careful to let their ships take enough water in their holds to make plausible their entry into French ports under the pretext of an emergency. Vergennes collaborated in the sport. He would always order the privateer and its prizes out of port within twenty-four hours, which gave the privateersmen (the British called them pirates) enough time to dispose of the cargoes. He would occasionally appease the indignant Lord Stormont by arresting the offending captain, but drew the line at turning him over to the British for trial as a pirate. Thus Vergennes preserved a tenuous neutrality that harried and provoked Lord Stormont. The British minister knew all the details of the Franco-American conspiracy, but dared not act on that information, because a fictional French neutrality was far preferable to outright belligerency.

He did his best to counter Franklin by spreading the rumor that the Americans were being defeated and that a reconciliation of England and her naughty American children was imminent. Though the rumors were not altogether without foundation, Franklin dismissed them with a pun that quickly went the rounds and stuck to Lord Stormont like a troublesome tick. He tortured the French word *mentir* (to lie) into "stormontir." It had its effect in a capital addicted to word play and was all the more appreciated because it was such a noble effort by a man whose spoken French was still rudimentary. Actually Franklin found a use for Stormont's rumors of impending reconciliation. Without in any way confirming them he let them seep into the consciousness of Vergennes, because they bolstered a threat he himself was fond of making in his meetings with the Foreign Minister. Though always couched in diplomatic velvet, the threat—indeed the only threat Americans could make—was to come to terms with England if France and Spain withheld support. The point had to be made delicately. The French had to be assured that American resistance would continue with their support but would probably collapse without it.

At the moment France was showing no inclination to accede to Franklin's suggestions of a military pact, and the undercover traffic in arms and supplies was plainly inadequate, particularly because so much of that nourishing trade was bottled up by the British fleet.

That circumstance troubled most bitterly another member of the American team, Deane's secretary and favorite emissary, William Carmichael of Maryland. He was an engaging fellow who carried a recommendation for loyal American sympathies from William Lee in London. It is not likely that they were personal friends because Lee could not have approved Carmichael's taste for waterfront pubs and whores. (His habits and the names of the tavern ladies to whom he was most partial were all neatly recorded in the dossiers of the British Secret Service.) Carmichael set out for America but ran into Deane in Paris and was persuaded to serve in the "militia diplomacy" of Deane's staff. Of all the guerrilla salesmen of America then trying to wangle money, men, and ships out of Europe, none was more elegantly articulate than Carmichael.

Carmichael's frenzied activity, enthusiasm, hope, fear, and literary flair are exemplified in a letter he wrote from Le Havre to his colleague Charles Dumas in Holland: ". . . from the heart of Germany I am now on the borders of the Atlantic. . . . I have been on the gallop ever since I parted with you at Leyden. No St. John apostle, or Saint in the Calendar, ever run through countries with more zeal to gain inhabitants for heaven, than I have to do miracles on earth. But unfortunately, it is not an age for miracles, nor can I even have the presumption that, it is said, was granted to Satan, of entering into the bodies of animals as sluggish as swine; for with great deference, be it whispered, as such do I begin to look on kings and the servants of kings . . ."

Concerning Franklin's arrival, Carmichael wrote: "You will, no doubt, have our Paris news from the prophet who draws down fire from heaven, or Emanuel; I shall, therefore, only give you my comment on the text, which is, that France has done too much and much too little. Too much since she has alarmed England, and made that country put itself in a better posture of defence than before; . . . much too little, because, depending even on that little, we looked not elsewhere in time. . . . Do you not think that we are particularly unfortunate that we could not find one wind in any quarter of the sky, that would blow the Spanish fleet to New York?"

Though Carmichael's efforts to raise funds were fruitless, he was nonetheless eminently useful in expediting the flow of whatever goods could get through. In that connection his predilection for waterfront saloons came in handy, inasmuch as he could recruit ship captains with a taste for smuggling. However, one such man, a fellow Marylander whom he recruited in London, proved an unmitigated disaster. He was Captain Joseph Hynson. William Eden of the British Secret Service received a flow of reports on the ripening friendship of Carmichael and Hynson, and his agents noted that so close were they that their respective mistresses shared the same house in London. To King George, Eden wrote that Hynson was "an honest rascal, and no fool though apparently stupid."

Carmichael persuaded Hynson to take a packet boat from Dover to a French port, where he would be given all the dispatches of the commission in France to deliver to Congress. Knowing precisely what was planned, Eden devised a pretty trap. At the end of one of his numerous lines he was dangling an ambitious parson named John Vardill, whose dream it was to become a professor of divinity in New York. The parson, who had heard of the Carmichael-Hynson scheme through a young lady-love of the loquacious captain, offered a counterproposition: Hynson was to sail to France as Carmichael proposed and under guarantees that the British fleet in the Channel would contrive to avoid noticing him. He was to pick up the packet of correspondence from Franklin and then sail into a trap of British cruisers which would be waiting for him. It would be a contrived mischance. His reputation with the Americans would be untarnished and he would live to serve two masters yet again, and to be paid by both.

The plan worked well and Hynson got as far as France, where he met the commissioners. But while his ship was being fitted out, Franklin and Deane heard of a packet under Captain John Folger that was to sail earlier. They gave Hynson the correspondence to deliver to Folger. On his way to the port Hynson neatly substituted wads of blank paper for the dispatches. When Captain Folger delivered the dispatches in America, Governor Richard Caswell of North Carolina remarked wryly that he "did not know the service of sending clean paper so far."

Further disturbing Franklin's life was another American in Paris, a self-styled "gentleman of fortune" named Ralph Izard, a close friend of Arthur Lee, exhibiting all of that cross-grained diplomat's disposition to suspect his colleagues and to vent upon them the wrath of his own self-conscious virtue. For the preceding five months Izard had carried a commission from Congress to represent the United States at the Court of the Grand Duke of Tuscany. Unfortunately no one in Congress had seen fit to ask the Grand Duke whether he would accept such an envoy. Izard had therefore been spending his time in Paris engaging Deane—and now Franklin—in a series of shrill controversies. He wanted support for his insistence that the French exempt all of his household goods from import duties, although he was in no way accredited to the French Court. He wanted to be paid for his services in Tuscany, although he had never set foot in the place, and he was demanding to be consulted as a full-fledged member of the commission in Paris, although he had never been invited to serve in that capacity. He also fed Lee's insatiable appetite for suspicion with reports of scandals, real and imagined, involving Franklin, Deane, Carmichael, William Temple Franklin, Beaumarchais, Chaumont, and all.

In this welter of skulduggery, rancor, and gossip, Franklin established the first full-fledged American Embassy on European soil. It was fitting that this should be a wing of the Hôtel Valentinois, belonging to that man of business and diplomacy, of charm and the freest of free enterprises, Chaumont.

It was located in the village of Passy, a half mile from Paris. From the terrace Franklin could see the Seine, the houses of the town, a group of villas belonging to wealthy citizens who had flown to the suburbs, four gracious royal châteaux, vineyards, a church, and forested hills. On the grounds was an octagonal pool, long avenues shaded by linden trees, and the formal gardens so in fashion with the aristocracy. On the roof of the wing allotted to the Americans, Franklin hoisted his lightning rods. They became his personal banner symbolizing his idiosyncratic adherence to the Enlightenment.

Chaumont declined to take any rent from his favorite republic and excellent customer. Franklin insisted on paying for his meals and his wines, which were served in elegant style by Chaumont's staff. Young Benjamin Franklin Bache was enrolled in a fashionable boarding school in the village but would come home on Sundays. William Temple Franklin, listed on the rolls as his grandfather's secretary, dressed in the height of fashion and cultivated the neighbors so assiduously that he advanced his own illegitimacy to yet another generation.

It was a pleasant spot from which to wage a revolution, but few—excepting Arthur Lee and Ralph Izard—begrudged this septuagenarian a bit of comfort. He handled it so gracefully. Franklin customarily rose at eight, breakfasted, exercised, visited, talked, wrote, and dined prodigiously (on beef, veal, or mutton followed by a course of chicken or game, and topped off with sweets, fruits, bonbons or ices, and cheese).

"Frugality," Franklin wrote years later, looking back on his days at Passy, "is a virtue I never could acquire in myself."

Franklin's reception by the French surpassed his and all other American expectations. In that year of 1777, his first at Passy, he had not yet become the darling of those women of the Enlightenment, beautiful, talented, charming, witty, and influential, to whom he was to pay such gallant court. But pilgrimages of intellectuals, both men and women, were pleasantly filling his afternoons and evenings. And when he went to the theater crowds of plain people gathered in the streets to cheer him as the symbol of a vaguely delineated but promising future. The medallions of Chaumont were now picked up and imitated by other ceramicists, who did a thriving business in Franklin motifs. The fad pleased the Queen, who was always willing to follow fashion in ornament as in politics. It irritated the King, however, whose spirits and wit, like his somewhat flabby frame, were heavy. In a moment of pique he ordered the court ceramicist to engrave an image of the fur-hatted American sage on the inside of a chamber pot and presented the handsome facility to a lady of the Court known for her Franklinophilia.

Louis's indelicate gesture was in response to a sensation of being pushed by people and currents he could not control—difficult circumstances for any king and particularly for a monarch supposed to preside over the most powerful country on the European continent. He had to contend with salon philosophers echoing Rousseau; nobles clinging to outworn privileges of feudal lords and protectors though in fact they had become absentee landlords offering no protection whatever; mobs huzzahing for Franklin and liberty; an extravagant wife; and the terrible prospect of a dwindling exchequer. Frederick the Great of Prussia and Maria Theresa of Austria, Louis's mother-in-law and supposedly staunch ally, had carved great chunks out of Poland, France's traditional protégé. And Louis, who had inherited a role as arbiter of Europe, had known nothing of this partition until it was too late. Russia had edged its way to the Black Sea at the expense of Turkey without so much as a nod to Versailles. The world was thumbing its nose at Louis. He seemed unable even to produce an heir. And there was England with its colonies, its businessmen, and its unrivaled fleet.

On the other hand, there was his uncle, Charles III of Spain, bound to him by the Bourbon Family Compact. Yet even here there was trouble, for Charles had a besetting appetite for his neighbor, Portugal, and a positive infatuation for his sprawling empire in the Americas, a matter which Louis thought a vain distraction from the serious business of the balance of power in Europe, the only suitable arena of diplomacy.

While Louis worried and tinkered with his collection of locks, Vergennes (whom Thomas Carlyle belittled as a mere "clerk") was busily trying to put his monarch's house in order. England was the enemy, but war with England, in the existing state of France's finances and naval power, was unthinkable. Vergennes looked upon peace as a last resort. When England sought a peaceful settlement of the Portuguese question (Portugal was a British ally) Vergennes had commented: "We share the wish, rather from necessity than inclination."

Ever since he had been convinced of the seriousness of the colonists' fight for independence, Vergennes had looked upon America as the key to his puzzle. The various memoranda of his agents and of Beaumarchais had persuaded him that with help the Americans could unhinge the British, to the greater glory of France and her restoration as the first power of Europe. But the Bourbon kings of France and Spain had to be sold the idea, and both were averse to entering a conspiracy with rebels who might one day stir nasty repercussions in the empires of their royal sponsors.

Vergennes therefore disguised his motives, pretending that he sought only to embroil England in America, not to assure an American victory, which, he agreed, might have dangerous effects. He counseled covert aid to Americans and an ostensible air of cool correctness toward England.

In August 1776, however, with Deane in Paris and the news of the Declaration of Independence freshly arrived from the French ambassador in London, Vergennes felt emboldened to take the wraps off his strategy. He went before the King and Council and called for an open alliance with the Americans, even at the risk of war with England. He carried the day against very little opposition, and a messenger was sent off to win the approval of Uncle Charles in Madrid. Just at that moment, however, dispatches arrived from America telling of the rout of Washington's forces on Long Island. Thereupon, Vergennes fell back on the cumbersome policy of sending secret aid to America—aid that was of course no secret at all to Lord Stormont and the British Secret Service.

The arrival of Franklin seemed to Vergennes to compensate for the fiasco on Long Island. A man who could stir the hearts of the ladies of the Court, and the minds of the Académie, as well as the spirits of peasants, milliners, tradesmen, and soldiers, was precisely the sort of battering ram that Vergennes needed to break down the resistance of his monarch. Thus it was that Louis felt the pressure growing and petulantly tried to exorcise the American spirit with a chamber pot.

Into this tangled web Franklin stepped gingerly. His original mandate was summed up in the "Plan of 1776," devised by the members of Congress, those whom a contemporary called "their highnesses, the Princes of the Wilderness." These men were insulated by an ocean from the realities of Europe. The plan called for the rights of each nation to trade. Let there be an end to restrictive tariffs, it declared, and even in wartime let neutral shipping use the ports of belligerents so long as they brought only food, naval stores, and the ordinary products of a free commerce. The only prohibited articles would be those plainly designed for war. It was a plan derived from European models, formulated by neutral commercial nations with small navies. It was aimed at England, whose warships prowled all the sea lanes and who saw no reason to blink the reality that food, clothing, and commerce are factors in the warmaking potential of a nation, hence subject to blockade.

Franklin and Deane were originally confined to the Plan of 1776, but as military catastrophes succeeded one another in America, they were given freer rein to entangle their country, albeit with bonds of cobweb fragility, in the ambitions of Europe. Following the invasion of New York State by Burgoyne, Richard Henry Lee wrote to his brother Arthur in London that independence itself would be doomed without an alliance with France and Spain, one sweetened by a massive loan. Gloomily Arthur Lee read the news to Franklin and Deane at Passy.

Congress underscored the doleful report of the Lees by suggesting that almost any inducement Franklin might make would be acceptable if it brought French and Spanish help. Franklin then formulated a grand scheme for a Triple Alliance—the two Bourbon absolute monarchs and the American rebels, whose rhetoric had challenged the far gentler tyranny of the British Parliament.

The proposal called upon France to join with the United States in the "conquest of Canada, Nova Scotia, Newfoundland, St. John's, the Floridas, Bermuda, Bahama and all the West India Islands." In return for thus driving the British from the American continent, the United States would concede to France half of the Newfoundland fisheries and those "Sugar Islands" of the Caribbean which France already held. The rest of the continent would go to the United States. Spain would also enter the war effort, in return for which the United States would declare war on Portugal and fight for the "Conquest of that Kingdom, to be added to the Dominion of Spain."

Furthermore, each of the three would bind themselves to make no separate peace until all their objectives were won or by mutual consent. All this and the profits of the American trade were laid on Vergennes's table.

For the conquest of the Caribbean, Franklin and Deane offered on the part of the United States to put up two million dollars. But in a postscript they asked for a loan of two million sterling, to be secured by a 300-square-mile parcel of Indian land on the shores of the Ohio or Mississippi rivers.

France was given a very short time for consideration, and it was indicated that if the answer was negative or dilatory, the Americans, wishing "for nothing so much as Peace & Liberty," might make their peace with Britain. That was the only weapon in the American diplomatic arsenal.

The document must stand as a monument of boldness or of desperation. Franklin and Deane could scarcely be said to represent a country. It was rather a loose confederation of quarreling ex-colonies, with a determination that still spun like a weathervane and an army not much better than a militia, which had fled from Long Island, was routed from Philadelphia, and had been ignominiously driven from Canada. It was this government, up to its ears in debt and clamoring for fresh loans, that now asked the kings of France and Spain to win an empire for it. It was this minuscule power with a well-publicized aversion to participating in Europe's quarrels that was offering to lend its services for the conquest of Portugal.

To Louis Bourbon it must have seemed as if his *valet de chambre* was offering to buy Versailles if His Most Christian Majesty would be so kind as to lend him the money.

Still, the threat of an Anglo-American reconciliation that would leave Britain supreme in Europe and on the seas was formidable enough to give Vergennes pause. He declined to swallow the bait but continued to play at the end of the line.

The Spanish ambassador to France, the Count de Aranda, seemed delighted with the proposal, as he would with any notion that could frustrate England and drive its flag forever from America. Unfortunately, the Count de Aranda was almost wholly without influence in Madrid. Actually he was not so much an ambassador in Paris as an exile, sent there to keep him out of the way of Spanish politics. In his eagerness to please Americans he suggested a secret mission to Madrid, and Arthur Lee was chosen for the assignment. Franklin suspected that the mission was doomed, whoever was chosen. The secrecy was blown before Lee left Paris. He was met at Burgos by the Marquis de Grimaldi, Spain's Prime Minister, who urged him not to go further into a Spain unwilling as yet even to acknowledge the existence of a rebel government in America. Grimaldi, it is said, sweetened his advice by hinting at a secret Spanish loan that might be forthcoming if Lee would pursue his diplomacy by a tactful retreat.

Grimaldi had been pro-American until the retreat on Long Island. He cooled perceptibly after the Americans began to seem a very bad risk. In a memorandum to Aranda designed to damp down that enthusiastic but powerless diplomat, he had written: "The rights of all sovereigns to their respective territories ought to be regarded as sacred, and the example of a rebellion is too dangerous to allow of His Majesty's wishing to assist it openly."

Actually it was not only the pernicious example of rebellion that alarmed the Spanish Court. It was also the fact that Americans had had a very high birth rate and a long-established willingness to make war. Those traits, which could be expected to grow stronger with the nourishment of nationalism, would make them unpleasant neighbors on the American continent. "I think that we should be the last country in all Europe to recognize *any* sovereign and independent state in North America," wrote the Marquis de Castejón of the Spanish Royal Council. Moreover, he pointed out, the Americans would probably always remain pro-English, would probably combine with the former Mother Country, and in that case, "the kingdom of Mexico would be compromised, in fact lost."

Grimaldi, whose Italian ancestry made him unpopular with the more insular courtiers in Madrid, was forced out in the spring of 1778 and replaced by the more astute and wily Don José Moñino y Redondo, Count de Floridablanca.

The courtier Aranda lost little time in mending his fences. In a letter to Floridablanca he recalled how distasteful it had been to serve under a man who could not pronounce Spanish correctly. "Thank God we are all now one." To Aranda, Floridablanca urged a policy of *"disimulo y la Frescura"*—cool and deceptive.

Although there was much to be said for humbling England, Spain was not yet ready for war, Floridablanca felt. Moreover, it would not do to risk war while gold-laden Spanish galleons were still on the high seas from America. Finally, he made it clear to Vergennes, the Americans must be placed under some control if they should win their independence. He suggested that they be coaxed into the conviction that only France and Spain could guarantee their independence once it was secured so that they might accept treaties of amity and commerce that would dilute their independence with wholesome restraint. Otherwise the Bourbon kings might have to face a power in America more troublesome than England.

Vergennes, whether out of conviction or tact, agreed with the Spanish analysis but thought the Americans in Paris too cagey to exchange the status of a colony for one of a permanent dependency on the Bourbons. "Ready enough to enter into the closest kind of union if the two crowns would consent to war, they are apparently determined to decline any other sort of diplomatic connection," he noted. "I have had more than one occasion to observe that their art looks not only to interesting us in their cause, but also to compromising us with England." Still, he agreed to see if Franklin and Deane would "nibble at that bait."

Franklin declined to nibble. He accurately gauged the dilemma of Vergennes and Floridablanca and their respective Bourbons. He felt that war between England and France was inevitable, that an Anglo-American rapprochement was anathema to France and Spain, that the consummation of an alliance of some sort with France needed only time and a signal from America that the rebels could break their string of defeats. He saw no point in compromising the post-independence course of America.

In September he reported to Congress that the French Court "privately professes a real friendship, wishes success to our cause, winks at the supplies we obtain here as much as it can without giving grounds of complaint to England, privately affords us very essential aids and goes on preparing for war. How long these two parts will continue to be acted at the same time, and which will finally predominate, may be a question."

Franklin kept up a brave front, trying to gloss over the gloomy news from the fighting front with quips. When told of the reports that Howe had taken Philadelphia, he said, "I beg your pardon, sir, Philadelphia has taken Howe." He could only hope that the city would be a trap for the British.

He fought the war at dinner parties, winning the day with the free-thinking libertarians by joining a French Masonic lodge. (The Freemasons were popular with revolutionaries, liberals, and children of the new Enlightenment.) He attended balls and showed himself at the Comédie, to the delight of the Paris crowds, though he could only with difficulty follow Molière's French. He sought to dispel the gloom cast by Lee and Deane, who foresaw the collapse of all their efforts, all their bargaining, wheedling, bribing, smuggling. In vain had Deane ordered a pair of Narrotoheganset horses and an American-made phaeton for Marie Antoinette, who, as he wrote to John Jay, "is fond of parade, and I believe wishes a war, and is our friend." In vain seemed all the American walnuts, butternuts, and apples they had distributed among the courtiers of France.

On November 27, Deane suggested that the commissioners tell Vergennes that they must have an immediate alliance or they would at once open negotiations with England. It would sound too much like an ultimatum, Franklin warned, and, in any case, it did not reflect the reality. America might fight on without help from abroad. Lee worried about the possible effect of too much boldness on the French Court, which might cut off all aid. It was plain to them all that a record of military defeats is not the firmest ground on which to take a heroic stand. A change of fortune in America could give them more solid footing in France.

The three-week lag between events and the report of them in Europe was nerve-wracking. How could one act diplomatically not knowing what news might be traveling across the Atlantic? On December 4, word came that an American packet had put in at Nantes with dispatches for the commission. Chaumont and Beaumarchais came to Passy to keep the vigil with the three Americans. When the coach bearing the messenger, young Jonathan Loring Austin, rattled into the courtyard, all five went down to meet him. All that was needed was one victory; a reliable report that Philadelphia had not been taken would do the trick. Austin shook his head. Philadelphia was indeed in British hands, but "I have greater news than that—General Burgoyne and his whole army are prisoners of war."

Actually Franklin's whistling-in-the-dark dinner-party quip about Philadelphia having taken Howe had proved accurate. Lord Germain, who was presiding over the American Department at Whitehall, had masterminded a plan for the sure destruction of the rebels. If carried out it might well have accomplished the purpose. Gentleman Johnny Burgoyne was to sweep down from the north. Howe was to come up the Hudson from the south. They were to meet in Albany, cutting off New England from her sister states and leaving the divided country to be mopped up at leisure. The difficulty was that the armchair general Germain scarcely bothered with the problems of terrain and, what was worse, seemed to suffer from an almost unbelievable lapse of memory.

Burgoyne, having picked up his orders in London, proceeded with his Hessian, Indian, and British troops to put the plan into execution. He competently fought his way down from Canada through hundreds of miles of forest and mountain, amid difficulties scarcely comprehensible in a London drawing room.

General William Howe had meanwhile conceived of a plan of his own: capture the capital, Philadelphia, and demoralize the rebels. Unaccountably, Germain told him to go ahead, disregarding the role he was to play in the grand strategy so carefully outlined to Burgoyne. In due course and with very little trouble, Howe took Philadelphia, routing Washington and his ragged troops. He was confident that he had won a great victory, and secure in the belief that London had authorized his mission, presumably canceling that crucial appointment far up the Hudson Valley. When Burgoyne, wearied by the long trek, reached Saratoga, just north of Albany, he found, instead of Howe, the American army of Horatio Gates and Benedict Arnold, vastly outnumbering the British and newly supplied with guns and munitions from one of Beaumarchais's ships, the *Amphitrite*, which had run the British blockade and landed at Portsmouth, New Hampshire.

Thanks in large part to the dash and generalship of Arnold (who fell wounded in the battle), the Americans forced Burgoyne to surrender everything—his troops, artillery, equipment.

Congress was then meeting disconsolately at York, Pennsylvania, surrounded by unfriendly German settlers whom John Adams described as "a breed of mongrels or neutrals, and benumbed with a general torpor." A three-day rain swamped the delegates and some worried that the surrender terms made on the field of battle would prove too generous.

Adams, however, greeted the victory rhapsodically. "The news lifted us up to the stars," he wrote. The grumpy delegates proclaimed a day of "public thanksgiving."

Europe, too, resounded with the news from the Hudson Valley. In the coffeehouses of London the question was asked: "Who will replace Lord North?" And the answer: "The first hackney coachman in the street." In Paris, Vergennes knew that this was the moment to win Louis to a policy of alliance with the rebels, and so decide the war. He waited to see whether Louis's uncle in Madrid had sniffed the change in the wind.

At Passy celebration and diplomacy had to wait on some private business. Beaumarchais dashed off to London to apply the victory of Saratoga to some stock-market trading before the news became too generally known. (Excited by the political and commercial possibilities, he drove at such a rate that his carriage flipped over on the road. He suffered an arm injury but still reached London in time to cash in.) Bancroft also interrupted his assiduous spying at Passy with a quick trip to the London market. He tried to cut out his fellow American in the British Secret Service, Paul Wentworth, who nevertheless heard the news in time for a quick speculative stock maneuver.

To King George this scurrying of his agents to cash in on state intelligence was unseemly. Buying up Members of Parliament seemed to him a gentleman's game, but lining one's pockets as a sideline of diplomacy was a tradesman's gambit. It deepened his loathing of the tools he had to use, such as Bancroft, whom he described as "entirely an American." He could say no worse of any of his agents. With Louis he shared a certain respect for the etiquette of kings and wished the game could be played without the moneygrubbers. He was particularly irritated with Wentworth and Bancroft because they had the effrontery of being proved correct in their warnings of the possibility of an open French alliance with the American rebels, a prospect the King had dismissed as absurd whenever the reports of his spies pointed in that direction. Now George, like Lord North and all the politicians of Britain, was engaged in an urgent reassessment of colonial and foreign policy.

Franklin and his team at Passy proceeded to complicate that reappraisal by playing the kings of Europe as if they were pawns.

The game that was to prove decisive for the Revolution lasted two months. This is the fateful chronology:

December 6, 1777: King Louis authorizes Vergennes to convey officially the royal nod of approval to the Americans, and to indicate that the Bourbon kings of France and Spain would favor a proper understanding with the rebels. No commitments, he cautions. Only encouragement.

December 7: Franklin and Deane spend the afternoon at Passy preparing a note to Vergennes suggesting no more than a treaty of "amity and commerce." Arthur Lee is asked to draft a similar note to the Spanish ambassador, Aranda.

December 8: Sir George Grand comes to dinner at Passy. He is a banker of tangled international connections: a naturalized Frenchman who sports a British title and acts as the political and commercial partner of the Americans. He has just received a note from Vergennes in which he reads a subtle augury of success. The precise but cautious Foreign Minister in his correspondence with the banker had always referred to the American envoys as "your friends." Now, in his first communication since the news of Saratoga reached Europe, he uses the expression "our friends." Franklin and Deane dwell upon that change of pronoun as a man might scrutinize the slightest lift of a woman's eyebrows for a promise of things to come.

December 10: Conrade Gérard, Vergennes's secretary, calls at Passy to congratulate the Americans on their victory at Saratoga. Now, he suggests, would be the time to formulate the American proposals for a treaty. Franklin writes out in organized form his draft of a commercial treaty and sends his grandson Temple with it to Vergennes at Versailles. Vergennes reads it while the young man waits, then tells him: "In two days an answer shall be sent to you and you will see how much disposed I am to serve the cause of America." The mood at Passy grows euphoric.

December 12: The three American commissioners—the aging Franklin, his disciple Deane, and the austere and aloof Lee—climb into a carriage that takes them in the direction of Versailles. Before they reach the town they alight and wait for a coach dispatched by the Foreign Ministry to take them to a rendezvous presumably hidden from the eyes of Stormont's agents. At a private house half a mile from Versailles, they find Vergennes and Gérard waiting for them. Vergennes is all smiles but finds the American concentration on a commercial treaty a bit disingenuous. Obviously there must be political implications. Franklin demurs. He says he sees no necessity for France to be embroiled in war, though he knows that for the American cause this is a consummation devoutly to be wished.

Vergennes calls for Franco-American ties that "would have all the solidity of human institutions." Franklin is wary, but the conference ends in the greatest cordiality. Nothing can be done, however, Vergennes makes clear, without the active assistance of Spain, for Louis will not move without his uncle Charles. And the Americans must be prepared to fix a boundary between themselves and the Spanish colonies. Remember, warns Vergennes, the independence of the United States is "yet in the womb." Vergennes promises to dispatch an urgent message to Madrid; they can expect to hear a reply by courier in three weeks' time.

December 15: Paul Wentworth, the New Hampshireman who turned British agent in the hope of a baronetcy, asks for a dinner dialogue with Franklin but must take Deane instead. England has sent him to sound out Franklin on a possible reconciliation to forestall the French alliance. He tells Deane that the British now see the war as a tragic mistake, that they are willing to repeal all the laws passed since 1763 to which the Americans object, and to go back to the halcyon days when Englishmen on both sides of the water could harmoniously harry the French and carry on the booming trade of yore. If Deane would promote this happy ending, he would have not only the "honor of pointing out the mode and means of salvation" but more tangible rewards. Cooperative Americans, Wentworth continued, might become "Governors General, Privy Seals, Great Seals, Treasurers, Secretaries, Councilors, local Barons and Knights."

Deane offers not the slightest encouragement.

December 16: Wentworth repeats the performance with the same results. He is baffled. He has tried to persuade his superiors that "the highest degree of political profligacy already prevails [in America] and perhaps a well-timed offer of indemnity and impunity to these Cromwells and Barebones may serve, like a strong alkali, to reduce the effervescence in the mass of the people, or turn their fury on their misleaders." Now in a disconsolate dispatch he calls Deane "vain, desultory, and subtle," unaccountably impervious to offers of "honours and emoluments."

While Deane dines with Wentworth, Franklin activates the grapevine so that all Paris will know that England is seeking to negotiate with the Americans. It is Franklin's spur to Versailles, and it has its effect. In vain Stormont lets it be known that Wentworth is a private traveler and presents him as such to the King. Vergennes has already had Wentworth to dinner to study the specimen more closely. Still, to offset the British approach he sends Gérard to visit Deane again and "make glitter before his eyes all that may be needed to keep the delegation in the lap of France."

December 17: Gérard "glitters" at Passy as per instructions. Even before hearing from Spain, he tells Deane, France has decided to recognize the American republic, requiring nothing more than an ironclad pledge to fight until independence from Britain is won.

December 18–31: The fate of the Franco-American alliance is being worked out not in Passy or Versailles but in Vienna, Berlin, St. Petersburg, and Madrid. At the Pardo Palace the young French ambassador, Count Armand de Montmorin, confronts the choleric Spanish Prime Minister, Floridablanca. Montmorin has come with firm instructions from Vergennes to convince Spain of the motto: *"Aut nunc aut numquam"* —now or never. His mission is to persuade the Spanish Court that posterity would never forgive the Bourbon kings if they neglected "the most interesting conjecture that heaven could present us" in which to humble England.

He finds Floridablanca fuming because he has just heard from the overenthusiastic and somewhat impolitic Aranda that France is already dickering with the Americans. "To negotiate with the Americans and to declare war is one and the same thing. . . . They have always wanted to compromise our position with the English," Floridablanca thunders. There is no need to recognize the rebels. They are already committed to independence and the British are committed against it. Better to give the Americans money and let them both destroy each other. Soothed by Montmorin and pressed to say what circumstances might move Spain to support the Americans, Floridablanca says that King Charles is the stumbling block. "You cannot easily change the mind of a sixty-two-year-old king who has had his head stuffed with Don Quixotism." It is a charming characteristic, says Montmorin, but "sometimes dangerous on the throne."

And from the middle of Europe comes the threat of a land war that may distract France from the American adventure. The aging Elector of Bavaria, Maximilian Joseph, is dying. Fredrick II of Prussia and King Louis's mother-in-law, Maria Theresa of Austria, wait to pounce, each waving texts of ancient claims to that land. The Tsarina Catherine, yearning to be called Great, is raising an army in Galicia to keep the Austrian Hapsburgs in their place. On such affairs does the fate of the Franco-American alliance hang and the fate of the United States as well. Some Englishmen, at least, feed their hopes. "Perhaps," writes the Duke of Marlborough to William Eden, "the Elector of Bavaria's death may be of use to us by setting the gentlemen upon the continent at variance."

In the end Vergennes decides that the prestige of France and the armies of Russia may be depended upon to keep Europe's peace and allow him to take up the cause of American independence and the ultimate defeat of England.

December 31: Official word comes from Madrid that Spain is not ready for war. It is a bleak New Year's Eve at Passy. Franklin must prod the

French into going it alone and he can only do so by another threat of Anglo-American reconciliation. The means for such a display are at hand.

Genial, honest James Hutton, sixty-two-year-old head of the Moravian missions, a man who holds all war in horror and a friend of Franklin's London days, is in Paris. He carries messages from the frantic Lord North, who will use any road to Franklin's good graces. Hutton, who used to charm Franklin with pleasant philosophical discourse and plans to convert Pennsylvania to the Moravian creed, is invited to Passy. There he spends two hours earnestly seeking to convince Franklin that the Americans may have anything from England—except independence. Franklin's reply verges on the frivolous, if one may judge by the summation he makes in a letter to Hutton after his departure. He advises England to send all its war leaders into disgrace, drop "all pretensions to govern," and "throw in" Canada, Nova Scotia, and the Floridas as "an indemnification for the burning of [American] towns." The flip tone of Franklin's defiance is not leaked into the Paris grapevine.

January 1, 1778: Vergennes ponders three urgent messages: The banker Sir George Grand reports that Franklin has held a "very animated" conversation with Hutton. "If this is still another emissary [from England] I regard him as the most dangerous of all." He adds his hope that Franklin will not be "converted" by the missionary. From Beaumarchais comes a note reporting Hutton's arrival, urging Vergennes to be on guard. "As you see, I do not keep too bad a vigil myself," he notes. And from Chaumont, Franklin's landlord: "M. Hutton, a Moravian leader of superior cunning and an integrity beyond all doubt, a favorite of the King of England, has come to Paris to confer with his old and intimate friend, Dr. Franklin." He assures Vergennes that Franklin will stand fast and asks him to keep the information secret, for Franklin does not know of Chaumont's letter.

All Paris seems to be chattering the "secret" of Hutton's visit. Is this because Franklin is surrounded by spies or does he use his friends to play on Vergennes's nerves? Now still another tool lies ready for Franklin. Wentworth, the frustrated loyalist, still waits in Paris desperately hankering to see him. He will come to Passy at the crook of Benjamin Franklin's finger.

January 6: Wentworth comes to dinner at Passy. Only one condition has been laid down for the talks: there is to be no suggestion of bribery. The setting is deliberately undiplomatic. Wentworth finds Franklin playing the grandfather role, and talk must be delayed until young Benjamin Franklin Bache is trundled off to bed. The dialogue goes very well at the start, as Wentworth is to note in a report: "I introduced the conversation by some compliments to which he is very open." After that the interview is all downhill. Wentworth recalls the recommendations for a united and loyal empire which Franklin himself made so eloquently a few years ago. If they were accepted then, it might have averted the war, says Franklin, but all he got for his pains was his own humiliation. This puts him in mind of far greater "barbarities" wreaked upon his country, and he flies into a towering rage. "I never knew him so eccentric," Wentworth notes. Wentworth produces a secret letter from Eden, whose sweet tone prompts Franklin to remark acidly that he is "glad to find honour and zeal so close to the throne" if not precisely in it. But to Eden's warning that Britain is prepared to fight for ten years to prevent American independence, Franklin tells Wentworth: "Americans are ready to fight for fifty years to win it."

The mood changes abruptly when Deane enters the room at dinnertime. There is a foursome at the table: the American envoys Franklin and Deane facing Wentworth, the known British agent, and Edward Bancroft, the spy still under wraps. The talk is lighthearted. Franklin and Deane lay odds that America will win her independence, that Vandalia —that cherished land of Franklin's speculations—will yet be "a paradise on earth," and that their good French friends will one day join them in America.

January 7: Vergennes's agents report a meeting between Franklin and Wentworth, and the minister is disturbed because Franklin himself has not seen fit to inform him of it. At the meeting of the Royal Council, Vergennes calls for an immediate and decisive commitment to a treaty of alliance with America that will confer recognition and all the commercial rights desired by the Americans. In a separate pact, to become operative in case of war, the Americans would be committed irretrievably to independence, to safeguard French rights in the West Indies, and to leave the way open for Spanish adherence. He wins the Council's unanimous approval.

January 8: At six in the evening, Gérard meets with the three American commissioners at Deane's apartment in Paris. Gérard poses two questions: (1) "What is necessary to be done to give such satisfaction to the American commissioners as to engage them not to listen to any propositions from England for a new connection with that country?" and (2) What could induce a similar stiffening of the spirit in the Congress and the American people? Gérard waits in the anteroom for a written answer. While Deane and Lee talk, Franklin writes his draft. He has time only to discuss the first answer before Gérard returns. Gérard is on the point of leaving when Deane asks him to read Franklin's reply: "The commissioners have long since proposed a treaty of amity and commerce which is not yet concluded. The immediate conclusion of that treaty will remove the uncertainty they are under with regard to it, and give them such a reliance on the friendship of France as to reject firmly all propositions made to them of peace from England which have not for their basis the entire freedom and independence of America, both in matters of government and commerce."

The response is all Gérard needs. He can wait for the second question to be answered later. Gérard announces that France is prepared to grant both treaties at once. Under questioning by Franklin, Gérard dismisses any thought that France might seek to monopolize the American trade as a reward for her aid. His Most Christian Majesty, Gérard declares, is "too great, too just, and too generous" to take unfair advantage of the hard-pressed Americans. America will be able to trade with any country on terms equal to those given France. The American idea of running the nation like a country store would be thus honored.

Gérard hedges on Franklin's proposal that France conquer Canada for the benefit of the United States. He is aware that Vergennes rather fancies the notion of a British presence in America to keep these bumptious rebels in line.

Beyond the agreement to leave French possessions in the West Indies untouched, Gérard disclaims all other territorial interests in America. It seems to Franklin a very low price to pay for French aid. On Spain, however, Gérard can make no commitment. On that score the Americans must wait. "The deputies applauded this recital in a sort of transport," Gérard notes.

January 11: Deane transmits to Gérard the commissioners' answer to his second query. The American people and Congress will turn their backs on England if France either enters the war or furnishes the backing for the American war effort and guarantees that when victory comes the United States will remain in possession of all the continent it can conquer with French help.

January 22: Lord Stormont calls on Vergennes, as he has done repeatedly in recent weeks, to protest warlike preparations in France. He is completely informed on the negotiations between Vergennes and the Americans but dares not press the question lest he get the answer and thus precipitate the war he fears. Vergennes knows that British agents have already picked up a story that the second answer of the Americans regarding Congress is a bit stiff and that Lee is lukewarm about it. Vergennes also ponders the rumors afloat in Paris that Lee is a British agent and that England is considering a 500,000-guinea bribe to members of Congress to wean that body away from ratification. And so they fence, neither wishing to go beyond the customary exchanges over minor issues.

January 28: Lee and Izard are storming between Paris and Passy. They mistrust the eagerness of Franklin and Deane for an alliance with France. Izard complains that he was not consulted and demands to review the entire treaty and all the negotiations. How, at this moment, can Franklin and Deane exempt West Indian molasses from duty? Do they not know that he was instructed to negotiate with the Grand Duke of Tuscany (if he can ever get there) on the molasses question? Franklin agrees that he will ask Vergennes to reconsider the molasses clause in the commercial treaty and let the question be decided by Congress.

January 29: At the Pardo Palace, Montmorin presents a message from Louis to Charles informing him of the impending Franco-American alliance and expressing his hope that uncle and nephew might be joined in the enterprise for the greater glory of the family. Floridablanca can scarcely speak. He trembles with rage, the French ambassador notes. When he recovers from the blow he tells Montmorin: "You think this moment a most auspicious one for the two crowns; I think it the most fatal for Spain; but it would be the fairest day of my life if the King would let me retire."

King Charles receives the news mournfully but expresses affection for his nephew. It is now too late to do anything because Vergennes— through oversight or design—has sat upon the message for several days before dispatching it. Whatever Charles's answer might be it will not come in time to prevent the signing, set for February 5.

February 5: The three American commissioners arrive at the Ministry of Foreign Affairs to put their signatures to the treaty, but find that Gérard has a bad cold and begs to be excused.

February 6: The commissioners are again at the ministry and all is ready, including Gérard. The ubiquitous Bancroft is on hand, noting that Franklin is unbecomingly attired in an old suit of brown velvet. When he is asked about his suit, the doctor smiles and says that it adds a note of revenge to the proceedings. It is the very suit he wore on January 29, 1774, when he stood in the Cockpit at Whitehall and heard himself denounced and humiliated by the Solicitor General while members of the Privy Council jeered.

The treaties are yet to be proclaimed by the King of France and ratified by Congress. Spain must be brought around. Lee and Izard must be appeased. It is plain that a diplomatic coup is a highly perishable flower if it is worn in the buttonhole. It is meaningful only if it can furnish seed for further victories. Troubled England, it seems to Franklin, is fertile ground for seeding. Using Bancroft as a courier, he sends a flurry of notes to his friends in and out of Parliament to make political hay in the sunshine of the new alliance so that Britain's will to war might be weakened. Peace between England and an independent America might yet be possible and not inconsistent with the obligations so recently entered into with France.

Four days after the signing of the treaties with France, Franklin writes: "America has been forced and driven into the arms of France. She was a dutiful and virtuous daughter. A cruel mother-in-law turned her out of doors, defamed her and sought her life. All the world knows her innocence, and takes her part; and her friends hope soon to see her honorably married."

While waiting for a marriage to be consummated it does no harm to look about for other offers.

V

THE GREAT TRANSATLANTIC RACE
TO WOO AMERICA

To FREDERICK LORD NORTH the news of Saratoga came like the tolling of a funeral bell to a hypochondriac. Physically, mentally, and politically, the King's First Minister had known few seasons of reassuring good health. Even on bright days he was aware of clouds to come. And when they came he begged to be relieved of his martyrdom.

North bore like a cross the personal loyalty he owed to George III. The King had bailed him out of debt and they had known each other as children. (The two boys when they played together were said to be so much alike as to suggest a common paternity.) Now the King, even with all his infirmities, cut the better figure by far. North, paunchy, with quivering fleshy jowls and protuberant eyes that rolled in excitement, was not an attractive leader. Still, he could fence with some adroitness in parliamentary debate and he had mastered the skills of the factional game. His prime attribute, however, was that he stood almost alone on the political horizon as a man of unquestioned devotion to the King. George therefore leaned upon him. The difficulty was that North tended to collapse under the royal weight, so that the King had constantly to support his staunchest supporter.

In a flow of memoranda to the King, Lord North regularly closed by urging a change of Prime Ministers. He pleaded ill health, incompetence, and the need for a government based on "a broader bottom," one that might include the Whig opposition. That heterogeneous band of dissident politicians opposed His Majesty's government chiefly on constitutional grounds. They were anxious to reassert the prerogatives of Parliament against the royal itch to rule. On the American question, however, the gap was closing rapidly between Whig and Tory. The probability that disaffected English colonists were joining with the Bourbon powers in league against England drove even the staunchest pro-Americans into a tight corner. While they could not sanction independence, they demanded an investigation of the war, denounced the use of Indian forces, and in other ways gave what comfort they could to the rebels. The Americans responded by heaping their abuse on the King instead of Parliament, a reversal of the attitude that had prevailed some five years earlier.

The administration was spared a full-fledged parliamentary investigation into the fiasco at Saratoga by the death of Lord Germain's wife and the unwillingness of the gentlemen of the opposition to break in upon his bereavement with a demand for explanations. Burgoyne was on his way home to tell his side of the story. (Consistent with the antique gallantry of those days, the Americans had returned the vanquished Burgoyne's sword to him instead of breaking it, and Washington had freed him from imprisonment to go back to England on his word that he would return if summoned. His troops were to be shipped home as well if they promised that they would not fight Americans again. Eighteenth-century honor countenanced bribery and profiteering but not the breaking of a promise.)

A panicky reappraisal was going on throughout Britain. North wrote to the King that "a pacifick proposition" appeared necessary but that the best he could think of was a measure repealing almost every bit of legislation to which the Americans had ever objected and a promise to negotiate any other grievance they might have. He doubted, however, that this would wean them away from their obsession with outright independence. In all of which he saw "additional proof . . . of his [North's] incapacity for the high and important office in which he is placed . . . whatever he does must be attended with some disgrace, and much misery to himself, and, what is worse, perhaps with some detriment to the public. In this case perhaps a change . . ."

Two days later the King tried to glue together his crumbling Prime Minister. He argued against proposals that might be too sweeping. This

position, he insisted, did not stem from "any absurd ideas of unconditional submission [by the Americans] which my mind never harboured."
Concessions, he said, would not appease the Americans, now glowing in
the hope of open French support, and would only "dissatisfy this country
[Britain] which has in the most handsome manner cheerfully carried on
the contest, and therefore has a right to have the struggle continued, until
convinced that it is in vain."

Within days, however, the King had second thoughts about the struggle. No doubt the warnings of war with the Bourbons flooding in from
Bancroft worried him, though he continued to look down his nose at the
spy. ("He is certainly a stock jobber and is not friendly to England.") On
February 6, Wentworth and Stormont reported—in a dispatch marked
"most secret"—that a Franco-American alliance had actually been
signed. And three days later the King's tone reflected the urgency of the
hour:

"The intelligence communicated by Mr. Wentworth if certain, shews
the veil will soon be drawn off by the Court of France, which makes me
wish you would not delay bringing your American Proposition . . . into
the House of Commons; and should a French war be our fate, I trust you
will concur with me in the only means of making it successful, the
withdrawing the greatest part of the troops from America and employing
them against the French and Spanish Settlements but if we are to be
carrying on a Land War against the Rebels and against these two Powers
it must be feeble in all parts and consequently unsuccessful."

The formal signing of the pact between the rebels and France was still
a top secret when the House of Commons met on February 17, 1778, in a
chamber jammed to the doors. Only the King, the Cabinet, and those
whom Franklin had alerted knew for certain that the alliance had been
made. Shortly before the start of the crisis session, Horace Walpole and
his cousin Thomas, Franklin's friend, whispered to the pro-American
opposition leader Charles Fox that the treaty had been signed.

North spoke for two hours, beginning with a humble expiation for past
misjudgments and closing with a proposal of two bills that would send
peace commissioners to America. These would be empowered to treat
with Congress "as if it were a legal body," and with Washington or any
other officer. They would be authorized to order a truce, suspend all
existing laws to which the Americans objected, and grant "all sorts of
pardons, immunities and rewards." Parliament would acknowledge its
willingness to give up the right to tax, and consider accepting American
MPs in the Commons. All leaders elected by the Americans since the
Declaration of Independence would be confirmed in office by British law.

To the landed gentry, worried as ever about taxes, North held out the hope that Americans might voluntarily vote to contribute a share of the burden. In short, anything for peace, except outright independence. If these proposals had come before the spring of 1775, there would have been no skirmishing at Lexington and Concord. If they had come before the summer of 1776, there would have been no Declaration of Independence. If they had come before the autumn of 1777, there would have been no French alliance and very likely no war, and the world would have seen the first prototype of a dominion within the British Empire.

Now these propositions, exceeding all the concessions the most rabid pro-American had ever envisaged in ten years of mounting crisis, appeared to the Commons to betray some deep unknown anxiety in the government. "A dull melancholy silence" gripped the House when North had finished.

Then Fox rose to hurl his bombshell, furnished indirectly by Franklin through the Walpoles: Was it not true that American agents had signed a treaty with France within the last ten days? And if so did it not follow that the incompetent North administration had again been beaten by events? Now it was adopting a course the opposition had urged before history had nullified its effect. Lord North was quiet until from the opposition benches came cries of "An answer, an answer."

His reply came haltingly. Yes, he had heard reports that the pact had been signed, but they were not official. They might be later denied, as other such rumors had been denied by the ministers of France. He could give no more explicit answer.

The opposition could criticize the timing but not the very measures they had long advocated. In London's political salons the gossip hummed. At Lady Gower's dinner table, Lord Mansfield bluntly affirmed that the ministers were lying; they knew that the treaty had been signed. Lady Elizabeth Montagu, a cousin of North's, whose home was a fashionable political arena, noted: "Strange things have happened this week. The Ministers are gone over to the American side."

Horace Walpole called it a day of "confession and humiliation." He declared that North had gone so far as to sanction even independence, "not verbally, yet virtually."

Though there were grounds for such an interpretation, North, in the days and weeks that followed, spent considerable time and heat denying it. Having boldly charged forward, he now tiptoed backward. Independence? Never, he assured Parliament. The Americans "must treat as subjects or not at all." He clung to the hope that the treaty with France had not actually been concluded, although Stormont's dispatches from

Paris left only the most minuscule room for doubt: "There is now an almost universal persuasion here, that there does exist some treaty or convention between this Court and the rebels . . . to the best of my judgment and belief, France has signed this treaty of alliance, and consequently thrown the die." At question time in the Commons on March 3, North came closest to admitting the worst: "It is possible, nay too probable," that the dread alliance had been forged. Still, he added, the report "had not been authenticated by the ambassador." To such straws did the King's minister cling. The King sent North off to his country house at Bushy to "recruit his mind."

The country air did little good. North wailed to the King that credit, "the principal source of the greatness and weight of Great Britain," was running out and would be exhausted in two years. He cited the opinion of Israel Mauduit, former agent of Massachusetts, now "one of the most zealous friends of Great Britain," that the Mother Country would be sadly "overmatch'd" in a war with France, Spain, and America. Peace with America, said the Prime Minister, and his own removal from office were "the only steps that could save the country. . . . Lord North's diffidence of himself is grounded upon seven years' experience, and will forever render it fatal to His Majesty to continue him at the head of affairs."

The King, despairing of men weaker than himself, would still not let North off the hook, however he might wriggle there. For the alternative was to turn the country over to the Whigs, and he would rather forfeit the Crown than face that prospect. North sought royal approval for still more missions to Passy to sound out Franklin, despite the failure of the Moravian preacher Hutton. The King in reply spoke of Franklin's "inimical conduct" and "hatred to this country," but added: "Yet I think it so desirable to end the War with that Country [America], to be enabled with redoubled ardor to avenge the faithless and insolent conduct of France that I think it may be proper to keep open the channel of intercourse with that insidious man."

David Hartley, Whig MP and old friend of Franklin, turned up at Passy in April and got nowhere, though the two parted as friends. Hartley left with a warning to Franklin that he was surrounded by spies and in danger. To which Franklin replied: "I thank you for your kind caution, but, having nearly finished a long life, I set but little value on what remains of it. Like a draper, when one chaffers with him for a remnant, I am ready to say: 'As it is only the fag end, I will not differ with you about it; take it for what you please.' Perhaps the best use such a fellow can be put to, is to make a martyr of him."

An Irish MP stopped by for a chat, ostensibly on his way home from Nice, spent an affable hour or two, and went away empty-handed. Franklin reported all these conversations to Vergennes because in any case the French agents could be relied upon to do as much, and an account of the feverish wooing of Britain might be useful in stimulating France's ardor. "On the whole," Franklin wrote to Vergennes, "I gather from these conversations that the opposition, as well as the ministry, are perplexed with the present situation of affairs, and know not which way to turn themselves, or whether it is best to go backward or forward, or what steps to take to extricate that nation from its present dangerous situation."

Another, more mysterious emissary popped an anonymous note into the mansion at Passy suggesting a rendezvous in the Jardin des Eaux under cover of night, an invitation which Franklin declined. A packet of letters and documents was thrown over the gates of Passy by someone who signed himself Charles de Weissenstein. It contained arguments for settlement of the American war, offers of peerages and pensions to all rebel leaders, and proposed a deliciously melodramatic scenario for a meeting in the choir of the Cathedral of Notre Dame. "You will ascertain my friend by his having a paper in his hand as if drawing or taking notes. On any one's coming near him he will either huddle it up precipitately or, folding it up, tear it with an appearance of peevishness, and walk away. At that very altar where he stood, place your packet within reach, or if there is nobody else near, throw it on the ground and walk away instantly." The messenger, who could further be identified by a rose in his hat or buttonhole, would later retrieve Franklin's answer.

Franklin drafted a long and eloquent letter which he did not send to the mysterious stranger but showed to Vergennes and allowed to drift into the propaganda stream. Referring to Weissenstein's suggestion of "Places, Pensions and Peerages," Franklin wrote: "This offer to corrupt us, Sir, is with me your credential and convinces me that you are not a private volunteer in your application. It bears the stamp of British Court character. It is even the signature of your King."

The French secret police showed up for the rendezvous in Notre Dame. There they found a short, thin, tanned, gloomy-looking foreigner scribbling on a paper. They tailed him to the Hôtel de Hambourg, found that his name was Jennings and that he was a captain of the King's Guard. They chronicled his movements. (He walked about the city alone by day and went to the theater in the evening; he dressed in gray, blue, and black, was given to reading posters and dreaming on his solitary walks.) The police did not prevent his return to England. Whether crank, amateur peacemaker, spy, or royal envoy, he served his purpose as an occasion for Franklin's patriotic prose.

Franklin's rebuffs to these and other British overtures cast a pall of doubt over the prospects of the Peace Commission which North was piecing together. For once there was unity of a sort in Parliament but it was a unity of despair. Few thought that the commission could carry much weight in America if Franklin treated their proposals with such scorn. America, secure in the affections of the Bourbons, was hell-bent for independence, and this not even Lord Chatham, the elder Pitt, that longstanding friend of Franklin and America, could stomach.

This hero of the London radicals and erstwhile scourge of George III, now ill and enfeebled, rose on April 7 to curse American independence and pledge his dying breath to the King in crisis. "My lords," he said, "I rejoice that the grave has not yet closed upon me; that I am still alive to lift up my voice against the dismemberment of this ancient and most noble monarchy! . . . My lords, his Majesty succeeded to an empire as great in extent as its reputation was unsullied. Shall we tarnish the lustre of this nation by an ignominious surrender of its rights and fairest posses-sions? Shall this great kingdom that has survived whole and entire the Danish depredations, the Scottish inroads, and the Norman conquest, that has stood the threatened invasion of the Spanish Armada, now fall prostrate before the House of Bourbon? . . . my lords, any state is better than despair. Let us at least make one effort; and if we must fall, let us fall like men!"

His peroration was cut short by a stroke that left him paralyzed. He was carried from the chamber. A fortnight later Chatham was dead.

The grim picture drawn by Chatham was not born of a deathbed apocalyptic vision. Britain suddenly seemed no longer the mistress of the world. It was no formidable tyranny defied by pipsqueak rebellious minutemen, however valiant. It was an isolated island kingdom fighting for its life, knowing that it could not battle simultaneously against ene-mies across the ocean and across the Channel. Moreover, Ireland was setting up a clamor in chorus with America, its Protestants demanding a greater political and economic autonomy, its Catholics hoping for deliv-erance by France. (Beaumarchais was indeed advising his King to land in Ireland.) And an invasion across the Channel was thought by many to be not only possible but imminent. The hostilities begun in Boston might end in England itself.

The Dutch were funneling money to the rebels through Franklin's friend Dumas. Frederick of Prussia was said to be considering aid to

America. Catherine of Russia was going beyond her refusal to let Britain hire her soldiers and was now considering ways and means of breaking the British embargo of American ports in the name of free trade, while taking advantage of the moment to whittle away Britain's interests in the East.

Saratoga seemed to have wakened the people of England and Scotland from a dream of British glory, of the invincibility of British arms, and of unquestionable British prestige. Now they began to look upon the war in a wilderness overseas as a drain of money and lives. They felt its consequences in high taxes and high prices, and saw themselves standing alone against the world.

Some rallied to King and country. Enlistments, particularly in the North, spurted upward. The London Common Council, however, speaking for a more radical constituency, balked at contributing money to send troops overseas so long as "offers of just and honorable terms are withheld from America." And many volunteers for the armed forces stipulated that they would fight only against Europeans, not Americans. For there was, curiously, little popular rancor against those overseas English who might have seemed to be betraying their homeland. Englishmen tended rather to blame their own politicians.

It was now assumed that there would be a commission to carry Britain's terms to America. But those terms had passed through committees and in the process had been largely emasculated. North and Parliament continued their graceless dance, which consisted of a bold step forward followed by two half steps backward. In the end the commission was empowered to do little more than offer pardons to the rebels. John Wilkes sneered that the bills seemed designed only "to keep the minds of the people quiet here." Edmund Burke commented: "What the infatuated Ministry may do I know not; but our infatuated House of Commons, as far as lay in them, have begun a New War on America."

In mid-March, France formally notified England that a commercial treaty had been signed with the Americans. No mention was made of the political treaty to come into force in case of war. There was no need to. Even the most optimistic in England had to accept the likelihood of such a pact. The King clung desperately to the hope that the chronic bickering in America and Passy might yet open a gap in the enemy's lines. Perhaps the peace overtures presently contemplated by Parliament might stretch that gap wide enough to encompass Britain's salvation. North's conciliation bills, as yet unvoted, had been put aboard the *Andromeda* bound for British headquarters in New York. If these reached Congress before the official text of the French treaties, there was a chance that tender messages from an old love might yet forestall a fateful marriage. True, Franklin had already seen the actual bills and dismissed them. (Hartley had rushed a copy of them to Passy as soon as North had introduced them.) Franklin, committed to the French alliance and, by its terms, to unconditional American independence, belittled the proposals, proposals he would eagerly have jumped at a year earlier. Now, he said, they were no more than "little arts and schemes for amusing and dividing us." But America was a month or more behind the news. Congress, without Franklin's advice and lacking certain knowledge of the French alliance, might be more pliable. Such hopes were skimpy fare to feed an embattled empire but they were all there was.

While Parliament debated the bills, grown every day more watery, William Eden, the master of Britain's intelligence system, and Solicitor General Wedderburn scouted the field for potential peacemakers. The most prominent politicians found reasons to evade the assignment, which looked more chancy with every new dilution of its mandate. At last they found a likely prospect: the Earl of Carlisle, a promising young man, not quite thirty, an Eton school chum of Eden's, a dabbler in poetry, a gentlemanly gambler, a cousin of Lord Byron, a friend and gaming companion of Charles Fox, the opposition spokesman. His credentials as a statesman were admittedly slim, but his style was elegant. Acidly, Horace Walpole remarked that he was "very fit to make a treaty that will not be made."

The Howes—both general and admiral—were to serve as well, but those appointments were meant solely to avoid giving offense. To lend the experience of a political heavyweight to the commission, Eden offered himself. He accompanied his offer with protestations that personally he would rather not take the assignment but would do so only if Lord North could find no better, etc., etc. This was taken for pure political ritual and Lord North leaped at his offer, for Eden had a reputation as a negotiator. Thus persuaded, Eden at once put in a bid for £1,000 to cover personal expenses, plus a seat on the Privy Council for all commissioners by way of enhancing their prestige in America. The King, no great admirer of Eden, or any others in the slightly unsavory career of intelligence gathering, balked at both demands. In the end he granted the £1,000 out of the general war budget but turned down the Privy Council notion, reminding both North and Eden that "parade is not the object of the mission, but business."

Franklin's one-time colleague in the Pennsylvania agency, Richard Jackson, "the omniscient," was nominated but at once displayed a total lack of enthusiasm. He told Eden at one evening session of the commission that "it was idle and ruinous to go to war with France . . . that we should proceed immediately to give independence to the colonies . . . that it did not signify when [the commission] arrived and was of no consequence except to satisfy the people of this country." He also demanded the right to withdraw from the commission if Congress should receive it badly. Eden described "the omniscient's" remarks as "a deal of skimble-skamble stuff" and cheerfully set about replacing that "delicate defeatist."

In a vain effort to head off political repercussions, Eden looked for another member of the opposition to replace Jackson, and so hit upon George Johnstone, a man with a history of unmanageability and unpopularity. Despite his opposition credentials, his parliamentary declamations for "liberty," and his American origin, he outdid the North administration in his virulent antipathy to the very notion of American independence. He was therefore disliked by the Americans and their friends in Parliament. He had always proved difficult as an underling (during the Seven Years' War he had to be court-martialed for insubordination); and he was impossible in a position of authority (when he was royal governor of West Florida his staff officers denounced his "cruel treatment" and "tyrannical behavior"). As an MP he had scandalized the House by casting aspersions on the personal courage of Germain and as a result had had to fight a duel (quite bloodless, as it turned out). Horace Walpole characterized him as "brave, brutal, overbearing, litigious and rather clever."

George Johnstone was, in short, the most unlikely candidate for a commission designed to calm the waters. To make matters worse, his brother (who used the name of William Pulteney) had already made two pilgrimages to Passy as yet another suppliant of Franklin's. Somehow, he and Bancroft received the impression of encouragement, though judging by Franklin's subsequent comments there was little or no foundation for such optimism. Johnstone, saddled with his brother's illusions, was thus in a position to compound the commission's troubles.

Moreover, the Carlisle-Eden team had the misfortune to be briefed by that ambitious clergyman-spy Vardill and the would-be baronet Wentworth as experts on America. Vardill steered them to John Jay as a man who could be lured away from the rebellion by the promise of judicial advancement. At one time Vardill had been instrumental in putting Jay on the Crown's payroll and thought he might be grateful. Accordingly, he gave Eden a letter of introduction, which turned out to be worthless. He steered the commission to a list of those he thought to be likely defectors—some of whom had already defected and therefore lost their value. Above all, Vardill advised, offer peerages. He described Americans as lusting after titles and rank.

Wentworth suggested that the commission play on Washington's alleged jealousy of Franklin and the aversion he held for Franklin's republicanism. He thought Samuel Adams worth a try as well. Though he admitted that for that fiercest of rebels "independency was a constant prayer," Samuel Adams was vulnerable, Wentworth thought, because he was ambitious and "an unprincipled man in his morals." If he could be persuaded to act the double agent, Wentworth suggested, he would be invaluable because he was "cool in deliberation, impetuous in the execution. . . . His conclusions are forcibly drawn and his language though not always chaste is often beautiful."

Thomas Paine, "naturally indolent and led by his passions," could be played upon. And Rutledge, according to Wentworth, was "a man of business" and as such approachable. He thought the economics of the patriots crucial and noted for the benefit of the commission which were rich, which of middling fortune, which were financially embarrassed, which owed their wealth to the Revolution and which had it despite the Revolution.

With such a briefing on the financial standing of the American patriots, it was understandable that Eden made arrangements to draw on a fund for judicious bribery, should all his fair arguments encounter difficulties in Congress.

The commission, too, was to have the aid of two irregulars, men unattached in any formal way to the Eden team but operating in close concert. One was a physician named Dr. John Berkenhout, who had tried in vain to subvert Arthur Lee. The other was John Temple, who had worked with Franklin on the Hutchinson letters, had lost his job in the customs house as a result, and regarded himself as a conscientious American who had already suffered for the Cause. Both Temple and Berkenhout were to follow the commission in another ship. Once in America they were to exhibit "an active exertion of notoriety and weight," supplementing the commission's efforts, though with a show of independence. Temple lent his services at a particularly handsome rate: £2,000 down, an expense fund of £2,000, a pension of £2,000 a year for life, and a baronetcy—all to be paid regardless of the commission's success or failure.

After the commission had been put together, their pay agreed on, their loose instructions drafted, North seemed to lose all interest. In March, Carlisle confided to Eden: "Lord North . . . had rather . . . meet the Devil sooner than a Commissioner." The Earl came away from one meeting in mid-March "not a little shocked at the slovenly manner in which an affair so serious in its nature had been discussed."

Eden was further miffed by the appointment of the Howes but not of General Clinton to the commission. He thought that this would so alienate the top military man in the American command that the mission was "half-damn'd" before it started. Germain, the minister for American affairs, shut himself off from the commission, offering no help whatsoever.

Before leaving London, Carlisle did get in to see Germain to ask why the commission was being ordered to New York instead of Philadelphia, then still held by Howe. He received an enigmatic answer: ". . . perhaps that city [Philadelphia] may not by your arrival be in our hands." This was worrisome because it had been understood that the commission would be laughed out of America if it were not bolstered by a continuing show of British military strength.

The truth, withheld from the negotiators, was that British troops were being pulled back to a few readily defensible coastal points in order to make them available for the seemingly inevitable war with France. Orders had already been dispatched to evacuate Philadelphia and "conduct no offensive on the Continent." It was plain that the peace effort had already been written off as hopeless and was being used only as a sop to public opinion. Eden described his final session with Lord North on April 12 this way: "He finished all his Conferences on this side of the Atlantic with me very much in the stile of a common acquaintance who is stepping from your Room to the water Closet and means to return in five minutes."

On April 16, 1778, the commissioners went aboard the H.M.S. *Trident*. It seemed more like a cruise of the *Pinafore* than the start of a doomed political mission to a war zone. Eden's wife, Eleanor, four months pregnant, had decided two days before sailing time that she would go along for the trip and was packed into a post chaise to get her to the pier. Johnstone had brought along a close chum, a professor of moral philosophy, to act as the commission's secretary. Carlisle and Eden had decided to ring in another Eton man, Anthony Storer, whose principal contributions seemed to lie in a talent for dancing, ice skating, and marathon whist games. Then there were several private secretaries, some twenty footmen, and a bevy of maidservants. The poor captain of the *Trident* (who happened to be Eleanor Eden's uncle) had to accommodate not only the commission and their retinues but General Cornwallis' as well. He was returning to the front, accompanied by his own personal staff. The skipper complained that "the servants and baggage is past all belief." There were in fact six hundred people aboard, counting the crew, and all had to be fed, catered to, and amused for five to six weeks.

There was much festive firing of salutes in the harbor as the *Trident* swept out to sea. Six hours out Eden noted happily, "We have not yet begun to be sick. . . ." That expected complication came in due course, affecting Eden and Storer in particular.

Adding to the general excitement was the discovery of sabotage that might have meant the toppling of the mainstay and bowsprit in the event of a storm. Once the damage was repaired the mission proceeded in festive spirits. When high seas washed through Mrs. Eden's porthole, dousing her in her bed, she laughed it off as an unsolicited but welcome cold bath before breakfast.

The gay throng aboard the *Trident* were unaware that a transatlantic race to decide the fate of their mission had in fact been run already. When the *Andromeda*, carrying Lord North's sweeping concessions, as yet undiluted by debate, had set sail in early March, a French vessel, the *Sensible*, was also putting out to sea with Silas Deane's brother Simeon aboard, carrying copies of the Franco-American treaty for ratification by Congress.

The *Sensible* arrived off the American coast considerably ahead of the *Andromeda* but found most ports sealed off by British men-of-war on the prowl for her. Her skipper headed north and on April 13 put in at Casco Bay on the Maine coast. The courier was landed with his precious documents and then had to ride overland across New Hampshire, down through the Berkshires and the Catskills to York, Pennsylvania. A day later, on April 14, the *Andromeda* came safely to anchor in New York Harbor.

Governor William Tryon of New York took the sweet-sounding British proposals and rushed them to the printer. Copies hot from the loyalist presses in New York were sent by courier to the key British posts along the coast. From Philadelphia, the Howes forwarded a batch through the lines to Valley Forge, where Washington and von Steuben were endeavoring to maintain a modicum of Prussian discipline in the underfed, underclothed, and thoroughly miserable irregulars who had wintered there.

Washington took a highly suspicious view of the olive branch that was held out to him. At first he considered the documents as forgeries, probably concocted in Philadelphia rather than in London, "to poison the minds of the people and detach the wavering, at least, from our cause." Then, granting for the moment that they might be genuine, he was nettled by the prefatory note from Tryon suggesting that the offers be circulated throughout the American forces. He called it "an extraordinary and impertinent request," but accepted the challenge. In a letter to Tryon he declared he would willingly publicize the offers to his men, "in whose fidelity to the United States I have the most perfect confidence." Actually, Congress voted to publish the offers because they were already being "industriously circulated in a partial and secret manner."

The peace offensive clearly was off to a very bad start, its thunder stolen by news that the French treaties were on their way. Washington relaxed his dignity sufficiently to permit himself a pun, which was an indication of the scorn he felt for the proposals. "Nothing short of independence, it appears to me, can possibly do," he said. "A peace on other terms would, if I may be allowed the expression, be a peace of war."

On May 1, advance couriers brought word that Simeon Deane was on his way with the French treaty in his kit bag. Washington confided the news to a few of his officers and noted that "no event was ever received with a more heart-felt joy." When Lafayette heard the news, he dashed off an ecstatically boyish letter to the president of Congress, Henry Laurens: "Houra, my good friend, now the affair is over, and a very good treaty will assure our noble independence. . . . I hope a grand, noisy *feu de joy* will be ordered, it will give high spirits to our soldiers, it will run through the whole continent, it shall reach the ears of our good friends in Philadelphia. I wish'd Mss Commissioners may arrive from England that very same day, where we shall let them know that we have discovered their jesuistical meanings . . ."

After a week's hard riding from Casco Bay, Simeon Deane reached York late on Saturday, May 2, where Congress was waiting for him in a late night session. The delegates convened on Sunday to consider the treaties, and on Monday, May 4, they ratified the alliance by unanimous vote. The festivities were marred only by the action of Congress in humiliatingly snubbing Washington. The delegates decided that they could spare no copies of the treaties, nor, for security reasons, trust them to be carried by courier from York to Valley Forge, even though they had made the trip safely from Paris. Washington was resentful, and Henry Laurens thought his reaction not unreasonable. After all, he noted, the full text of the treaties might have been entrusted to the "Commander-in-Chief of all the forces of the United States of America . . . with equal propriety and safety as they have to the Members [of Congress] who lay snoring fuddled on one of the benches while those papers were reading."

Though there was no opposition to the French alliance, there were undoubtedly some regrets as the Americans embraced the Bourbons. The enemy, England, was preferred by many to the ally, France.

John Jay, for example, serving as a judge in Albany and regretfully finding it necessary to be unmerciful in the face of a rising crime wave, summed up the mood of thoughtful patriots. In a letter to Gouverneur Morris he wrote: "The influence of Lord North's conciliatory plan is happily counterbalanced by the intelligence from France. . . . What the French treaty may be, I know not. If Britain would acknowledge our independence, and enter into a liberal alliance with us, I should prefer a connexion with her to a league with any power on earth. Whether those objects be attainable experience only can determine."

He hoped that North might not have closed the door to independence and that the British peace commissioners, when they arrived, would "have instructions to exceed their powers, if necessary. Peace, at all events, is in my opinion, the wish of the minister."

The grant of American independence in that spring of 1778 would have given England an unshakable ally and probably a trading monopoly as tight as any to be had with a colony. "I view a return to the domination of Britain with horror, and would risk all for independence," Jay continued, "but that point ceded, I would give them advantageous commercial terms. The destruction of Old England would hurt me; I wish it well: it afforded my ancestors an asylum from persecution."

It was clear that two years after the Declaration of Independence, Americans were still transplanted Englishmen, and very likely to remain so.

Unfortunately, Carlisle, Eden, and Johnstone were empowered to offer less, not more, than was embodied in the North propositions. They had but one hope: that perhaps unremitting British military pressure might make the Americans more susceptible to sweet and gentle words. That hope was blasted in short order. The *Trident* headed not for New York, as instructed, but up the Delaware to Philadelphia. On the way the British commissioners saw the river crowded with warships and transports, heavily loaded with loyalist refugees, fleeing Philadelphia. Civilians loyal to the Crown, who had passed a safe and cozy winter under British occupation, saw the evacuation of the city, which was not even under attack, as a betrayal by their protectors. Still they fled with them, fearful of the reprisals that might follow a return of the rebels.

The *Trident* put in at New Castle and the peace commissioners made the rest of their way to Philadelphia aboard an armed sloop sent out by General Howe. The Earl of Carlisle seemed dismayed at the sporadic rifle fire from American snipers on the shore. It indicated to him a certain "malevolence . . . of their intentions," a surprising observation on a visit to a war zone.

The atmosphere in Philadelphia fitted in with a more decorous idea of war and revolution. The city was as festive as a royal jubilee. There were dances, charades, theatrical performances, all of which climaxed in the grand "Mischianza," a fete which included a mock tournament, a regatta, a grand ball, and an admirable display of fireworks. This elegant celebration, profitably catered by the merchants of the town, marked the end of a brilliant social season, and a farewell for General Howe, the genial leader of the revels; a Mardi Gras dividing the splendor of British folly from the Lenten austerity of American patriotic virtue, soon to take over.

Rarely had the capital of a country been yielded with such fanfare. The fact that the evacuation had been ordered before the commissioners had left London and had been kept secret from them dampened the commissioners' ardor. The mere threat of a war with France had already permitted the Americans to regain their capital without a shot, and had undercut any leverage the Carlisle commission might have hoped for. Washington's cold reception of the North drafts that had been brought aboard the *Andromeda* and Congress's ratification of the French alliance were duly reported to the commissioners and convinced them that they had been sent on a pointless propaganda mission for home consumption. It was another charade of the Mischianza.

There was no hurry to evacuate Philadelphia since there was no enemy in striking distance. And the commissioners lingered in the city. They rode out into the pleasant country and were deeply moved by its marvels. The early summer brought heat which recalled that of Italy to the English visitors, and mosquitoes which they described as being big as sparrows. But Carlisle also admired the beauty of the place. And the wildlife so intrigued him that he bought raccoons, a gray squirrel, and a fish hawk to take home as souvenirs. He thought of bringing along a black servant, though in England he would be a free man. Eden mournfully noted in his diary: "It is impossible to see even what I have seen of this magnificent country, and not go nearly mad at the long train of misconducts and mischances by which we have lost it."

On May 27, the bills of reconciliation were sent to Congress and drew the coldest of responses from Henry Laurens, president of that body: "When the King of Great Britain shall be seriously disposed to put an end to the unprovoked and cruel war waged against these United States, Congress will readily attend to such terms of peace as may consist with the honour of independent nations, the interest of their constituents and the sacred regard they mean to pay to treaties."

The commissioners then went beyond the instructions—as Jay had hoped—but not quite far enough. They offered what amounted to dominion status for America, with American MP's sitting in Westminster and British representatives participating in American legislatures; with a guarantee against the presence of any British troops in America without American consent; with full freedom of trade and English help to liquidate American debts. All these terms were negotiable and could be still further modified to suit American wishes. Everything was possible—except independence.

Unfortunately the letter containing the offer took a swipe at France, referring to its "insidious interposition" in the family affair, and warning Americans against such an "insincere and unnatural foreign alliance." Congress refused to listen to the letter, formally resolving that it would not hear "any language reflecting upon the honor of his most Christian Majesty, the good and faithful ally of these states."

Sadly the commissioners went aboard the *Trident* and journeyed to New York. The Edens moved into a house on the Bowery owned by Eleanor Eden's uncle—there to await the birth of their child—a daughter, as it turned out. Carlisle set up headquarters on Cherry Street, from which he issued a stream of unavailing letters to Congress, all in the same tone of complete surrender on every grievance ever cited by the rebels. He continued to assail the French alliance as odious. Lafayette answered one such attack by challenging Carlisle to a duel, but the embattled Earl had enough problems without seeking to satisfy Lafayette's touchy honor. "You ought to have known," he wrote to the Marquis, "that I do and ever shall consider myself solely answerable to my country and my King and not to any individual for my public conduct and language." Washington consoled Lafayette: "The generous spirit of chivalry, exploded by the rest of the world, finds a refuge, my dear friend, in the sensibility of your nation only."

Johnstone meanwhile went out on his own, dangling the usual promises of emoluments to a number of high-echelon American leaders, including Robert Morris. He suggested to Francis Dana of Massachusetts that Franklin had approved the British terms, a claim which caused a stir but ended by discrediting Johnstone more than Franklin. In a personal note to Laurens, Johnstone asked that Congress, if it "should follow the example of Britain in her hour of insolence and send us back without a hearing," allow him to "see the country and the worthy characters she has exhibited in the world." It was an extraordinary request from an envoy of the enemy and seemed like an application for a license to hunt for promising defectors.

At this point Washington suggested that Congress might very well open the mail which the commissioners were dispatching to individuals. After at least one attempt at bribery seemed to be conclusively proved, Congress in effect declared Johnstone persona non grata. Taking great offense, he withdrew from the commission.

Dr. Berkenhout, the commission's irregular, proved to be even more of a liability. With Eden's very reluctant permission and a purse of about £300, Berkenhout headed for Philadelphia, now in American hands again. At Elizabeth, New Jersey, he talked an American brigadier general into giving him a pass through the lines. In Philadelphia he posed as an ardent American seeking to set up a medical practice, and played on his acquaintance with Arthur Lee to open doors for him. Then he suggested to various leaders that he be given the assignment of arguing the American cause in England. He was finally tossed into jail, then paroled and put aboard a sloop bound for Trenton. He made his way back to Elizabeth, still on his American pass, picked up some minor, and probably inaccurate, intelligence from three Irish officers in the American Army, chatted again with his friendly brigadier, concluded that Americans would be easy pickings for any serious British effort, and implied that the present British command must be thoroughly incompetent or traitorous not to have managed the victory before.

Eden and Carlisle now felt that they had done all that they could do. Only one gesture was left. They issued a manifesto to the American people denouncing Congress for irresponsibly continuing a war which would bring destruction upon them all, although England was now offering to satisfy all demands of the colonists. It offered full pardons for rebellion, military posts in the British Army for soldiers, religious liberty to clergymen, and peace to the "free inhabitants of this once-happy empire." Copies were printed in German as well as English to appeal to the Pennsylvanians, and sent out by British ships to all parts of the country. Congress branded the papers as "seditious," and most were confiscated before they could be distributed.

It was now October, and Carlisle marveled at his first American autumn: "There are some trees when touched by the night frost have their leaves turn to a bright red which has a very extraordinary effect among the different shades of green and yellow which predominate. . . . Everything is upon a great scale upon this continent. The rivers are immense;

the climate violent in heat and cold; the prospects magnificent; the thunder and lightning tremendous."

Regretfully the commissioners prepared to leave what seemed to them a bounteous and beautiful world, lost beyond redemption. They left John Temple to win converts to reconciliation within the Empire. As it turned out, he found it easier to be converted than to convert. He became an advocate of independence, and won a minor bit of acclaim when he revealed to the world that it was he who had stolen the Hutchinson letters and delivered them to Franklin. He thereby forfeited the baronetcy for which he had contracted.

On November 27, Carlisle and the Edens, with their maidservants and secretaries and footmen, boarded the *Roebuck* in New York Harbor. They made a near-record passage, reaching England in twenty-two days. The failed missionaries of peace there reaped their rewards. For Carlisle, there was the presidency of the Board of Trade and the post of Lord Lieutenant of Ireland. Eden was made his chief secretary. He declined to resume his seat in Parliament out of disgust with British policy but won a post for Mrs. Eden at Court with a salary of £600 a year. The bungling briber Johnstone was given a commodore's rank and titular command of a naval squadron based in Portugal. Knowing nothing of the Navy, he proceeded to a comfortable life ashore in Lisbon. The inept Dr. Berkenhout was pensioned off to his satisfaction and far beyond his deserts. He wrote to Arthur Lee in Paris: "I hate all your bloody-minded rogues on both sides of the question. Peace, everlasting peace is my hobby-horse."

The epitaph of Carlisle's commission and all such untimely diplomacy was written by Laurens when he first read the letters of the would-be peacemakers. "If all the fine things now offered had been tended some time ago, admitting their solidity, there can be no doubt but that the people of America would joyfully have embraced the proposition, but now what answer can be given but that which was returned to the foolish virgins: 'The door is shut.' . . . Here's a card house tumbled down by a breath."

V I

JOHN ADAMS CONFRONTS
THE SEPTUAGENARIAN DARLING
OF PARIS, AND CONGRESS
INVESTIGATES THE STRANGE
AFFAIR OF SILAS DEANE

IN SEPTEMBER 1777, Philippe Tronson du Coudray, a French artillery officer who had contracted with Silas Deane to become a major general in the American Army, rode his horse onto a ferryboat for a trip across the Schuylkill River near Philadelphia. The horse, unaccountably disturbed by the idea, galloped clean through the ferry and out the other end, taking the unfortunate major general to an inglorious death by drowning.

"Perhaps a happy accident," commented the Marquis de Lafayette.

"This dispensation will save us much Altercation," noted John Adams.

The readiness to look upon the bright side of the major general's watery end was not a comment on his military merits but a reflection of the resentment felt by ambitious American patriots toward the honors accorded to foreigners recruited by Deane and Franklin at Passy. Deane not only had promised Coudray a command position in the American artillery but had assured high rank to at least a dozen of his aides and full pay and allowances for some seventy of his men.

When the Coudray party arrived to claim their rank and emoluments, the affair blew up into a major scandal. Generals Knox, Greene, and

Sullivan threatened to resign their commissions and go back to their farms.

The fiery Samuel Adams complained that for a long time Deane had been sending us "Majors, Colonels, Brigadiers and Majors General in abundance and more than we knew what to do with, of his own creating." The fires of Samuel Adams' indignation had been carefully stoked. As a favorite correspondent of Arthur and William Lee, he had been served up a steady diet of atrocity stories concerning the high life at Passy. In letter after letter Deane was reviled, Franklin implicated, the French suspected, and Beaumarchais denounced.

The understanding with Beaumarchais, Lee insisted, was that Hortalez and Company was to be no more than a front, a channel through which the French Court was to pour money, munitions, and supplies to the rebels as pure gifts without any expectation of payment. Now, according to the Lee brothers, Beaumarchais, with the complicity of Deane and the indifference of Franklin, was trying to *sell* the Americans what they had been promised free of charge. The flood of foreign officers added a tinge of xenophobia to the brewing scandal.

The Coudray contingent was the last straw. Congress debated the matter, trying to appease the outraged American officers without discrediting their own representatives abroad. Then Coudray's horse obligingly solved the problem and everyone breathed easier. Coudray was given a hero's burial; his officers and men were eloquently thanked and shipped back to France at American expense.

In November 1777, Congress, prodded by the Lees and their friends, voted to recall Deane. Ostensibly, he was to report on the situation abroad. At the time, John Adams had taken temporary leave of politics. His friends told him that he was "losing a fortune every year," and he himself observed that "young gentlemen who had been Clerks in my Office and others whom I had left in that Character in other Offices were growing rich" in the war boom. Now he was back in his law practice attempting to recoup some of the time and money he had lost in four years of working for the Cause.

He was just delivering the peroration in a case of admiralty law in a courtroom in Portsmouth, New Hampshire, when word arrived that Congress had decided to ask him to take Deane's place in Paris. The formal notification of his appointment awaited him when he arrived home at Braintree. His wife, Abigail, had already opened the dispatches and was trying to resolve in her own mind—as flinty as John's though set in a far more attractive head—whether she should surrender her husband again to the Revolution. She had decided to make the sacrifice even before John rode up to the door.

James Lovell of the Committee of Foreign Affairs followed the official news with a personal letter underscoring the importance of Adams' mission: "Dr. Franklin's age alarms us. We want one man of inflexible integrity on that embassy." No doubt Lovell was thinking only of the importance of having Adams in Paris, but he had also made no secret— to Adams or to others—of his admiration for John's wife, Abigail, in a series of ardent letters seasoned with salacious eighteenth-century puns. (It was after John had gone that Lovell tenderly consoled Abigail by pointing out how fortunate it was that her husband's "rigid patriotism" had not made her pregnant again before he left, and assuring her that he, Lovell, would "take pleasure in her escape.")

John, quite justifiably, trusted the Puritan fidelity that lay like a whalebone corset stay beneath the flirtatious humor of his Abigail, and listened receptively to his country's call. His neighbors urged him to go because he knew so well the interests of the cod fishermen and, whichever way the war went, he would be able to safeguard their fishing rights off the Grand Banks of Newfoundland. More potent dignitaries journeyed up to Braintree that winter to assure themselves that John Adams was not part of the anti-Washington faction and that he would uphold the reputation of the Commander in Chief abroad even though it was suffering somewhat at home.

At forty-two, John Adams was an orthodox rebel. He was committed to the Revolution, but not to the radical fringes that would seek to establish republicanism as a global principle, upset the hierarchic order of society, and open the way to democratic experiments. The British system of a constitutional monarchy as it then existed seemed to him to guarantee the likeliest balance of freedom and stability. His inflexible morality, which meant more to him than partisan loyalties, had led him to defend the British officer charged with the Boston "massacre."

He looked upon Europe with a mixture of awe, derived from his classical education, and suspicion, derived from his Puritan antecedents. Reluctantly but excitedly he came to the decision already reached by Abigail. For a while Abigail thought of accompanying her husband abroad, but when it became plain that her expenses would not be paid by Congress, she resigned herself to the prospect of waiting in Braintree. Their oldest son, John Quincy Adams, aged ten, who had precociously assumed all the grave deportment and high morals of his father, would go instead. It would be good for the lad's education and character development, and he would be a comfort to John.

That winter the Adams family had to outfit John for his diplomatic career. Wartime shortages had made dress shirts scarce, and fabric that would pass Abigail's critical inspection cost forty-five dollars a yard. Abigail and the young Abigail (Nabby), by dint of hard bargaining, put together the ingredients of a diplomat's baggage: Indian meal for pancakes, six chickens (all live and promising egg layers), fourteen dozen eggs, seven sugar loaves, fresh meat, bushels of corn, apples, six dozen barrels of cider, casks of rum, pepper, wafers, brown sugar, tea, mustard, reams of paper, two copybooks, homemade ink (in a bottle that once held stout), twenty-five quills, madeira and port wine, two mattresses with bolsters.

American officers and politicians loaded John Adams with advice, often conflicting. French officers journeyed to Braintree to give him letters of introduction and to ask him to carry personal messages to their families. He personally selected a few instructive books, including some French grammars.

On a February morning in 1778, John Adams said his farewells to friends, advisers, cod fishermen, and family—including a somewhat unbalanced cousin who chilled the travelers with a prophecy of dire commotions of the heavens and seas—and went with his son, servant, and copious cargo aboard the frigate *Boston.*

Waiting for them on board was a young boy, John Quincy's age, who bore a letter from his uncle asking that John Adams take him under his protective wing for the journey to Paris. The boy was the son of Silas Deane. Dutifully the patriarchal Adams assumed the role of father and tutor of young Jesse Deane, agreeing to follow the wishes of the lad's uncle to keep him from "associating with the common hands on board" even as he would his own son. He was also charged with seeing that William Vernon, Jr., a young man fresh out of Princeton, the son of a member of the Continental Navy Board, was suitably apprenticed to a merchant "of Protestant principles" in Nantes or Bordeaux. Seeing nothing odd in thus disposing of a fellow patriot's able-bodied son in the midst of the Revolution, Adams noted in his diary: "Thus I find myself invested with the unexpected Trust of a Kind of Guardianship of two promising young Gentlemen, besides my own Son. This benevolent office is peculiarly agreeable to my Temper."

The five-week voyage was a horrendous experience for the landlubber Adams and prompted him to a great many righteous observations. During an *"épouvantable orage"* (a terrible storm)—Adams used his diary to practice his schoolbook French—he was horrified at "the practice of profane Cursing and Swearing" indulged in by the seamen and pleased "to recollect that I was myself perfectly calm." He was horrified at the stench that came up from the crew's quarters and deplored the lack of pistols aboard "because there is nothing but the Dread of a Pistoll will keep many of the Men to their Quarters in Time of Action." In short, he found the same lack of discipline, cleanliness, piety, and propriety that offended him in the camps of the rebel soldiers. Adams felt it his duty to instruct the captain on these points.

When it came to a showdown, however, during a brief engagement with a British ship (which quickly surrendered), the captain was amazed to see John Adams ready for battle along with the crew. And when a gun aboard the *Boston* exploded, shattering an officer's leg, John Adams was on hand, holding the still conscious and agonized man in his arms while the doctor amputated the limb.

On less exciting days he found it "a dull scene . . . no business, no pleasure, no study. There is nothing I can eat or drink without nauseating. We have no Spirits for Conversation, nor any Thing to converse about. We see nothing but Sky, Clouds and Sea, and then Sea, Clouds and Sky."

They sighted the lighthouse off Bordeaux on March 30, and the next day Adams dined sumptuously aboard a French man-of-war in the harbor while the guns boomed in salute. The festive welcome was continued on shore: a night at the theater to see a Molière play, a round of lunches and dinners, all amid wit, elegance, and shocking depravity. He found the French language incomprehensible to him, despite his book learning. The French ladies were even more so. He blushed when a young and handsome woman at a supper party asked—through an interpreter—for clarification of a vexing problem: "Mr. Adams, by your Name I conclude you are descended from the first Man and Woman, and probably in your family may be preserved the tradition which may resolve a difficulty which I could never explain. I never could understand how the first Couple found out the Art of lying together."

In his autobiography he noted: "This is a decent story in comparison with many which I heard in Bordeaux . . . concerning married Ladies of Fashion and reputation." He decided on that first encounter with France that such free manners would never suit a republic and must never be imported into chaste America.

If the table talk at Bordeaux shocked Adams, the political rumors alarmed him. He was told of a certain "dryness" that existed at Passy, which, he quickly gathered, was an understatement for a bitter, divisive rancor setting Franklin and Deane on one side, the Lee brothers and Izard on the other, each faction with its own allies among the French. The rumors grew more ominous as the Adams party traveled across France.

But the countryside delighted him. By contrast with the harsh American wilderness France seemed a garden. "Every part of it is cultivated," he wrote in his diary. "The Fields of grain, the Vineyards, the Castles, the Cities, the Parks, the Gardens, every Thing is beautiful. . . ." However, he also observed the rot below the surface: "Yet every Place swarms with Beggars."

John Adams, John Quincy Adams, Jesse Deane, and the manservant brought from America rode a hundred miles a day across France. Often the streets of cities on their route would be draped with welcoming banners and there would be the invariable glittering banquets, the toasts, the extravagant compliments. John Adams smiled ruefully when he realized that he was being mistaken for "*le fameux Adams,*" his cousin Samuel, whose impassioned rhetoric was known far more widely than John's sober speechmaking. In his diary he consoled himself with the fact that once the confusion was unraveled and the newspapers ceased to describe him as the "famous Adams," nobody "went so far as to say I was the infamous Adams."

On the night of April 8, 1778, their coach crossed the Seine, rattled through the Louvre, and entered Paris, its streets jammed with carriages and servants in gay livery, the hotels crowded and bright. On the next morning, with the air filled with church bells and the cries of street vendors, they rode out to the Bois de Boulogne and Passy, where the magnificence of the first American Embassy dazzled and scandalized the plain man from Braintree. Only the bitter feuds of the American commissioners reminded him of the Continental Congress in its tempestuous deliberations amid the mud and squalor of York.

In short order John Quincy Adams and Jesse Deane were packed off to M. Le Coeur's private boarding school, where Franklin's grandson, Benjamin Bache, was already absorbing a classical education seasoned with dancing, fencing, music, drawing, and French. John himself moved into the apartment on the Passy grounds formerly used by Deane. He found it "every Way more elegant than I desired, and comfortable and convenient as I could wish." He decided to forgo Deane's town house in Paris as well as his coach and horses, "determined to put my Country to no further expense on my Account."

He tried to persuade Arthur Lee to give up his Paris apartment and join his fellow commissioners at Passy, a move that would not only save money but provide at least the appearance of unity. Lee balked because, he said, he mistrusted the landlord, Chaumont. In actual fact he mistrusted Franklin but thought it poor tactics to reveal his misgivings to Adams so quickly. "He must be let to lead or at least to think he does so," his brother William wrote to him, summing up the family tactics on the manipulation of John Adams.

Franklin was more direct. He quickly outlined his view of the divisions then tormenting the Embassy. Arthur Lee, he told Adams, was the type of man who would spend his life amid suspicions and drive himself mad with incessant quarreling. Ralph Izard, "a man of violent and ungovernable passions," who was supposed to be in Tuscany as a minister to the Grand Duke, was instead maintaining an apartment in Paris with his wife and children, nurturing Arthur Lee's deepest, darkest fears and interfering with the commission at every turn. As for William Lee, said Franklin, even though he was at the moment off in Vienna, he was nonetheless a key partner in the faction. In sum, the group had been bitterly hostile to Deane and openly mistrustful of the French—and in turn mistrusted by them.

Izard himself came out to Passy for a private conference with Adams and confirmed at least some of Franklin's report on him. He scathingly denounced Franklin, Deane, Carmichael, Beaumarchais, and Chaumont as corrupt, treasonable, or worse. (Bancroft, actually the only genuine traitor in the lot, was described as an honest man who had been duped by Franklin and Deane, becoming as unprincipled as they.) Izard's heaviest barrage of vituperation was reserved for the venerable Franklin, whom he described as master of the cabal. As Adams later recalled the conversation, Izard referred to Franklin as "one of the most unprincipled Men upon Earth . . . a Man of no Veracity, no honor, no Integrity, as great a Villain as ever breathed: as much worse than Mr. Deane as he had more experience, Art, cunning and Hypocricy."

The harangue, Adams noted, "was extended to a great length." Though horrified, John Adams still balanced the two factions, concluding that the "rancour in [Franklin's] heart was not less though his Language had not been so explicit." He was neutral, but found himself perplexed.

His impartiality was curious because one might have expected that Adams' knowledge of Franklin and the doctor's overwhelming prestige would have added some weight to the scales in his favor. Franklin was in fact the only commissioner whom Adams had known personally. They had served together in the Congress for two years. More important, one might have thought that Franklin's record of service, his age, and the fact that he had just brought off the alliance which had saved the American Revolution would have outweighed the rather slender prestige of the other side.

Izard was known to Adams only as a scion of wealthy South Carolina gentry who had married into the even greater wealth of the De Lancey family of New York, who had traveled for his own amusement before the Revolution, and whose attractive wife, it was said, had given him "a Son or Daughter in every great City in Europe." These seemed to be his only qualifications for a diplomatic post at the Court of the Grand Duke of Tuscany.

Adams knew Arthur Lee as a valued source of information from abroad and as one of the celebrated Lees of Virginia. Despite Lee's obsessive suspicions of those around him, he carried himself with a certain sobriety that Adams valued in a man. "His manners were polite, his reading extensive, his Attention to Business was punctual and his Integrity without reproach," Adams wrote.

Such attributes counted much with Adams. At forty-two, he was far more sedate than Franklin at seventy-two. Certainly Franklin's manners were polite enough to meet the Adams standard, and none but the Lee faction had ever doubted Franklin's integrity (beyond some mild carping by the Penn family at his expense accounts in London). On the score of punctuality and the minutiae of embassy management, however, there was no doubt that Franklin could never get a passing grade with his stern junior colleague. His bookkeeping was as informal as a billet-doux. Indeed Adams' first requisition was for two ledger books so that he could begin to grasp the arithmetic of Franklinesque diplomacy.

There was, for example, the matter of rent for the Passy quarters, luxurious by Braintree standards but modest by the measure of European embassies. There was, alas, no lease, and hence no rent. The hospitable Donatien Leray de Chaumont, who had bought the Passy estate only four months before Franklin arrived, and who owned several more like it, was not only a businessman with an eye for the main chance but a politician very close to the ministry. In fact, he had turned down an official post because he thought he could be of more service to France as unofficial liaison with the Americans. If the connection was too delicate to allow Chaumont a Cabinet title, it would certainly not stand the strain of a landlord-tenant relationship. Franklin seemed to have grasped this subtlety from the start. The arrangement, however, left a gap in the ledger and appeared to Adams, as to Lee, to be unpardonably irregular.

In time Adams sought to put Passy on a business basis but found it as difficult as cutting silk with a meat ax. "As our finances are at present in a situation seriously critical," he wrote to Chaumont, "and as I hold myself accountable to Congress [Adams seems to have ignored Franklin as a stern uncle might take over the management of a household left too long in the hands of a wayward nephew] . . . I must beg the favor of you to consider what rent we ought to pay you for this house and furniture, both for the time past and to come." He argued that it was not reasonable that the United States should be "under so great an obligation to a private gentleman" for "so elegant a seat, with so much furniture, and such fine accommodations." He thought his constituents might not understand their commissioners living so well and that the world at large might think they were abusing their host's hospitality. He pleaded for a bill "as soon as possible, as every day makes it more and more necessary for us to look into our affairs with the utmost precision."

Chaumont forcefully brought Franklin back into the picture from which Adams had erased him. He observed that he had never expected compensation when he "consecrated the house to the use of Dr. Franklin and his associates who might share it with him," because he understood that "you had need of all your means to send to the succor of your country, or to relieve the distresses of your countrymen escaping from the chains of your enemies."

On the matter of what others in or out of America might think, Chaumont wrote, "There is no occasion for strangers to be informed of my proceedings in this respect. It is so much the worse for those who would not do the same if they had the opportunity, and so much the better for me to have immortalized my house by receiving into it Dr. Franklin and his associates."

Adams was thus frustrated in his efforts to approach diplomacy with a strict eye to cash-flow accountancy, but he was considerably enlightened as to the unshakable position of Franklin in France and his own status as a humble "associate." If he could not fly in Franklin's exalted orbit, he could at least put some order into life at Passy. He tried in those first months, and found the attempt a daily exercise in frustration.

Adams could scarcely pin Franklin down for a few minutes to sign the business correspondence which he and Lee would painstakingly prepare. Adams soon regretted that he did not keep Deane's coach and horses, because the septuagenarian Franklin was forever commandeering the commission's vehicle for lunches, dinners, levees, the theater, picnics, garden parties, meetings of the Academy of Sciences, and intimate evenings with friends.

Within weeks Adams gave up trying to keep pace with Franklin on his daily and nightly rounds. Aside from Adams' inability to construe partygoing as a diplomat's work, he grew weary of living in Franklin's shadow, of being introduced as *"le collègue de M. Franklin."* Franklin had so set the fashion that it seemed to Adams that French ladies had "an unaccountable passion for old age." Once when Adams asked a lady to dance she laughed gaily and cried out to her companion, "Oh, he is much too young."

It was undeniably hard for a man in his forties to realize that he might have to grow up another thirty years before he could be accepted by the witty young women of the most frolicsome Court in Europe. Quite aside from the chagrin he felt at being upstaged, Adams blushed for righteous America when he beheld some of the goings-on of his dashing elderly colleague. A chess game with a neighbor might seem a harmless diversion, but not when the neighbor was the enchanting Mme Brillon and when the game was played while the lady was taking her bath. Allowances had to be made for foreign customs, but must Mme Brillon sit on Dr. Franklin's lap of an evening with company present?

How much of Franklin's amours were mere exercises in gallantry or literature is a matter for conjecture. (Once, the chroniclers of such things report, when Mme Brillon was perched on his knee, combing his somewhat straggling hairs, Franklin asked why she had so often invited him to spend the evening but never the night. Smilingly Mme Brillon suggested that he stay that very night. Whereupon Franklin, taking out his appointment book, remarked: "I'll make a note of the invitation, Madam, and when the nights are longer, will have the pleasure of waiting on you.")

Adams rebelled against this life style, although he found some things to admire in France. He noted that Frenchmen chose their mistresses not for their beauty but for their "wit and sense." He enjoyed French opera, after a fashion. "There is everything to please the eye and the ear," he acknowledged, but added: "I always wish, in such an Amusement to learn something."

After an evening with Mme Helvetius, perhaps the most serious love of Franklin's lighthearted senescence in Paris, Adams was shocked at the discovery that a handsome abbé shared the widow's house. "Oh Mores," he exclaimed, "what absurdities, Inconsistencies, Distractions and Horrors would these Manners introduce into our Republican Governments in America; no kind of Republican Government can ever exist with such national manners as these. Cavete Americani." Americans, beware.

John Adams found not only France but Franklin appallingly un-American. Still, vastly more perceptive than the Lees and Izard, he realized that only such an American as Benjamin Franklin could have won the hearts of France. Parisians would pay for a grandstand seat to see a Franklin pass in his coach and wave. Not so for an Adams or a Lee. In the eyes of Europe, Franklin embodied the free American spirit.

Adams grumbled at Franklin's "affectionate and insinuating Way of charming the Woman or the Man that he fixes on," but he came to acknowledge its effectiveness. "It is the most silly and ridiculous Way imaginable, in the Sight of an American, but it succeeds, to admiration, fullsome and sickish as it is, in Europe."

Seen through the stern New England eyes of John Adams, even Franklin's triumphs took on a decadent appearance. When the distinguished audience at the Academy of Sciences enthusiastically shouted for a public meeting of those two philosophers of the Enlightenment, Voltaire and Franklin, Adams found the exhibition frivolous. He sneered at their unmanly embrace *à la française:* "The two Aged Actors upon this great Theatre of Philosophy and frivolity then embraced each other by hugging one another in their Arms and kissing each other's cheeks, and then the tumult subsided. And the Cry immediately spread through the whole Kingdom and I suppose all over Europe. . . . How charming it was! Oh! It was enchanting to see Solon and Sophocles embracing!"

Whatever the infatuated world might imagine, Adams thought the Sage of Philadelphia was not "so deeply read in Philosophy as his name imputes." There was, indeed, a paradox in the conflicting political and philosophical views of these two American rebels. The rock-ribbed Adams, who disdained the frivolities of European aristocracy, was himself less than fond of mixing with the common man. And he thought Franklin much too harsh on the values of the monarchical principle. Franklin shared the spirit of the French Enlightenment which laughed at royalty while reveling in the delights of aristocracy. He had grown more radical with age and had shed his earlier respect for kings. Adams, on the other hand, proudly disclaimed "any general Prejudice against Kings, or in favour of them." He thought them necessary in many countries of Europe, though unsuited to America. And in later years he came to feel that perhaps even in America a monarchic-aristocratic order might be necessary ultimately to rescue the nation from the distractions of party politics. The darling of the Paris salons and the staid patriot of Braintree were not easily fitted into ideological pigeonholes.

Though Adams left the gaudier aspects of diplomacy to Franklin, he went through the required Court formalities of attending the King and receiving a nod and a word from His Most Christian Majesty. He was allowed to watch the Queen eat publicly on state occasions and found the performance edifying. He would himself dine out now and then with

Franklin at palaces like La Chaise, the home of that truly international banker, Sir George Grand of Amsterdam, Stockholm, Paris, and Vienna, who was so obliging to the American cause.

(The relationship between such international financiers and royalty was forever enshrined in the name of banker Grand's château. While hunting on the estate, Louis XV had found himself in urgent need of a facility of convenience. A seatless chair reserved for such occasions was brought from the house and set in the fields for the royal emergency. Afterward a small equestrian statue of the monarch was erected to mark the site and thus the banker's castle took the name La Chaise. Such were the tributes exchanged between wealth and royalty. Sir George did not in fact owe his knighthood to that timely chair, however. He received the title of Chevalier de St. Louis for his cooperation in establishing a helpful monarchical government in Sweden.)

When Adams turned from the great world of Paris to the day-to-day work of the American mission, he found no relief from the besetting theatricality that either vitiated any thought of business or turned simple transactions into a masked ball. He tried to work in the early morning but soon found that Franklin slept late or lingered in his "tonic bath," nude before the open windows of his room, as he had in London. After Franklin's breakfast the carriages would begin to arrive, bringing scientists, philosophers, ladies of fashion, humbler women with their children —all bent on paying homage or hoping to cull some scrap of wit or anecdote from which to fashion a dinner's conversation. At eleven Lee would arrive from Paris just in time to see Franklin drive off for an early luncheon meeting.

Adams' impression of playing a sober role in a riotous farce was reinforced by the bizarre characters who haunted Passy and took up his time. The new envoy thought Dr. Edward Bancroft helpful in propagandizing the American cause though he objected to his atheism and his predilection for "tittle-tattle." He particularly bridled at Bancroft's "very improper" gossip concerning Marie Antoinette's intrigues with the Duchesse de Polignac, attributing such a taste for scandal to the habit of seasoning one's food with cayenne pepper and washing it down with too much Burgundy. That Bancroft was keeping a woman in Paris, who never appeared in public, bothered Adams far more than the fact that he enjoyed friendly relations with personnel of the British Embassy. It never occurred to Adams—or to anyone else—that Bancroft might be a double agent.

There was another medical man on the scene, Dr. James Smith of New York. He had attached himself to the Passy circle by exhibiting some flaming articles he had allegedly written for the British press on the nature of liberty. After his prose received a somewhat cool reception, he turned into a savage heckler of Franklin and all things French. Once at breakfast Franklin, complaining of the corrosive backbiting in his official family circle, told Adams: "This envy is the worst of all distempers. I hope I shall never catch it. I had rather have the pox and Dr. Smith for my physician." The Smith brand of venom was too much for Adams; he once threatened to have him thrown out of the house.

There was also a clergyman, the Rev. Hezekiah Ford. Ford turned up at Passy in the spring of 1778, claiming to have seen combat as a chaplain with a couple of North Carolina regiments. By the summer Lee had taken him on as his private secretary, replacing Major John Thornton, who later proved to be a British agent. Although the pathologically suspicious Lee seemed to have had a predilection for spies on his personal staff, it is only fair to say that he had no way of knowing that the Virginia legislature had formally branded the Rev. Ford as a renegade and traitor before he left America. It was not until the spring of 1779 that the parson came down with a venereal disease, thus disenchanting both Lee and Adams.

Off in the wings was the commercial agent William Lee, working a species of militia diplomacy in Frankfurt, Vienna, and Berlin, and by his letters feeding the near paranoia of his brother in Passy. William Lee sprinkled his correspondence with references to Franklin as "the old buck" and "this old creature." He freely announced: "In my mind, there is no doubt of the criminality of Franklin."

True, much of William's vituperation was confined to correspondence with his brothers (Arthur and Richard Henry Lee) and to friends in Congress, but echoes of it found their way to Adams and saddened him. He concluded that American diplomacy hung on "a rope of sand." Adams used the occasion of the Fourth of July to try to bring all the Americans together "and compel them if possible to forget their animosities." The effort failed miserably.

Those animosities flowed back and forth across the Atlantic. Bancroft, who had been instructed by the departed Deane to open his mail, showed Adams a letter from John Hancock, renewing his respects to Deane, deploring his recall, and indicating the dark forces that had been at work to replace him with Adams. Adams "resented the malice of this letter," called it "a persecution against me," and attributed it to Hancock's "jealousy and envy."

To further bedevil him, Adams had the dashing, eccentric privateersman John Paul Jones. Jones was Franklin's protégé and therefore highly suspect to the Lees. His high style, his popularity among the French, and his undisputed skill bore all the hallmarks of what by July 1778 Adams came to call "the Cabal of Paris." Adams did his best to trim Jones's financial demands if not his sails. This in the light of Jones's flashy victories at sea, seemed to Jones, to the French, and to Franklin to indicate a pettifogging approach.

Adams managed to straighten out some of the commercial tangle and poured out his general disgust in letters to Congress. He was worried that America might become the tool of France. Not only was he afraid that France might export its morals to the New World (in which case, he remarked, "our governors, our judges, our senators or representatives and even our ministers would be appointed by harlots for money") but he feared also that politically the United States would find a snug refuge in France's pocket. The state of the Embassy alarmed him most, however.

"Our affairs in this kingdom," he wrote to Samuel Adams, "I find in a state of confusion and darkness that surprises me." He complained that the public and private business of the American representatives were hopelessly intertwined and recommended that diplomats be relieved of commercial duties, and commercial agents ordered to stay out of diplomacy. Finally he suggested that the whole diplomatic establishment be limited to one representative in France and one in Spain. For the French post, he concluded, there could be only one candidate, Franklin. He wrote to Lovell that "it would do great harm to recall him—and one alone is enough." However Adams felt about the "old conjurer," as he called him, he had the perception to see where the interests of the nation lay. Adams saw no future in France for Arthur Lee; he was unpopular there and could only serve to undercut Franklin. And as for himself, Adams pleaded with congressional leaders only that he be kept out of the Deane-Lee imbroglio. Personally, he fancied he might be useful in Holland, but, writing home, he asked only that he be recalled from Europe's charms. They were, he assured Abigail, no match for Braintree's.

Adams could not speak at first hand about Silas Deane, and his sense of fairness was hard put to withstand the tirades of the Lee faction against him. That Deane had accomplished his mission effectively seemed beyond doubt. That he had lived high on the hog—at least by the standards of Braintree—was evident. That he lined his pockets in the course of his patriotic duties was at least plausible. But beyond such conclusions nothing else could be confirmed, for Deane had left before Adams arrived.

Though news of Deane's recall had come in November, it was not until March that he sailed. In a secret letter to Vergennes, Beaumarchais attributed the move, quite rightly, to the machinations of the Lees. They were motivated, he said, partly out of envy but also out of a partiality to England and a dislike of France. He suspected Arthur Lee of being "a two-edged sword." Why else, Beaumarchais asked, did he dispatch his *valet de chambre* to London as soon as news arrived of Deane's recall?

Beaumarchais was, of course, heavily involved in Lee's charges against Deane, for they centered on the purchase orders to Hortalez and Company, all signed by Deane. Lee insisted that these were mere window dressing, the bills never submitted in hope of payment. Actually, the fact that Beaumarchais could in his letter report those charges to Vergennes seems, in retrospect, to be substantial proof that his version of the story was accurate, and that Lee was either mistaken or lying. For Vergennes knew the truth of the deal.

Beaumarchais told Vergennes that Deane was likely to be vindicated and Lee humiliated in any congressional investigation. But he thought that some indication of the King's esteem for Deane would be useful.

"I would desire a particular mark of distinction," he wrote Vergennes, ". . . the king's portrait or some such noticeable present—to convince his countrymen that not only was he a creditable and faithful agent, but that his personality, prudence and action have always pleased the French Ministry." Whether or not the King was reacting to Beaumarchais's suggestion is not known, but the King did give Deane as a parting present a gold snuffbox with his portrait on the lid as a sign of favor. More impressively, he was allowed to sail with Conrade Gérard, France's first ambassador to the United States. Silas Deane thus left France to all appearances a much-honored ambassador instead of a culprit being brought back to answer charges of corruption.

To Arthur Lee, the grand manner of Deane's departure came as a new personal affront. He dashed off an angry note to Franklin complaining that he had not been consulted: "Is this the example, you, in your superior wisdom, think proper to set, of order, decorum, confidence and justice? I trust, too, Sir, that you will not treat this letter, as you have done many others, with the indignity of not answering it. Though I have been silent, I have not felt the less the many affronts of this kind which you have thought proper to offer me."

It is not certain that Lee ever received an answer, though Franklin vented his indignation in at least two drafts of a response. In one he pointed out that Deane wished his departure to be kept secret: "I shall account to the Congress, when called upon, for this my terrible offence of being silent to you about Mr. Deane's and M. Gérard's departure. And I have no doubt of their equity in acquitting me. . . . I saw your jealous, suspicious, malignant and quarrelsome temper, which was daily manifesting itself against Mr. Deane and almost every other person you had any concern with. I therefore, passed your affronts in silence, did not answer, but burnt your angry letters, and received you, when I next saw you, with the same civility, as if you had never written them. Perhaps I may still pursue the same conduct, and not send you these. I believe I shall not, unless exceedingly pressed by you; for of all things, I hate altercations."

To the president of Congress, Franklin wrote a testimonial for Deane, which, he pointed out, was unsolicited. He ascribed Deane's recall to "misrepresentations from an enemy or two." Of Deane he wrote: "I esteem him a faithful, active and able Minister, who, to my knowledge, had done, in various ways, great and important services to his country, whose interests I wish may always be, by everyone in her employ, as much and as effectually promoted. . . ."

Deane thus sailed on Gérard's coattails armed with the knowledge of Franklin's warm endorsement and carrying the King's snuffbox. He shared in the grand ceremonial reception for the first foreign ambassador sent to the United States. The rigamarole, the flourishes, and the fireworks were gaudy enough to suit an Imperial Court rather than the Congress of an austere fledgling republic.

A committee of Congress went down from Philadelphia to Chester to greet Gérard—and inevitably Deane, who stood at the envoy's side. The welcomers were rowed out to the vessel on a barge manned by twelve oarsmen dressed in scarlet trimmed with silver. And fifteen cannon roared in salute. Gérard—with Deane in tow—was escorted to Philadelphia in a cavalcade of four coaches, each with four horses. When the procession entered the city, the American artillery boomed a welcome and crowds followed the ambassador, the congressmen, and the social and political cream of Philadelphia to the apartment on Market Street set aside for Gérard. Then came the official reception in Congress, to which Gérard was brought in a state coach drawn by six horses. After formal addresses were read to and from His Most Christian Majesty came the grand banquet in which twenty-one toasts were drunk to the roar of cannon. The republican patriots toasted the King of France, the Queen of France, the King of Spain, and the everlasting union of France and the United States.

The fruits of that union were not hypothetical or relegated to some rosy future. They were there in the tangible, visible presence of Count d'Estaing's fleet. It lay off the coast of America to aid the rebel cause, even though France had not yet officially declared war on England.

The *Pennsylvania Packet* (July 14, 1778) summed up the triumphant mood of Americans: "Who would have thought . . . that the American colonies, imperfectly known in Europe a few years ago, and claimed by every pettifogging lawyer in the House of Commons, and every cobbler in the beer houses of London, as part of their property, should in the course of three years of a war with Great Britain, receive an Ambassador from the most powerful Monarchy in Europe."

Another ceremonial welcome, with gala parades, fireworks, and roaring artillery, was extended to the Count d'Estaing and the French fleet. Although the press and public whooped it up, the performance nettled the more sober and less Francophile patriots. Why, Samuel Adams demanded, did the "Monarch and Kingdom of France" take precedence over the Congress in the order of the toasts? "Nations and independent sovereign states do not compliment after the manner of belles and beaus," he complained. And why did General Washington and the Army rate a thirteen-gun salute but the Congress none at all? When James Warren asked Washington to explain, the Commander in Chief said the Congress was included in the toast to the United States. To which Warren replied that if Washington and the Army "were not included also in the United States I wish they were disbanded."

The deep divisions among Americans were visible in this argument over the protocol prescribed for the first full-dress diplomatic function on their own soil. It drove Samuel Adams to a denunciation of military power and a solemn warning: "Tyrants have been the scourges and plagues of mankind, and armies their instruments. . . . The time may come when the sins of America may be punished by a standing army; and that time will surely come when the body of the people shall be so lost to the exercise of common understanding and caution, as to suffer the civil to stoop to the military power."

If constitutional, diplomatic, military, economic, moral, and political questions could so easily surface in arguments over trivia, such as the conduct of a ceremony, the Deane case seemed designed to provide a cause célèbre and a battleground.

The Deane camp gathered in not only the pro-French but those who were willing to settle for peace on reasonable terms, limiting territorial ambitions to what the infant state with its minuscule military might could reasonably be expected to win and hold. To the Lee banners flocked those who wanted the Mississippi and its delta in American hands, who chafed at seeing Florida still Spanish and Canada still British. The debate, far surpassing the importance of Deane or the Lees or Beaumarchais, forecast the currents of American diplomacy in the years immediately ahead and in the century to come, down to the unfolding of that destiny which required that the continent be cleared for its new tenants.

In November 1778, Samuel Adams, a partisan of Arthur Lee, wrote: "We never shall be upon a solid footing till Britain cedes to us what Nature designs we should have, or til we wrest it from her." He made it clear that Nature had included in her designs for a United States all Canada, Nova Scotia, and the fisheries of the Grand Banks, and he added, "Florida, too, is a tempting object at the South."

The Lees rallied to their side stern men like James Warren who were dismayed that the war had provided a windfall not only for the aristocratic landowners but for the lower orders in America. Bitterly Warren complained, in a letter to John Adams, that "men who would have cleaned my shoes five years ago have amassed fortunes and are riding in chariots." The enemy, as his wife, Mercy Warren, put it, were "the gamblers, courtiers and stock jobbers . . . the votaries of pleasure . . . the Deaneites."

Distrust of France was one bond that helped to hold together the Lee faction. Dislike of Washington was another. It was suspicion of the Chief that joined the Lees of Virginia with the Adamses of Massachusetts in what John Jay termed "the family compact." Much, indeed, of the factionalism that tore apart the Congress and the Army was based on the politics of the great American families. For in America the crusted feudalism of Europe had been replaced by those clans, dignified by property and wealth, which were considered the likeliest ingredients to nurture leadership in the republic.

The Morrises, the Livingstons, and the Jays were among the clans that declared for Deane, for Washington, and for the French alliance. They saw their opponents as narrow provincials, pettifogging bookkeepers blowing the envious libels of Arthur and William Lee into a storm that threatened the nation's diplomacy.

With the snuffbox of King Louis in his waistcoat pocket, with the support of the charming Gérard, to whose opinion patriots listened with the attention due to the representative of a generous benefactor, with the friendship of the revered Franklin worn like a boutonniere in his lapel, Deane played his hand too confidently. He struck an overly righteous pose that irritated Congress. He denounced the Lees not only as envious conspirators and defamers but as simpletons as well. Had not Arthur Lee let the British ambassador steal his papers while in Berlin? Undeniable. Had not the Lees made themselves disliked and suspect in the Courts of France and Spain when they ought to have wooed them? This was true, though some Lee partisans either denied it or pretended to see a rugged American virtue in their behavior.

Telling heavily against Deane was his and Franklin's disdain for book-keeping. He had only the scantiest records with him, and it did no good for him to explain that he had left his accounts back in Passy. John Adams had already confirmed the fact that the accounts were either nonexistent or in such sloppy shape as to be worthless. Without documentation it was hard to refute charges that Deane had grown rich in the service of his country. Most damning of all, he had no way of proving that the deal with Hortalez and Company was in fact an out-and-out business arrangement. Congress found it impossible even to consider that matter, inasmuch as France, which was not officially at war with England, would be embarrassed by an open debate on the question. Discussions were held offstage, and everyone believed what he wanted to.

Soon both sides began to feel that the Deane affair was far too hot to handle. Gouverneur Morris wrote to Jay: "Your friend, Deane, who has rendered most essential services, stands as one accused. The storm increases and I think some of the tall trees must be torn up by the roots." Congress hesitated between condemning Deane, an action which would cast a shadow over Franklin, and acquitting Deane, which would taint the Lees. They pussyfooted throughout the summer and would gladly have let the entire affair blow over, allowing time and the excitement of other scandals to bury the awkward mess that had been stirred up in Passy. Deane, however, deprived by an ocean of the sage political advice of Franklin, boldly rushed down his road to ruin.

He went over the heads of Congress and published a wildly inflammatory "Address to the People" in the *Pennsylvania Packet,* excoriating Congress, attributing horrendous personal and venal motives to the Lees and his other detractors, and challenging Congress's authority. The reaction of Americans at home and abroad verged on the hysterical. It was the first —and certainly not the last—time that Europeans were astonished by the shrill way in which Americans aired their domestic scandals and imposed their own political passions on the world.

John Adams, for example, when he read Deane's address, exploded. He told the astonished Franklin that the statement was "one of the most wicked and abominable productions that ever sprung from an human heart," that if it was tolerated "no evil could be greater" and "it was no matter how soon the [French] Alliance was broke."

To Bancroft, who as a British agent must have been richly amused by the crisis, Adams declared that the publication of Deane's address was "evidence of such complication of vile passions, of vanity, arrogance and presumption, of malice, envy and revenge, and at the same time of such weakness, indiscretion and folly, as ought to unite every wise man against him." Silas Deane, Adams said, seemed to him "a wild boar that ought to be hunted down for the benefit of mankind." Now all of Adams' past efforts to be fair to Deane gave way, and he was ready to yield him "up to Satan to be buffeted."

Adams confided to his diary that he trembled for the government of the United States and its future, for its reputation in the Court of France and in all the world, if Deane were not promptly punished. He drafted and redrafted a letter to Vergennes which in its earlier form read like a scream of panic. In it he told the French minister that he was not showing the letter to Franklin, who had "unhappily attached himself to Mr. Deane, and set himself against Mr. Lee." It expressed an oblique criticism of the King for honoring Deane and the hope that this had not "emboldened" Deane to take this step which, Adams thought, might tear the United States apart. Fortunately, Adams thought better of that first, utterly tactless draft. The letter he actually sent contained no reference either to Franklin or to the King. It was confined to an attack on Deane and a defense of Lee, to which Vergennes replied politely, discreetly. The minister showed no signs of having been ruffled by the uproar or to have lost any confidence in the ability of the American states to survive. One wonders whether Adams' first draft might not have shaken that confidence.

The crisis further exacerbated relations at Passy. Franklin, who made no effort to defend Deane's impolitic appeal to the people, could only repeat in mild language his admiration for the way in which his former colleague had acted in Europe. Although Adams was growing increasingly irritated with Franklin, he did not alter his conviction that the Philadelphia sage should be allowed to hold down the Embassy in France alone and unimpeded even by the upright Lee, whose "prejudices and violent tempers," Adams wrote, "would raise quarrels in the Elysian fields . . ." Adams felt himself hopelessly inadequate in the crisis: "The wisdom of Solomon, the meekness of Moses, and the patience of Job, all united in one character, would not be sufficient to qualify a man to act in the situation in which I am at present; and I have scarcely a spice of either of these virtues."

France gossiped about the affair but seemed unshaken until Deane's gaffe was overshadowed by a far greater one. A furious battle had been raging in the American press. The invective was so loud that it drowned out the pros and cons of the Deane and Lee charges and magnified their injustice. The secretary of the Committee on Foreign Affairs felt moved to answer Deane in the pages of the *Pennsylvania Packet*. He was Thomas Paine, and his reply was characteristically eloquent and intemperate. He claimed to have evidence that all the deals with Hortalez and Company were merely fronts for what were in effect gifts to the United States by the King of France, and that Deane and Beaumarchais had been trying to make profits on the royal Bourbon generosity.

Even if Paine's charges, inspired by the Lees, had been true—and they were not, as subsequent history disclosed—they would have been nonetheless wildly irresponsible, incriminating an ally and offering to prove that France's King and minister had lied to Britain and the world.

Gérard had to demand that Congress disown Paine and all his works. He thought this could best be done by firing him on the spot. (Gérard, however, considering him both talented and on the make, offered to engage him in the service of France. Paine took the job but held it only briefly, after which he returned to the Lee camp.)

Now it was the turn of the Deane faction to blunder. Gouverneur Morris took the floor in Congress to denounce Paine as "an adventurer" who had proved himself untrustworthy. The circumstances, said Morris, called for his immediate dismissal without so much as a hearing. If Morris had stopped there, it is likely that none but the most ardent Lee partisans would have objected. But Morris had an abiding disdain for Paine which he could not conceal. He went on to denounce Paine's political principles, his grammar, and his plebeian birth. In so doing he confirmed the popular impression that the Deaneites were patrician snobs dreaming of an American aristocracy.

Though Morris' sneers at Paine exacerbated the split, Congress had no choice but to vote for the dismissal of their embarrassing employee. Only seven of the thirteen states voted to deny Paine a hearing, which, if it had been held, would have compounded the embarrassment to France.

The sessions of Congress were theoretically closed, but the results of the debate were run through the gossip mill of Philadelphia as quickly as if they had been proclaimed by a herald. When on the morning following the vote a letter from Tom Paine arrived quoting from the confidential *Journal* of Congress, a new uproar developed. Who had leaked the word to Paine? Who had shown him the *Journal*?

A resolution was passed requiring the president of the Congress, Henry Laurens, to ask each delegate upon his solemn honor to reveal whether he had broken the secrecy rules. Then Laurens—a confirmed and vehement supporter of the Lees—declared that it was he who had told Paine. He offered no defense but instead attacked Robert Morris, Gouverneur's brother, charging that this champion of Deane had brought in fifty hogsheads of tobacco for his own commercial purposes on a vessel chartered for public business. The scandals rippled out in ever widening irrelevancies. Deane waited while a committee probed the affair of the fifty hogsheads. Such investigations could go on indefinitely. For Arthur and William Lee had certainly used American government transports to carry the merchandise of their private sidelines. And Richard Henry Lee had created ugly talk by exacting rents from his tenants in the form of tobacco and wheat to hedge the family fortune against inflation, thereby debasing the American currency.

All this must have been well known to Gérard, who was wining and dining congressmen in his home on Market Street. It is not likely, therefore, that he, Vergennes, or any of the royal Courts in London, Paris, St. Petersburg, Berlin, Vienna, or Madrid could cheerfully contemplate the world's future in the workings of the new American democracy.

On December 9, 1778, President Henry Laurens submitted his resignation, officially giving only "sundry reasons" for his decision to step down, though privately he made it clear that he was incensed because Congress had failed to censure Deane. He was replaced in the chair by John Jay, who had been among the targets of Arthur Lee's liveliest suspicions, who had been a classmate of Silas Deane at King's College, and who had engaged in extensive correspondence with him—frequently in invisible ink.

John Jay was a most promising politician in that year of 1778, and his career was being watched attentively not only by the jockeying factions of Congress but by those Europeans who made it a practice to study the strange men who boiled to the surface in the chaos of the American Revolution. Jay came from a Huguenot family and in his youth was fed on anti-Papist legends of Protestant martyrs and escape stories of refugees who had fled from Catholic France.

He was a student at King's College with Deane and John Vardill (not then either a clergyman or a British agent) when the Liberty Boys were tarring and feathering loyalists in Boston and Samuel Adams was appealing even to the mechanic class to demonstrate against the British Parliament. Jay called Samuel Adams' radicals "the mobility" and declared them absurd.

A lawyer with pronounced conservative tendencies but no political ambitions, he found himself chosen as a delegate from New York when he was scarcely twenty-nine. The delights of the political battle and the admiration stirred by his inventive and caustic oratory soon persuaded him that politics was not as dreary as he fancied. And as he warmed to the business he shed some of his conservatism. To the horror of his conservative friends, he went along with the radicals on the nonimportation association, clinging, however, to some prejudices, notably his horror of Papists and Scotsmen.

Jay had already strayed somewhat from the Huguenot tradition by marrying into the fiercely republican and freethinking Livingston clan. His bride, Sarah, was the daughter of William Livingston, the patriarch of Liberty Hall in Elizabeth Town, New Jersey.

Tall, slim, sharp-featured, hot-tempered, and proud, Jay on his way up won his share of enemies. Though his opinions could and did change, he was almost always dogmatically certain of them at any given moment. He was constant in his principles of Protestant rectitude but eschewed the temptation to hunt witches. When he presided over the Committee on Conspiracies at Connor's Tavern in Kingston, New York, he curbed the more vengeful patriots who would have hanged any of the loyalists named by neighborhood informers. And he sternly opposed slavery as sinful. In the stormy debates over the New York constitution he fought stubbornly, though unavailingly, for a clause that would have outlawed slavery in the state.

He rose swiftly in the politics of New York, blessed by the prestige of the Livingstons and by his own acumen. He was aided, too, by Sarah, a loving but ambitious wife with a keen political intelligence and a forceful Livingstonian republicanism. He strode the floor of Congress in the latter months of 1778 not only as a delegate but as an independent with an impressive legal career behind him and the distinction of having served as New York's first chief justice.

He was thus a man to be carefully watched and, if possible, wooed. Following with scrupulous interest the intrigues of Philadelphia, more labyrinthine and more fluid than those of Versailles, the astute Conrade Gérard carefully cultivated Jay. Assisting in the courtship was Juan de Miralles, the unofficial representative of His Most Catholic Majesty, Charles III of Spain.

Miralles had been running a discreet observation post in Philadelphia since the spring of 1778, shortly before Gérard's triumphal entry into the capital. Inasmuch as Spain's aid to the rebels had been extremely modest and much more closely concealed than France's, he could not hold court as Gérard did on Market Street. Moreover, Miralles had come to look upon the Americans with a more critical eye than did Gérard. He saw them as a geopolitical threat to Spanish holdings in America. He listened to speeches in and out of Congress in which the Mississippi was described as an American river—whereas in fact it ran through Spanish colonies into a gulf that had been designated as Spanish waters.

He heard the bold demands by the Lee faction that their republic ultimately embrace all Canada. How long would it be, wondered Miralles, before they would seek to push south and west as well as north, driving the Spaniards out of their present position in Florida? Gérard had no choice but to listen to the promptings of Miralles. He knew that France could not carry the battle against England in Europe and America without the help of the Spaniards, who were then offering to "mediate" the war.

Though the French had originally assumed that Americans should and would have the rights to ship the produce of their interior down the Mississippi, Gérard began to see that this could prove a sticking point with Spain, and he set about preparing the Americans for possible concessions in the west. He did this in long evening chats with the likeliest Deaneites, among whom Jay figured prominently. One such session went on from eight in the evening to eight in the morning, with Gérard expounding, pleading, and cajoling while Jay puffed on his pipe and remained polite, affable, and noncommittal. Jay later remarked on the extraordinary attention shown to him by the Spanish and French envoys but added, "I have every reason to think that both of them entertained higher opinions of my docility than were well founded."

If Gérard and Miralles did not consider Jay precisely in their pocket, they at least felt they had won him over to a frame of mind in which he could foresee a bargain whereby Spain would get the security it wanted for its colonies in exchange for active participation in the war. Thus emboldened, Gérard addressed Congress discreetly and tactfully as the representative of America's all-important ally. And when the delegates gathered around him afterward he sought to warn them that France was quite prepared to see the Mississippi as a Spanish river if that were necessary to keep Charles III as an ally.

Even the most arrant pro-French Deaneites, however, were less than fully convinced of the need to make so desperate a bargain. True, the military scene was a shambles, the patriots seemed ready to turn against each other as well as against the loyalists, and economic ruin threatened the infant republic. But few would willingly have seen the new nation —if there was to be one—hemmed in by the Alleghenies.

The value of such a concession depreciated still further in the summer of 1778 when the Chevalier de la Luzerne brought the news that Spain had at long last entered the war against England. Now it seemed pointless to pay the price of the Mississippi. The huzzahs at this happy turn of events were muted, however, when it was learned that Spain had pointedly allied itself with France and not with the United States. The Court of

Charles III still withheld recognition of the new country. At the moment the only relationship between Spain and the revolted colonies of England was that they shared a common enemy. All the rest—including Spanish gold—was still to be won by diplomacy.

If the issue of the Mississippi seemed removed from the original charges of Arthur Lee against Silas Deane, what should be said of the fish of the Newfoundland Grand Banks? Yet they figured hugely in how Americans thought of Silas Deane. In fact, James Lovell summed up the entire Deane-Lee battle as a "long struggle about cod and haddock." Beaumarchais and the allegedly fiddled bookkeeping of Passy seemed lost in the shuffle.

In general, the Lee forces favored the fishing rights as a sine qua non of peace. Gérard did not feel, however, that King Louis of France should commit himself to fight for the American jurisdiction over all fish to be found off the shores of Newfoundland and Nova Scotia. Nor would Spain, he fancied, regard this as a justifiable war aim for His Most Catholic Majesty. American independence would be sufficiently difficult for him to accept without throwing in cod, haddock, and the Mississippi as well.

So it was that all of these issues, which were to be among the burden of diplomacy in the years to come, rose to the surface of the boiling Deane affair. It was a stew in which Deane's alleged improprieties seemed like trivial, almost irrelevant flotsam.

Congress in due course disposed of the Deane investigation by accepting a committee recommendation that in view of the "animosities . . . prejudicial to the honor and interests of the United States," the commission in Paris would be dissolved and that henceforth there would be only one minister accredited to each foreign Court. Deane, neither exonerated nor condemned, would have to be allowed to lapse into obscurity. But what of Lee?

Samuel Adams and other anti-Deane-ites hurried around to Gérard to win at least silent acceptance for Lee as an ambassador to Paris. Gérard could not oblige and showed Adams a letter from Vergennes saying, "I fear M. Lee and his entourage." Lee was politically dead in Paris, it was clear. And Franklin would keep the post, henceforth unhampered by colleagues.

Congress proposed to put the rest of its diplomatic house in order, and in a rosy optimism, induced by the presence of the French fleet and French arms, thought it timely to name a commissioner to negotiate peace with the British when the moment of victory arrived. The Lee faction nominated John Adams; the Deaneites, John Jay. Congress split down the middle and neither could command a majority.

Then the Deane forces suggested postponing that decision and considering the appointment of an ambassador to Spain. Arthur Lee had held the title of commissioner to Spain under the old setup, but a minister's post carried different implications. The Lees put up their man again, and the Deane faction—now known as the Gallicans, the pro-French party —proceeded to split their opponents by nominating John Adams. Then the Gallicans tossed yet another hat into the ring by presenting Jay. The Lee people, torn between Arthur Lee and Adams, failed to carry the vote and Jay squeaked in.

Congress returned to the question of a peace negotiator and now Adams had a clear field. He won the unanimous vote of Congress for a post that called upon him only to stand ready, if and when.

As for Arthur Lee, he could now join Deane in diplomatic oblivion. His exit from the scene was noisy and rancorous, in keeping with his role onstage. James Lovell, that friend of the Adams family, charged metaphorically that Lee had been "murdered on purpose to make room" for Jay. And Laurens declared: "Our friend Arthur Lee will rise again." In actual fact, that most undiplomatic of diplomats, that patriot obsessed by his own virtue and the vice of others, had to content himself with obscure diplomatic missions to the Indians, although unofficially he continued his politics of paranoia by means of prolific correspondence.

As for Deane, his "murder" may have been not merely metaphorical. He first embarrassed his friends by an unfortunate association with Benedict Arnold, and then, in 1780, went into exile in Europe. Franklin continued to be friendly and permitted him to be involved in pursuing that will-o'-the-wisp Vandalia. Deane fell on hard times—which seemed to belie tales of the wealth he had amassed during his heyday. There were reports of him living in a slum in Ghent. He alienated even Franklin and Jay when for a purported bribe of £300 he wrote a series of letters to American friends urging them to give up the Cause, thus seeming to confirm the direst predictions of the Lees.

His only friend in the bitterest days of exile in Ghent was his erstwhile pupil Dr. Bancroft, whose role as a double agent was still a secret. After the war, Deane turned up in London, where he came to dote on a whore. She took him for his last shilling, plunged him into debt, and threatened to toss the first plenipotentiary of the United States into the gutter while he was almost comatose from a variety of ailments. He was rescued by friends, survived, and began to plan ways by which the steam engine could revitalize the mills of America. In 1789, at the age of fifty-two, buoyant once again, he went aboard the Boston packet to return home.

But while the ship was still in the Channel he fell mysteriously, agonizingly ill and died within hours. A rumor—traced to Dr. Bancroft—had it that Deane had committed suicide by taking an overdose of laudanum. However, why should he have taken his life at a time of returning hope, after enduring years of misery? Historian Julian P. Boyd, in a remarkable series of articles, has suggested an answer: Silas Deane knew many of Edward Bancroft's secrets. Edward Bancroft had much to lose if Deane chose to tell what he knew in America. Dr. Bancroft had been a student in the use of poisons. Dr. Bancroft was close to Silas Deane at his departure. Could that skillful double agent have been a murderer as well?

However Silas Deane may have died on that September day aboard the Boston packet, he had in fact been a political and diplomatic ghost for years. He and Lee were restless, troublesome specters who could not be exorcised from the politics and diplomacy of their times. Even after they vanished from the scene, the rattle of their feuds was to be heard again and again in the Courts of Europe, troubling diplomats in Paris, Madrid, Amsterdam, St. Petersburg, wherever Americans sought to create the image of a nation. Spleen, after all, may be as important as heroism in the making of history.

VII

THE AGONY OF JOHN JAY,
WHO CONTENDS WITH POLITICOS,
SPIES, AND FRACTIOUS AMERICANS
IN PURSUIT OF SPANISH GOLD

WHAT WAS NEW was anathema; what had been done should be done again; the Golden Age of Spain sat mummified in a seat of empire which was poorer, less comfortable, more backward, and more flea-bitten than the colonies which yielded up its gold and glory.

Spanish cities hummed softly with nascent industry, it is true, but the merchants taking their long siestas complained that the artisans were devoting too much time to the enjoyment of cafés, gambling tables and the bull ring. Only in Barcelona was there a faint echo of the eighteenth-century bustle that was stirring the rest of Europe, but the Catalans, like the Basques, were exceptional. However poor he might be, a Catalan usually owned a parcel of land, was entitled to attach the handle of "Don" to his name and announce himself as a "hidalgo." The rest of Spain, where a peasant was grateful to be praised as humble, breathed dust and called it air.

Still, even the most Spanish parts of Spain in 1779 were not immune to the effects of the Enlightenment. True, a book by the Abbé Rayneval criticizing the nature of colonialism had just been banned. True also that, the year before, an auto-da-fé had been arranged for Pablo de Olavide, a bright young Peruvian who had suggested that the Church was an obstruction on the road to urgently needed land reform. The ceremony, which led to the perpetual confinement of that hapless Peruvian in a monastery, had the desired effect on other intellectuals. One of them confessed publicly that he had read the forbidden books of Voltaire, Mirabeau, Spinoza, Hobbes, Rousseau, and other dissenters. To mark the sincerity of his confession he complied with the Inquisitor's request to name those who had procured the subversive literature for him. However —and here one may read the waning power of the Inquisition and the spread of the Enlightenment—the men he named were so highly placed in the Spanish government as to render them safe from the Inquisition.

The man who set them thus out of reach was that enlightened despot Charles III. One of those mentioned as a procurer of heretical literature was José Moñino, who had served his monarch well in persuading the Pope to accept the expulsion of the Jesuits from Spain and the suppression of the order as a political force. As a reward, His Most Catholic Majesty conferred upon Moñino the title of Count de Floridablanca and in 1776 had appointed him his Foreign Minister. Another on the list was the Count de Aranda, who had seen to it that the expulsion of the Jesuits was not attended by any domestic upheavals. He had sat in the state's highest councils, although in 1779 he was serving a genteel political exile as ambassador to France, where he basked in the fine talk of the Philosophes, smiled on the American rebels, gloried in Franklin's charm, carried on a lively affair with the star of the Opéra, and in short conducted himself as a man of the Enlightenment.

Having tamed the Inquisition, Charles resisted the temptation to outlaw it altogether. A mystical veneration still cloaked the Holy Office in the people's eyes. "The Spaniards want it and it does not bother me," he commented.

Under this rule of filtered enlightenment the royal academies were cautiously groping toward a more reasonable view of the world. Spanish history was up for sober reappraisal and even conservative writers were questioning whether the expulsion of the Jews and Moors almost three hundred years earlier had been just or wise. There was no question that the new age was dawning in Spain. Unlike the situation in England and France, however, where the sun of pure reason shone on cleared ground ready to bloom, in Spain it had to penetrate a rain forest, barely touching the tops of the trees with its warmth.

Charles, the guiding light of this cautious progress, was then in his sixty-third year and remarkably unprepossessing for a hero of the Enlightenment. He habitually stooped, though he was quite squat to begin

with. His huge aquiline nose loomed monstrously over a mouth disfig-
ured by execrable teeth. He underscored his personal unattractiveness
with a total scorn for anything approaching elegance. He usually dressed
as if for the hunt, which, in fact, was his only personal indulgence—
usually pursued at a breakneck speed.

Aside from that amusement he gave himself up wholly to his royal
duties, for he was Europe's hardest-working king. Relentlessly and skillfully he strove to stir into motion the gigantic, creaking Spanish bureaucracy, mired as it was in ingrained habit and vested interest. This most
austere king even begrudged his people the pomp and parade which
monarchies traditionally owe their subjects. On at least one occasion he
ordered that the sums allocated for a gala fete be used to provide dowries
for the daughters of impoverished families. In general he thought festive
folderol a needless distraction from the nation's work and a waste of
public funds.

Charles not only inhibited the Spaniard's love of theatricals but set
sharp limits to that other popular amusement, scandal. In an age and a
nation that took its loves lightly and talked of them incessantly, this
Bourbon monarch led a life of obsessive chastity. The Court admired, if
it did not emulate, the scrupulous fidelity of the King to his Saxon wife
even after she had died.

Before he ascended the Spanish throne Charles had acquired experience in the job by serving as King of the Two Sicilies. He knew how to
find the people for the hard job of governing, how to use the talents of
men whose life style did not match his own, how to cajole courtiers and
diplomats, how to nip factionalism, and, above all, how to judge all events
by the exclusive criterion of what was good for Spain.

He saw the rebellion in the English colonies of North America as
potentially useful and potentially dangerous. He could not share the
preoccupation of his nephew Louis of France, or rather of Louis's minister Vergennes, with such intangibles as revenge against England. Nor
was he concerned with the famous "balance of power" in Europe and the
delicate question of prestige in European diplomacy. These considerations, he thought, betokened the lightness and impracticality of the
French. They blinded Vergennes to realities, as Charles saw them. Prime
among the realities were Gibraltar and Minorca. If the American rebellion could help shake Britain's hold on these possessions, it was worth a
moderate support. On the other hand, what if these same American
rebels were to threaten Spanish possessions in Florida and Louisiana and
the Gulf of Mexico? Could they not pose a greater menace than the
British? And is not the encouragement of colonial rebellion as dangerous

a tactic as setting your neighbor's house on fire when you have scant means of protecting your own?

It was all very well for France, which had seemingly abandoned its ambitions overseas for the sake of domination in Europe, to smile at rebels across an ocean. It was different for the ruler of the world's most extensive empire. Hence the anguished correspondence between Paris and Madrid, between the two Courts presumably bound by the Bourbon family compact—a sentimental bond that held only when reinforced by national interest.

The family unity had been tested only nine years previously when Charles had tried to drive the British out of the Falkland Islands, so dangerously close to the tip of South America. Louis XV of France declined to lend a hand, and Charles had to give up the project. It was a failure that rankled. Then Louis XVI and Vergennes, without consulting Charles, had entered into the American alliance, with the independence of the colonies as a principal war aim. It was a step Charles thought premature, ill advised, and dangerous. Now France was calling as Bourbon to Bourbon for war with England.

Charles and Floridablanca listened to Vergennes's arguments. There was nothing to fear from an independent United States of America, Vergennes claimed, because the new nation would be burdened by the "inertia that is characteristic of all constitutional democracies." The Spanish leaders put up with the rhapsodic communications from their man in Paris, the Count de Aranda, and ascribed his enthusiasm to a Francophilia picked up in the course of too intimate contact with the Philosophes, Franklin, and the women of the salons. Charles and his ministers, their eyes on purely Spanish objectives, toyed with the diplomatic possibilities.

They knew that Spain was much in demand, possibly the linchpin of French and American hopes. Could France, emptying its coffers into the American Revolution, hope to maintain by itself a war against the British fleet in European waters? Not likely. And with the British fleet unchallenged, could the Americans ever hope to win their independence? If Charles was in doubt he had only to listen to the Americans themselves. Washington had declared: "If the Spaniards would but join their fleets to France and commence hostilities, my doubts would all subside. Without it I fear the British navy has it too much in its power to counteract the schemes of France." And John Jay, showing some of the effects of the long lectures from Gérard and Miralles, seemed prepared to pay a price for Spanish help: "Our empire is already too great to be well governed, and its Constitution is inconsistent with the passion for conquest."

Floridablanca raised the ante by open offers to England of mediation and by furtive negotiations seeking to buy Gibraltar away. When these seemed utterly fruitless, in the spring of 1779 Charles slowly heaved himself into action. He dispatched to England a final offer of mediation that read suspiciously like an ultimatum. (It would have given the United States de facto though not de jure independence.) Then, without allowing time for a response, Floridablanca met with the French ambassador in the royal palace of Aranjuez, made fragrant by its formal gardens. He declared that Spain's honor had been affronted by Britain's failure to respond, and pledged his country to war. The war aims, so far as they applied to Spain, were to include the conquest of Gibraltar. Quite pointedly, they did not obligate the Spaniards to fight until the Americans won their independence. Indeed Spain made no gesture of recognition toward the Americans, for this was not an adherence to the Franco-American alliance but a strictly Franco-Spanish alliance in which, ostensibly, Gibraltar was more of an issue than the thirteen colonies.

A secret article of the compact provided for a Franco-Spanish invasion of England. The secret was scarcely worth a spy's stipend. Ever since the Chevalier d'Eon tried to blackmail Louis XV with an invasion plan left over from the 1763 war, it had been assumed that in case of hostilities another Armada would threaten England. Indeed, it was the only possible gambit. Only details remained to be decided: which coastal points should be selected for the major invasion, which beachheads in Ireland and/or Scotland should be used for diversionary landings, and how thorough an occupation might be envisioned. Vergennes was adamant on restricting the invasion to the barest amount of territory needed for victory. That cautious man feared that too great a victory would be as disastrous as defeat, rousing other powers to England's defense. He would be gentle with conquered England.

Vergennes and Floridablanca probably could have harmonized their views, but each was bedeviled by confusion, ineptitude, and bitter personal divisions within their diplomatic and military staffs. The admirals and generals in both countries were old, vain, and inept. Vergennes had to struggle with a Minister of Marine whose prime qualification for the job seems to have been a career in the police force. His Minister of War was a leftover from earlier governments, an opponent of Vergennes's policy toward America, and thoroughly unconvinced that the whole war was necessary.

As for Floridablanca, his rivalry with the Count de Aranda had reached such heights of incivility that they scarcely conferred at all except in the icy tones of official memoranda.

All that spring the French fleet lay bottled up in the harbor of Brest and only monumental tardiness on the part of the British admiral—an elderly gentleman roused from a snug retirement as the governor of Greenwich Hospital—saved the French fleet from total destruction. Early in June the French ships put out to sea. Aimlessly they roamed up and down the Spanish coast waiting for their allies, while contending with an outbreak of smallpox that threatened to wipe out the crews. At last the Spaniards showed up—some two weeks late for the rendezvous —and the Armada of sixty-one warships headed toward England.

In Paris the Marquis de Lafayette, home from the American wars, itched to carry his revenge to English soil. He had the notion that an invasion of Ireland might rally the Irish to rebellion. And indeed he might have been right, because the Irish—both Protestant and Catholic —were raising demands that made them sound rather like Bostonians. Franklin and Lafayette chose the one man they felt they could trust to sound out the Irish situation—Dr. Edward Bancroft. He undertook the mission readily and, no doubt, broke his journey in London to report the matter to his superiors in the British Secret Service. By the time the fleets were massing near the English Channel, Bancroft was back in Paris with the gloomy news that the Irish were not yet ripe for revolution. Would it help, Lafayette suggested, if a handful of Americans were landed to subvert the Irish? Later, later, cautioned Bancroft, playing the British game.

The drama that was being acted out at sea was low farce. The fate of England depended on which side would prove the more inept. British admirals, frustrated by a shortage of knowledgeable seamen and a supply of cannonballs which did not fit their cannon, and baffled by the failure of the politicking Earl of Sandwich, Lord of the Admiralty, to order an interception of the invasion fleet, waited until the enemy ships rode just outside Plymouth Harbor. Then the defense fleet went out to do battle but managed inexplicably to avoid making contact with the enemy. The British admirals congratulated themselves on slipping back into port in a dense fog without firing a shot. It was said that some veteran seamen put a hood over the bust of George II on the deck of their flagship so that his spirit might not behold the Royal Navy at its worst.

The admirals of the invasion fleets of France and Spain, however, were more than a match for any British bungler. Up to the crucial hour they debated: Should the major beachhead be Plymouth or Portsmouth or somewhere in Cornwall? Although the invaders clearly outnumbered the defenders, they spent the crucial weeks debating whether to attack the British fleet, which through the sheerest dunderheadedness had been allowed to escape from the ports where it had bottled itself.

In this dreary performance only the weather, smallpox, and dysentery were decisive. At a moment when Portsmouth lay virtually open to attack, an incapacitating calm settled outside the harbor. When it lifted it was replaced by a gale that blew the French and Spanish fleets clear out of the Channel. As the summer ended and winds turned raw and cold, Vergennes lost heart. Let the issue be decided in America, he insisted. And the Spaniards lost interest in the French, who had pleaded with them to enter the war and now seemed stymied by philosophical and tactical doubts. In the end the French went back to Brest to salvage their disease-wracked seamen, and the Spanish galleons headed toward Gibraltar, where, the Spaniards were now more convinced than ever, their true interests lay.

In Berlin the philosophical Frederick the Great pondered the spectacle of England's glorious muddle and concluded: "There is a special Providence for Fools."

While the farce was being played out in the English Channel, and while Floridablanca and Charles III were beginning to regret the whole adventure, John Jay was setting out to bring the Spanish Court into a full-fledged alliance with the United States. For this quixotic mission he went armed with a lock of General Washington's hair, sent as an affectionate memento and received just as he boarded the *Confederacy* at Chester, Pennsylvania. With him went his wife, Sarah, a nephew Peter, William Carmichael, named by Congress as the delegation secretary, and young Brockholst Livingston, Sarah's brother, whom Jay had signed on as his personal private secretary. The *Confederacy* was also carrying Gérard and his wife home to France.

Franco-American good cheer lasted for eighteen days. Then a gale hit and in three minutes' time knocked over all the ship's masts, split the bowsprit, and severely damaged the rudder. For two weeks after that the ship rolled helplessly while the crew tried to make repairs. The spare sails turned out to be rotted and the supply of cordage was running low.

Gérard was all for pressing on toward France or some island where they could find another ship and a fresh crew. Jay, unwilling to abandon the *Confederacy* and the American seamen, favored setting a course for Martinique, where they could refit the ship and start again. It was an American ship and the last word would be Jay's. He had it, but at the expense of the French ambassador's good humor. To make matters worse, Carmichael openly sided with Gérard, thereby laying the foundations for a squabble that promised to re-create the dissensions of Passy in Madrid. William Carmichael's "cloven foot was not concealed as formerly," Sarah Jay later wrote to her father. Jay noted his own dismay for an eventual report to Congress: "I think Mr. Carmichael being my Secretary, ought not to give me open and avowed Opposition in Matters referred to my Discretion by Government . . ." At worst, Jay remarked, Carmichael should be silent and neutral if he could not conscientiously support his superior in such a situation.

Jay tried to calm the diplomatic waters on the way to Martinique by tossing a surprise birthday breakfast for Mme Gérard complete with band music and the boom of cannon. However, the noise served only to jolt the French ambassador out of an early-morning calm and caused him to bolt from his cabin to the deck ready for blood and battle. After he was soothed he displayed frosty politeness throughout a frenetic day: parlor games; playful ceremonies of passing the Tropic of Cancer which involved the ducking of initiates in the ocean; a formal dinner with ritual toasts and boom of cannon. And all the while the crippled vessel was taking him farther from Paris. As they approached Martinique arguments broke out again, with Gérard favoring a course along the northern coast, Jay the southern. They steered for the southern route, with Gérard and Carmichael in sullen opposition. As they rounded the island they spotted a British squadron cutting its way through the sea to attack a convoy headed for Port Royal. To the smug satisfaction of Gérard and Carmichael, the *Confederacy* promptly put about and headed for St.-Pierre on the northern coast. Jay's leadership had almost landed them in British hands.

During the ten days they spent in St.-Pierre, Jay was confirmed in two long-held convictions: that the position of a poor man in the company of a wealthy benefactor, however gracious, is galling; and that slavery is a repulsive institution, however profitable. His position in Gérard's company was similar to that of the American officers of the *Confederacy*, who had to avoid hitting the cafés of the town in the company of their French counterparts because they couldn't pay for their share of the wine. On Christmas Day, Jay gave a hundred guineas out of his own salary to the officers so that they could celebrate free of humiliation. He reported the matter to Congress, regretting that his own funds were so scanty that he could do nothing "towards covering the nakedness of the crew."

He also let sink into his mind and soul the sight of slaves rowing the lighters to shore or working on the docks, each shackled to his mate or to an oarlock, with iron chains about his neck and feet. The time would come to press for the abolition of slavery. But in the meantime he purchased a fifteen-year-old boy to take with him to Spain, perhaps to save the lad from a far more dismal destiny, perhaps because the eighteenth century was unashamed of paradox.

Deciding not to wait for the *Confederacy* to be refitted, the Jay and Gérard parties continued their voyage aboard the French vessel *Aurora*. They scudded nicely before a fresh wind all the way to Spain, thereby no doubt proving to the Gérards that somehow French vessels find more efficient winds and fewer gales than do American ships. They made Cádiz on January 22, 1780, planning to sail past Gibraltar and up along the east coast of Spain to Toulon. There Gérard could once again set foot happily in France and the Jays could set out for Madrid. Unfortunately the British Navy had just routed the Spaniards in the Mediterranean, making the last leg of the sea voyage far too risky. As it was, a British man-of-war had chased them just outside of Cádiz and they had to make a run for it into port.

No matter that the spectacle of the Royal Navy's supremacy over America's allies was far from reassuring. They were on dry land in Spain and faced only the perils of fleabites; they were saying farewell to M. and Mme Gérard, and the Huguenot John Jay was about to woo His Most Catholic Majesty.

There was, however, the depressing fact that the American mission was broke. Jay found American credit in the port of Cádiz absolutely nonexistent, with unpaid American bills already piling up. Fortunately the French anticipated the situation and, without waiting to be asked, advanced enough money to get their poor American cousins to Madrid.

Worrisome, too, was the fact that it had been three months since the *Confederacy* sailed from Chester, Pennsylvania. Jay knew nothing of what might have happened in that time to alter the course of the war. He knew nothing, for example, about the fiasco in the English Channel and the frustration of the grand fleets of the allies. And, of course, he knew nothing about the effects of that fiasco on the mood and strategies of Charles III of Spain. Conversely, no one could have known that Jay was still alive after a silence of three months. He might have been swallowed up by the sea or been seized by the Royal Navy.

The first job was to re-establish contact. He dispatched a letter to Benjamin Franklin in Paris which began: "You have doubtless been amused this month or two past with various conjectures about the fate of the *Confederacy*..." It went on to explore the matter of money and the embarrassment experienced by the representative of a shining new republic on confronting masses of bills, blithely incurred by Congress.

He wrote dutifully to Congress and to Vergennes and then sent Carmichael ahead to Madrid in the company of Gérard, who had decided to head home by way of the Spanish capital. He gave Carmichael a long letter, his first diplomatic approach to the skittish Spaniards, which proved to contain two egregious blunders—a bad start for any mission. First, it was directed to Don José Gálvez, General Secretary of State for the Department of the Indies; it should have been sent to the Count de Floridablanca, who normally would receive such accreditation and who was in any case the man with whom Jay would have to deal. (Apparently it was Gérard who advised Jay to be in touch with Gálvez, but Gérard had been as out of touch as Jay. It was one of the difficulties of working in a time when news traveled on horseback, muleback, or under sail. Diplomats were frequently operating weeks or months behind events.)

The second boner was that the letter invoked the clause in the Franco-American treaty of alliance allowing for Spanish adherence to the pact, which Charles had volubly disapproved and the mere mention of which was calculated to throw Floridablanca into a tantrum.

Carmichael obediently rode off with the letter toward Madrid. He also carried with him a set of pedantically drafted instructions from Jay which must have nettled him a bit and revived the nasty spirit of acrimony which had manifested itself at sea. Carmichael, after all, was a man of some experience in Europe, and Jay, however skilled a jurist and politician at home, was a rank neophyte in diplomacy abroad.

If Gérard showed signs of dallying on the way, Carmichael was to dash on ahead. In Madrid, Carmichael was to treat the French ambassador "with great attention and candour and that degree of confidence only which prudence and the alliance between us may prescribe." He was not to give him any idea that Americans were to take their "direction" from the French—a warning which indicated Jay's suspicions and sensitivities, apparently rubbed raw by the long voyage with Gérard.

Carmichael was told what to nose out at the Spanish Court—the state of Spain's finances, its military plans, its attitude toward England. He was told what tales to spread—atrocity stories of how the British were rousing the Indians to savage war, for example, which would not only encourage a salutary antipathy toward England but underscore the Americans' determination to fight. He was to handle Spanish fears about American expansion by pointing out that it would take ages to settle the wilderness and hence need not concern diplomats of the present generation. Jay, who knew no Spanish whatever, banked on Carmichael's fluency to set the Court talk in Madrid flowing in helpful channels. He closed with a selection of Polonius-like advice: "Command yourself under every circumstance; on the one hand, avoid being suspected of servility, and on the other, let your temper be always even and your attention unremitted . . . and commit nothing of a private nature unless in cipher."

Carmichael did as he was told, tracking down Gálvez, only to learn that he should be after Floridablanca. He found the French ambassador, the Count de Montmorin, extraordinarily helpful, generous, and the least devious of diplomats. The count, who had learned to walk the labyrinthine paths of Spanish diplomacy, was eager to guide the Americans and to smooth the way to Floridablanca. Carmichael picked up all that the grapevine had to offer: the Spaniards were preparing the conquest of Florida . . . the Dutch were arming. He dined with Montmorin and his family and was told that Louis was sending a fleet to the West Indies, and was making available to the Americans some £3 million a year for the duration of the war. Then, as if to shame Jay for his suspicions, Carmichael added to his report: "Judge after this, if attention, candor and apparent unreservedness were not the more necessary on my part."

What Carmichael apparently did not pick up from either the genial, optimistic Montmorin or from the small talk of Madrid cafés was the ominous tidings that Charles III had decided, while Jay was still at sea, that he would on no account recognize the United States of America as an independent country before George III of England did so. Floridablanca underscored that determination in a finicky display of protocol that tested Franco-Spanish cordiality.

Gérard, who had arrived with Carmichael, quite naturally expected to be received in audience by the King. To do otherwise would offend France, for Gérard was a senior diplomat and furthermore an ardent advocate of Franco-Spanish amity. But Gérard was still wearing his title as ambassador of France to the United States, that country which the King of Spain did not and would not recognize as a nation. How could Gérard be announced as he entered the King's presence without reference to the unmentionable land across the sea? The Court strategists therefore ruled that Gérard would be invited to appear at Court as a "distinguished guest" without reference to his function.

Gérard, nettled, declined on the transparently absurd grounds that he was traveling without clothes fit for so grand an occasion, although all the tailors in Madrid were ready to outfit him at a moment's notice. Vergennes and Montmorin were dismayed at the news and foresaw the frustrations to which the fledgling American diplomat would be doomed.

Unaware of what lay ahead, the Jays waited in Cádiz and enjoyed the hospitality of those wild geese, the Irish who for reasons of a common faith, a common romanticism, and a common enemy had settled in Spain as Irish grandees. (They made the most likable of all Spaniards, Sarah Jay remarked.)

Sarah was pregnant but nonetheless looked forward cheerily to the overland ride to Madrid. She had been warned of the rugged mountain roads, the fleabitten inns, and the austere, incomprehensible inhabitants of the Spanish hinterland. A trek through the forests of New York, it was said, would seem like a stroll in a garden by comparison with travel in Spain's backcountry.

The voyage started off in elegant style on a cushioned barge shaded by a crimson fringed canopy of damask, rowed by twenty gaily bedecked oarsmen to the sound of music. That carried them a few miles to Puerto de Santa María, where a coach brought them in regal style to the villa of the Conde O'Reilly, where they were sumptuously entertained for the evening and bedded down in comfort. In the morning the Jays were loaded aboard two large, cavernous coaches drawn by teams of mules, each with a collar of relentlessly jangling bells. They took aboard a supply of ham, chocolate, tea, and sugar, as if they were setting out into a desert or an ocean. Then the servants hauled up enormous trunklike objects which were in fact portable beds, complete with mattress, bedstead, and mosquito netting.

At their first stop, an inn at Xeres, they found a large room containing fourteen beds, but Sarah Jay refused to let anyone enter until a servant could go into the city and buy a broom. She later recalled that they had to remove the beds, which were filthy, along with several loads of dirt and some three thousand fleas, lice, and other insects. The retinue of servants Sarah carried with her then took down the trunks and set up the beds. They might have slept, despite the fleas that survived the sweeping, but the mules had been quartered in the next room and the drivers declined to take off their bell collars. In the morning John Jay, short of temper after a restless night-long serenade, and short of money as ever, was handed a bill for fourteen beds.

"How is it possible," asked the methodical Jay, "for eight persons to sleep in fourteen beds?"

"Señor," said the innkeeper, "is it my fault that you did not sleep in all the beds?" Jay had no answer, for the room had been furnished with fourteen beds, though none of them was usable and there were only eight in the party.

So, fleabitten and fleeced, they traveled until they came to Córdoba, where there were pleasant meadows, a marvelous town, goats, cattle, and engaging Irishmen who entertained them and sent them on their way. In their funereal vans they drove across the plains of La Mancha, past the rudely marked graves of travelers murdered by banditti who customarily took whatever the innkeepers left.

It was a strange introduction to Europe for these Americans who had the notion that they came from the wilderness to an effete continent wallowing in sinful luxury. Austere, impoverished, Catholic, and feudal, Spain was incomprehensible to this family from the comfortable hills and valleys of New York and New Jersey, imbued with their country's rectilinear moral standards and rosy optimism.

They passed through Aranjuez and so on to Madrid, whose spacious avenues, parks, and plazas had been designed by Charles III as if to let the sun and air of the Enlightenment into at least a corner of Spain. They settled down in a modest house on San Mateo Street and prepared to wring money from the dour, proud heart of the Spanish Empire.

In the mail that waited for Jay was a formidable letter from Floridablanca—a three-page questionnaire requiring data on the population, the attitude of political parties, the financial resources, and the military potential of each American state. Jay thereupon went into an intensive three weeks' work to provide as many answers as he could, devising in the process a state-of-the-union primer. There are solid grounds for the belief that this assignment was designed by Floridablanca as make-work to keep Jay busy and fend off his inevitable importunities. It was decidedly easier to supply Jay with questions than with answers.

No sooner had Jay finished the arduous task set by Charles III than he came under intense pressure from home. The Committee on Foreign Affairs sitting in Philadelphia had run up bills totaling £100,000, payable by Jay within six months. These were dated five months earlier, so that he had exactly one month in which to conjure that amount out of the Spanish till. He had closeted himself for three weeks to finish Floridablanca's quiz and had not even had his first interview with that minister of a Court known to be formal, leisurely, and parsimonious. Floridablanca, from all reports, was not the man on whose desk you could toss £100,000 worth of bills and expect him to produce the cash. Congress had plainly become accustomed to the openhanded ways of the French and assumed that Jay was as competent a conjuror as Franklin.

The emergency was underscored by a letter received by Carmichael reporting the grimmest winter of the war. At Morristown, New Jersey, the troops were barely surviving on half a herring and a gill of rice per man per day. The interior was snowbound. The coasts were lashed by a hurricane scattering troopships and convoys. The Commissary General had vanished and the troops were requisitioning whatever they could find in the farmers' barns.

Sarah's sister, Kitty, had written more cheerily, but she viewed the war from a vantage point in Philadelphia which overlooked sordid details: "The Virginia Brigades have passed through town on the way to Charlestown with Colonel [*sic*] Washington's squadron. We have never had so many troops in winter quarters as at present, and they are exceedingly well situated—good water and fuel all around them. As the General does not meet Mrs. Washington here she sets out early tomorrow for camp. We had yesterday a Christmas dinner in compliment to her at the Chevalier's [de la Luzerne, France's ambassador to the United States, who replaced Gérard]. Next Thursday he gives a ball to thirty Ladies; tomorrow evening we have a second at Mrs. Holkers [the French consul]. His Excellency intends having concerts once a week at his house. . . . Last Thursday the Assemblies commenced and there are private dances, once a week, at the City Tavern. . . . Mr. Penn is returned to Congress and with him a Mr. Jones in the place of Mr. Hewes who died shortly after you left America. I had very good reason to suppose the Lady in the bush had made a conquest of him. He had—poor man—amassed a great fortune in the Southern clime, but paid the price of his health and life without any enjoyment of it."

Jay sent along to Floridablanca extracts from the heart-wringing letter from the front received by Carmichael but not the gossipy chitchat from Kitty. Then he set out to find the minister. This was not an easy matter, since the Court of Charles III flitted about from the Pardo, just outside Madrid, to Aranjuez, some twenty-five miles away, to El Escorial, off in the hills, to San Ildefonso, near Segovia. There was no foreordained schedule for the Court, for Charles would be moved by the weather or his mood or the possibilities of the hunt, and his ministers would follow after.

When Jay and Carmichael caught up with Floridablanca in the gardens of Aranjuez, the enchanted air was poisoned for Jay by the omnipresent soldiery with drawn swords or fixed bayonets. The conversation, moreover, was baffling, beguiling, and frustrating. Floridablanca, who had bested the Jesuits at their own game, practiced his most genial art upon the Americans. He was known to have a volcanic temper, but in his cool and pleasant study he was all smiles. He began with an off-the-record confidence. It was a bad time to ask for money from Spain, he said. Ah, if only the Americans had come a year ago. Still, there was a plan which he would not advance officially but only as one private gentleman to

another. The scheme was simple: America would build
light frigates, load them with whatever they wanted t
them to Spain, where the cargoes could be profitably (
ships left for use by the Spanish Navy. If that were d
as the King's minister, might be able to offer £25,000 to ~,
£40,000 by the end of the year, some five months away.

Jay mentally noted that this would not even begin to meet his immediate critical need for £100,000, and would demand in trade a number of
ships which could fetch as good a price anywhere. It was, in short, a
proposal to do nothing, and even that unprofitable suggestion was
shrouded in a cloak of confidentiality which put it beyond the range of
sober business.

Officially, Floridablanca felt obliged to raise the question of navigation
rights on the Mississippi, to which, he said, his sovereign was very much
attached. He suggested that unless the United States was prepared to
concede the Mississippi as in effect a Spanish river, the Spanish Court
might find itself unable to pay the American bills. The rest was an
exercise in punctilio, replete with smiles and bows and graceful compliments.

Before Spain had entered the war, while Jay was being wined and
dined by Gérard in Philadelphia, Jay had thought the Mississippi highly
negotiable. He could not foresee that the river would be of any importance to the United States for "this age" and would cheerfully have
settled for a treaty that would give the Americans one free port along the
river, if in return Spain would recognize the independence of the United
States, send money, and join fully in the war. But now that Spain was
at least technically in the war and showed no great inclination to bail the
United States out of its near bankruptcy or even grant diplomatic recognition, he was in no hurry to give up the Mississippi, however negligible
its foreseeable use might be.

Floridablanca's proposal—if one might call it that—seemed the merest
shadow of a premonition of a diplomatic smile, nothing that a creditor
would take in lieu of cash. Jay was troubled, too, by the awkward off-the-
record nature of at least part of the conversation. He wanted to discuss
the matter with his one confidant in Spain, who, as an ally, should be
entitled to know all that had happened, the Count de Montmorin. But,
he debated with himself, would not this be "acting with exquisite duplicity, a conduct which I detest as immoral, and disapprove as impolitic?"
Jay was not a sophisticated Franklin, nor could he wrap a breach of
confidence in the flag of patriotism as Lee did on occasion. He was indeed
the virgin diplomat. He wrote to Floridablanca describing his dilemma:

But, Sir, my feelings will not allow me to permit the confidence due to one gentleman to interfere with that which may be due to another. Honour prescribes limits to each, which no consideration can tempt me to violate."

Floridablanca, plainly touched by the niceties and novelties of Jay's diplomacy, wrote: "The delicacy, which induced you to doubt, whether there would be any impropriety in communicating to the Ambassador of France the explanation we had in the course of our last conference, accords well with the idea I first formed of your character, and I am pleased with this mark of your attention." He released Jay from his bonds of confidentiality, adding, however, a cautionary note that might allow for future intrigue: "But if, hereafter, circumstances demand a more pointed reserve, by accidents we cannot now foresee, we shall always have time to agree upon those points which it may be necessary to keep secret."

The question of honor was thus neatly resolved. The question of the £100,000 was not. And beyond those bills, who knew what others the Continental Congress was drafting in the blithe confidence that their man in Madrid held the keys to the Spanish treasure of the Indies.

Money was one major concern, and, although Franklin ultimately bailed Jay out of the debt by tapping Vergennes, there were other worries. One was embodied in a middle-aged giant of a man, an Irish-Spanish priest whom Carmichael spotted at the inn where he and Jay were staying in Aranjuez during that anguished initiation into Spanish diplomacy. Carmichael briefed Jay on the black-robed Father Thomas Hussey, whom he described as possessing "a conscience as pliant as a lady's kid skin glove." Hussey's erratic career has been sharply sketched by the historian Richard B. Morris. Formerly a Trappist monk, he had been released from his vows of silence by the Pope himself and put to work in the shadowy field between espionage and diplomacy that suited his talents and his garrulity better than did the holy stillness of the monastery.

It is not clear whether Father Hussey was working for the Papacy, for Spain, or for England, but it was certainly obvious that he was working against the interests of the United States. In 1775 and 1776 he had been a familiar figure in London, where, under cover of his designation as chaplain to the Spanish ambassador there, he gathered masses of intelligence which he diligently forwarded to Madrid.

In 1779, only a year before Carmichael and Jay noticed him at the inn at Aranjuez, Father Hussey had been back in London pretending to be interested in the purchase of scientific instruments. Actually he was busy cultivating highly placed Englishmen who might be wooed into supporting an alliance with Spain leading ultimately to the dissolution of the Bourbon family compact and its stepchild, the United States of America. He hit upon Richard Cumberland, a man of engaging manners, aristocratic tastes, and conservative politics. Cumberland had been a mildly successful playwright but earned his living at the Board of Trade. Very early in the agitation of the American question, Cumberland had been viewed by American agents in London as a contact to be cultivated, even to the extent of a judicious bribe now and then, because he held the key to what the great men of the Board of Trade were thinking. But as early as 1770 he had turned decidedly anti-American and would have nothing to do with those who frequented radical coffeehouses or the Bill of Rights Society. In the following decade his virulent anti-Americanism had deepened and driven him to the illusion that the inept Prime Minister Lord George Germain was an inspired leader. As a faithful admirer of Lord Germain, of whom there were few in that year of 1779, Cumberland was charged with maintaining contact with the industrious Hussey. The playwright is generally credited with having prepared the script for Hussey's first diplomatic negotiations with Floridablanca. He was to sound out that minister on an Anglo-Spanish rapprochement that would scuttle France and America. He was given no bait to dangle, but the ingenious Hussey was quite capable of inventing inducements as he went along.

He arrived in Madrid in late December while Jay was still far out on the Atlantic. The Father announced at once to Floridablanca that Gibraltar could be had without a struggle if Spain would withhold support from the American rebels. Floridablanca's answer was characteristically tough. If England were willing to cede the Rock and toss into the bargain its holdings in Honduras, Campeche, and Florida, His Most Catholic Majesty might interpret the alliance with his nephew of France with a certain liberality. Charles III would be in a mood to mediate the conflict and prevail upon the Americans to accept a kind of dominion status very much like that proposed by Lord North through his emissary the Earl of Carlisle. If England did not accept such a plan, he reminded Hussey, John Jay—who was reported on his way to Spain—would meet with a more favorable reception. And, moreover, another invasion Armada was being prepared for that summer, and this time England could not expect to be rescued again by a combination of smallpox and Channel storms.

Back to London went the black-cassocked go-between, who, according to Morris, rendered a rose-colored description of Spain's eagerness to come to terms. Gibraltar, however, was then regarded by George III as a gem in the royal crown; the most that Hussey could promise in the coded messages he sent to Madrid was that if negotiations got under way the cession of Gibraltar might conceivably be discussed. In the meantime, the English insisted, there was to be no recognition of an American envoy.

While that envoy, completely unaware that he was being thus discussed, was in Cádiz dispatching letters and thanking the Lord that he had gotten so far on his mission, the Royal Council was deliberating on the English offer. Hussey was told that they had to move fast because, Floridablanca warned, "I shall not be able to detain the course of the negotiations of Señor Jay who is even now on the road to Madrid." (Actually there was no course which that master of the ingenious stall could not detain even if it meant keeping the American scribbling away in his study on an elaborate questionnaire.)

The upright John Jay would have blushed for his own innocence if he had known that while he was torturing himself about the "duplicity" of betraying the Spanish minister's innocuous "confidence," that same urbane diplomat was dickering with the enemy.

While Jay fretted in anterooms and drafted elaborately polite and unavailing letters to Floridablanca, he was totally unaware of the gigantic betrayal that was opening a chasm beneath him, into which at any moment he might fall and with him all hopes for American independence. For if Spain in fact could negotiate a peace with Britain, France, its resources already strained, would have to follow suit, and the Americans, deprived of French money, troops, and ships, would be forced to surrender. The Continental Congress in Philadelphia, busily writing more drafts on Jay and Franklin (in effect, on Paris and Madrid), knew little of the danger, and Jay, on the scene, could scarcely appreciate the true menace embodied in that hulking black figure of Father Hussey sitting in the smoking room of the inn at Aranjuez.

Hussey's intrigues were frustrated by the peculiar foibles of George III, who cordially disliked the men he used, so that he used them badly, and who generally came to the wisest political decisions a little too late for them to be effective. He thus let slip through his fingers the chance of retaining the North American continent at the price of a rock fortress in the Mediterranean. Hussey was told to offer the King of Spain West Florida instead, a piddling sort of bait.

But the ways of Whitehall were curious, and while Hussey was given one line of merchandise—a pathetically poor one—to offer in the Spanish market, another salesman was sent into the territory. This was that blunderer George Johnstone, who, after embarrassing the Carlisle commission by too obviously trying to bribe American leaders, had been put on the shelf in Lisbon. He was given the command of a naval squadron with the hope and clear understanding that he would never go to sea. It is not known whether Johnstone was acting at the instigation of Lord North or taking his own initiative to relieve the boredom of his Portuguese idyll, but in any case in the spring of 1780 messengers began to arrive from Lisbon at the Pardo.

The offers they carried, though unofficial, seemed too specific to be mere trial balloons sent up by Johnstone, merely to amuse himself. Spain could have Gibraltar merely for the price of neutrality, Johnstone's messengers reported. For active participation in the war on England's side, there would be other prizes.

In April came another unofficial envoy, Sir John Dalrymple, a man hitherto distinguished by his suggestion that the entire American problem might be solved by making George Washington a duke. His overtures were vague straws in a constant wind. Then in May the playwright Cumberland, on leave from the Board of Trade, turned up with his family—a wife and two charming daughters, who attracted the gallants of the Court. It was indeed a *drôle de guerre* in which envoys of the enemy came and went while Jay, representing a fighting, if unrecognized, ally, was kept waiting, hat in hand, for a few pesos which Floridablanca let drop from time to time.

Cumberland tried earnestly to keep Hussey from giving away Gibraltar and to persuade Floridablanca to a brisker pace of negotiation. He might have succeeded if word had not arrived that England was in the midst of what looked like revolution. It seemed scarcely politic for Spain to leap from an alliance with a somewhat romantic French government and its rebel protégés across the ocean to a partnership with a monarchy that might be toppled by uncontrollable street rioters.

What was disturbing England—and Spain—in that confusing spring were the Gordon riots. A most eccentric Scot, George Lord Gordon, though he was pro-American, antiwar, and antislavery, had one abiding prejudice, fear, and detestation: the Catholic Church. He carried a copy of the Old Testament about with him like a proper Scottish Calvinist and seized every parliamentary opportunity to inveigh—at a somewhat boring length—against "the Whore of Babylon," as the Papacy was then popularly known. (A quip of the time had it that this was the only whore that did not attract Lord Gordon.) So it was that this otherwise enlightened liberal broke from the ranks of his associates when it was proposed to restore a modicum of civil rights to the Catholics of England, a plan which neatly combined enlightened principle with a sop to the Irish that might make them more cooperative in the war effort.

Lord Gordon sought to bolster his parliamentary onslaught against the bill with a showing of popular support. He had gathered an impressive number of signatures to a petition and called for a demonstration to show Parliament where the people stood. Unfortunately, the demonstration led to a march which led to a riot. The riot raged for four days, with mobs burning churches and the homes of Catholics, and almost bringing the government to its knees. The rioters resisted every appeal from Gordon to give up and go home. Even John Wilkes, who had risen to power on the shoulders of rioters, now called for shooting the mob down. George III finally called out the troops, who suppressed the outburst at a cost of twenty rioters killed. "Examples must be made," he cried. Among those tried for treason was Gordon himself, but his ancestry and connections were so lofty that he got off lightly.

(By way of postscript: Gordon subsequently vanished from society into the Jewish quarter of Birmingham. He was attracted, he explained, by the hospitality rendered him at a Passover service as well as by the Jews' aesthetic sensitivity and scrupulous reverence for the Old Testament. He became a convert to Judaism, had himself circumcised, grew a beard, put on a kaftan, and called himself Israel Bar Abraham Lord Gordon. When he was later tossed into Newgate Prison for a pamphlet allegedly libeling Marie Antoinette, this bizarre Highland laird would entertain his fellow prisoners by playing the bagpipes still robed in his kaftan and wearing the ritual skullcap. His private cell became a celebrated gathering spot for his aristocratic friends, where they mingled with the bearded Jews of the ghetto who were Gordon's special friends and teachers. He continued to write pamphlets, including one advocating prison reform, and died in Newgate, a practicing Jewish laird to the end.)

Oddly enough, while Gordon was falling in love with Jewish life in Birmingham, Cumberland—whose mission was collapsing as a result of the riots—was happily discovering other Jews, the Marranos of Spain, who practiced their faith in secret. Cumberland made notes for new plays that would remodel the venerable image presented by stage Jews in the English theater, of whom Shylock was perhaps the most charitable example.

When he was not thus engaged, the resourceful playwright was gathering material for a definitive catalogue of Spanish art and escorting his fetching daughters to a round of parties. Jay, cut off from the high life of Madrid, marveled that this agent of the enemy was so well received; that the King of Spain should present a pair of magnificent horses to the King of England, with whom he was ostensibly at war, and that Cumberland should ride them proudly through the parks of Madrid; that Charles III should send his own musicians to a party at the Cumberlands' to celebrate the birthday of George III.

It bewildered the Jays, but in fact Floridablanca was playing with Cumberland as he played with Jay, as he played with the Count d'Estaing, who was trying to promote a new Franco-Spanish naval assault on Britain. Floridablanca let them all chase after him from Madrid to El Escorial to Aranjuez to San Ildefonso. He sent Hussey back and forth, played games with Johnstone's Portuguese emissaries, and soothed Montmorin with forceful assurances of unwavering loyalty to the Bourbon family compact. He played each against the others, while hoping that someone would offer him Gibraltar. It had become an *idée fixe* of Charles III. It was important that all the pawns remain in Spain to offset one another, and he was expert in giving each just enough hope to hang himself.

Floridablanca was a master at dropping the name of a rival into casual conversation, and if this failed to whet the fears of the diplomats around him, he would refer to vague stirrings in Russia and Holland, where, he suggested, diplomatic and military moves impended.

For John Jay, who glimpsed only the broad outlines of the drama being enacted around him, the mission was an unrelieved agony. Not only was he caught in Floridablanca's web and living in an alien feudal world he neither liked nor understood, but he had to contend with a troublesome mutiny among his own official household. The seeds that had been sown aboard the *Confederacy* ripened amid the frustrations of diplomatic life in Spain.

Although both John and Sarah Jay described Carmichael as an intriguer and mischief maker, they could ascribe no motive other than ill nature. It may be, however, that Carmichael, who was not impeded by Jay's somewhat straight-and-narrow approach to life, felt that he was doomed to serve a stuffy incompetent. He had, after all, been trained in the school of Franklinesque diplomacy and quite possibly considered Jay naïve. He also found Jay prissy, for Carmichael regarded the morals of politicians, whether American or European, as not much different from those he found in the waterfront taverns he loved to patronize.

In any case, he very soon sought to take the reins and at one point asked that he be allowed to countersign all of Jay's correspondence. Jay then trimmed the sails of his subordinate: "As I consider the affairs of the American Legation at this Court to be committed to my exclusive Direction, and consequently that I alone am responsible for the manner in which they may be conducted, I must object to your taking any measures respecting them but such as I may previously have approved of and assigned to your management. . . . I am a little suspicious that we entertain different Ideas as to the Extent of your Appointment."

After that Jay refused to show Carmichael any of his confidential reports to Congress. He found, however, that Sarah's brother, Brockholst Livingston, to whom he dictated all of his most important memoranda, was promptly reporting on them to Carmichael. Brockholst had become heart and soul a Carmichael man and denounced Jay's precautions as "damned nonsense." He also absorbed Carmichael's disenchantment with politicians and displayed a tactlessness about expressing these iconoclastic notions. He embarrassed both the Jays by describing to foreign guests the drunkenness of congressmen and their bureaucratic bungling. Young Brockholst was in fact glorying in the Anglo-American privilege of lambasting the leader. When on one occasion the Jays scolded him for airing the family dirt in a country from which they were trying to gain recognition, young Brockholst stormed out of the house, declaring that he was off to Carmichael's villa. "There's a man who can abuse Congress to a turn, though he was formerly a member of it. Thank God! there we can say what we damned please about Congress and the knaves who are in it."

To add to Jay's household problems, there arrived on the doorstep of the American Legation one October day in 1780 a dashing and impecunious American playboy entrusted by his uncle to Jay's tender tutelage. Lewis Littlepage was in his early twenties, with a flair for writing verse and pursuing glory whether in the bedroom or in military adventures. He had little interest in Jay's homilies on virtue and solid study. He ran up debts which Jay had to scramble to pay, indulged his youthful fancies, and quickly aligned himself with Carmichael and Brockholst Livingston against poor sober John and Sarah. Littlepage became a gnat in Jay's ear, vexing him at odd moments with abusive letters whenever he was inhibited in his more rash and expensive adventures.

The Carmichael-Brockholst-Littlepage cabal had none of the weighty political implications of the intrigues that ringed Franklin at Passy, but it unsettled the Jays, particularly Sarah, whose first child had died three months after she was born and who was in no mood to tolerate her husband's humiliations. In a letter to her father, Sarah vented her anger: "Good God! papa—so dearly as we love America! that all our unquiet should proceed from those who rec'd their birth in that favored Country."

There were still other troubles besetting the American Legation. Stranded American seamen were forever knocking at the Jays' door, broke and wanting passage home. American captains were demanding passage money for them and the Jays had nothing to spare. As Congress continued to pile up bills for him to pay, an embarrassed Jay had to admit to Floridablanca that such behavior could be considered "a desperate measure, prompted by our imbecility." And to compound the confusion, individual states were competing for whatever slim pickings there were in Europe. Marylanders shamelessly wooed the French. Philip Mazzei was sent with the blessings of Thomas Jefferson to try to raise money for Virginia and found, to his chagrin, that Benjamin Franklin, acting for Congress, was offering a higher interest rate in the money markets than Mazzei was authorized to do for his adopted state. The spectacle of American states bidding against each other and against the nation as a whole did little to smooth the way toward recognition, though it is unlikely that even with the most correct diplomatic behavior, Jay's mission could have succeeded fully. The confusion served, however, to perpetuate the notion that Americans were charming but rambunctious children who required the tutelage of their elders.

Jay tired of the game but dared not leave it while Hussey and Cumberland hovered at Floridablanca's call. Nevertheless, the humiliations ate into his soul.

Again and again Floridablanca would be away or indisposed when the American envoy called. Jay's letters would go unanswered, and in desperation he would consult Montmorin. That patient man bore the brunt of Jay's anger. Montmorin cautioned Jay that he represented "as yet only rising states, not firmly established . . ." He urged Jay to smother his rage over unanswered letters and write yet again, "praying" the artful Floridablanca for audience.

"Your excellency," Jay stormed, "I was sent to Spain by Congress to make propositions, not supplications." He followed this with a tongue lashing which Montmorin bore resignedly. When, at long dreary intervals, Jay was granted an interview with Floridablanca, the conversation ran a well-worn groove. Some of the bills might be managed in a year or two, perhaps. And as for recognition, His Most Catholic Majesty might be more approachable if Congress were less obstinate about the Mississippi.

Congress was, in fact, wrangling over that problem, under pressure from the energetic French ambassador, the Chevalier de la Luzerne, who wanted some concession that would carry weight with Charles III. The delegates were divided not so much by considerations of an ultimate western destiny for the United States, but by conflicting aspirations in the real-estate business. Maryland, for example, envisioned its future as a trading ocean port, and therefore supported the French view that mountains and plains could just as well be left to the Indians and Spaniards or at least to a federal government that could dispose of them. Virginia, on the other hand, saw its dominion reaching out to the Pacific. And many of the New England and Pennsylvania patriots had invested heavily in companies to develop the western wilderness, for which the Mississippi would be the prime avenue of commerce.

The debates and bargaining that raged in Philadelphia scarcely echoed in Madrid. Months would go by with no word at all for the perplexed and embattled Jay. He wrote to the secretary of the Committee on Foreign Affairs: "I would throw stones, too, with all my heart, if I thought they would hit only the committee, without injuring the members of it."

When mail did arrive—all opened en route by the Spanish intelligence apparatus—it contained little more than bills and bad news. The defeat at Charleston, for example, had the effect, Jay noted, "of a hard night's frost on young leaves." Whatever news there was, the French and Spaniards seemed to be aware of it long before Jay. When at last, in February 1781, Congress drafted new instructions to Jay allowing him to negotiate away all rights to the Mississippi save a single free port somewhere along its course, the news did not reach Jay for months, during which time he followed the old uncompromising line. He had to endure the sly suggestions from the Spaniards that they knew something he didn't, and that soon, no doubt, he would get word of the change.

The Spanish tone had grown more acerbic. At one point Floridablanca's secretary, Bernardo del Campo, told Jay: "You told us you were prepared to assist us in taking Pensacola, but instead of aids, we have heard nothing but demands from you. You are scarcely in a position to make demands. Your situation is deplorable."

(Jay later had a small, sweet moment of revenge on that issue when, after the Spaniards had seized Pensacola, he could scold Floridablanca because the entire defeated British garrison there had been permitted to sail to New York to fight again. "It was ill done," admitted Floridablanca. "It will not happen again." Such apologies were refreshing but rare in that parched season of American humiliations.)

When at last Jay got the word of Philadelphia's change of heart about the Mississippi, he thought it altogether too sweeping. It would make a present of the Mississippi at any time Spain chose to recognize American independence. Jay attached a small proviso: Spain could have the full navigation rights of that river if she recognized the United States of America and concluded a firm treaty of alliance at once, but if she waited until victory was won the offer would be considered nullified.

Floridablanca stalled and stalled, laid siege to Gibraltar, dangled Britain at arm's length, and in the process lost half a continent, as it turned out.

For Jay, with the future dimly perceived, and perceived to be dim, Spain had grown intolerable. As an unrecognized diplomat, he was cut off from the social swirl, except for a handful of Irish friends. When he was invited to Spaniards' homes, he declined for fear of being thought a sycophant. He detested the bullfights, though Sarah rather fancied them. He couldn't abide gazpacho or any other Spanish delicacy. The only creatures in Spain that truly elicited his admiration were the mules, which he found to be marvelously well trained, and the cabbages and onions, which he thought superior to the American produce. With those exceptions he saw nothing in Spain to envy. He was not a gourmet or an aesthete or a medievalist. He was a lawyer in a land where the law was ecclesiastical. He was a diplomat who believed in straightforward, hard-fisted bargaining, and he was given little to offer in the way of bargains. He spoke for a rising middle class of a quasi nation with excellent prospects, but had to beg for alms at the palace gates. He was an anomaly who found no place in Spanish reality except perhaps in the world of Don Quixote. Though unlike that knight in all respects, he excited the same mixture of amused and unavailing sympathy.

Reluctantly he turned for more substantial support to France. And even more readily he turned to Benjamin Franklin, who told him—and it was balm to Jay's soul—that "if I were in Congress I should advise your being instructed to thank [the Spaniards] for past favors and take your leave."

Jay pleaded for just such instructions from Philadelphia, but none came. Seemingly, he would have to wait until the hour of victory to be liberated.

VIII

HOW STAUNCH JOHN ADAMS BATTLED AGAINST AMERICA'S ALLY

WHILE JOHN JAY was trying to demonstrate that he could not be fitted into a French or Spanish waistcoat pocket, an American who was even more stiff-necked and less adroit was setting out to entice, if not demand, money from Europe. It was Henry Laurens, that North Carolina patrician and partisan of the Lees who had stepped down from his post as president of the Continental Congress at the height—or depth—of the Deane affair. He had been assigned to gather guilders from the Dutch.

Laurens was impatient not only with France and overly Frenchified Americans but also with the exigencies of wartime sailing. (Before embarking, he had watched the British move in on Charleston and his vast landholdings nearby, and this did nothing to cool his temper.) He waved away the promises of a convoy because one sloop assigned to protect him was too slow and the others were late for a rendezvous. His own brigantine was fast but no match for any enemy warship he might meet. Accordingly, when a British frigate spotted his brig off Newfoundland, there was never any doubt of the outcome. The American sailors began tossing over the side all the confidential papers they could find aboard ship. Laurens stubbornly guarded his trunk. Only when the British ship came within firing range did Laurens allow his papers to be put in a sack with a load of shot and dropped overboard. Unfortunately, in the confusion they put in too little shot and the sack floated to the surface in plain view.

It took only three cannonballs to convince the American captain to strike the flag, and the British crewmen swarmed aboard. They fished up the sack of papers which was bobbing temptingly on the waters and found therein evidence which made it impossible to pretend that Laurens was a private businessman on an innocuous commercial journey. They also found in the sack a document that would have momentous impact on the course of the war. It was a draft of a misbegotten treaty of alliance signed by William Lee and some Amsterdam burghers. No matter that neither Lee nor the Amsterdamers had authority to make treaties, no matter that the pact was never ratified by anybody and was only an airy effort by the amateurish Lees at what they called "militia diplomacy." It would make deadly ammunition for the British to use against the Dutch, struggling to preserve their neutrality. It provided solid evidence that Dutch officials were dealing with England's enemy.

Laurens was taken to England and given a cell in the Tower of London, where he whiled away his time copying out in a meticulous hand all of Gibbon's *History of the Decline and Fall of the Roman Empire*, a form of torture he devised for himself. There he met another hapless strong-willed man, Lord Gordon (not yet a fully accoutered and convinced Jew), but no record exists of any dialogue between them.

In that autumn of 1779, John Adams was also setting out to sea, assigned to make the final peace treaty with England. No one thought that victory was imminent, but in view of the mediation and appeasement efforts of Spain and the difficulty of communications, it was considered wise to have a minister plenipotentiary on hand in Europe. The Lee faction, now constituting an Anti-Gallican party, had strenuously vetoed Benjamin Franklin for the job. Reluctantly the French accepted Adams, though the Chevalier de la Luzerne and his aide François Barbé-Marbois had lobbied strenuously against him in the corridors of Congress. Vergennes had found Adams distinctly uncongenial, no doubt, recalling with distaste his somewhat hysterical behavior at the time of the Deane-Lee crisis.

Concealing whatever misgivings they may have had, the French put at Adams' disposal the *Sensible*, the same vessel that had brought him home just three months earlier. There was again the question whether Abigail should go along and again the reluctant decision to leave her behind because Congress would not pay her way. She accepted the verdict tearfully and prepared once again to endure the lonely life at Braintree, which, as it turned out, was to be cheered by the increasingly ardent (literary) lovemaking of Adams' friend and colleague James Lovell.

Adams, declaring that he regarded "the voice of my country as the command of Heaven," was again shepherding a covey of children on this expedition. There were John Quincy Adams, now twelve, embarking on his second mission to Europe with only mild misgivings about seasickness; Charles Adams, eight; and Samuel Cooper Johannot, eleven, dispatched by his family to get an education abroad. There was also John Adams' one-time law apprentice, John Thaxter, a gentle young man who, during Adams' first mission to France, had held down the law office, tutored the Adams children, and served as a correspondent, filling Adams in on the family news when Abigail was not disposed to write. Now he was to be Adams' personal secretary. As the official legation secretary, aide, and replacement if necessary, there was Francis Dana, a flinty lawyer of impeccable New England moral standards, a political view that tallied in all respects with Adams', and a lineage of solid republican virtue. (He could recall his father dictating a recantation to the Tory Andrew Oliver to sign while a mob howled for Oliver's blood beneath the Liberty Tree in the days of the Stamp Act crisis. Dana remembered the effigy of Oliver swinging from a tree along with a petticoat, representing the King's mother, and a cast-off shoe, the punning symbol of Lord Bute, her lover and political mentor.)

A ramrod of a man with hair in straight-cut bangs over his forehead and a forbidding, thin-lipped face, Dana had been abroad before. In 1775 he had gone to England as an unofficial American envoy to the Wilkes movement. On that occasion he had missed meeting Franklin, who had already left, but had mingled with the coffeehouse radicals. He had encountered a maverick self-appointed American agent, Stephen Sayre, who helped convince him of the necessity for revolution. Sayre was then an ardent follower of Arthur Lee and part of the cabal on Artillery Row that began the factional assault on Franklin. Thus indoctrinated, Dana was in a position to bolster Adams in his suspicions of the venerable sage of Passy.

Dana had also served in the Continental Congress, where he demonstrated an unflagging loyalty to Washington when the general came under attack by military men and a faction of the Congress.

They left Boston in mid-November with French sailors in the rigging, shouting, *"Vive le roi!"* Off Cape Ann the *Sensible* sprang a leak and all hands, including the minister plenipotentiary of the United States, had to man the pumps. The leak, which continued on and off throughout the voyage, became critical as the *Sensible* neared Cape Finisterre on December 7. Though they were almost in sight of France, the captain decided to head for the closest port, the Spanish harbor of El Ferrol. The diversion was a monumental nuisance, for it meant that Adams would either have to wait in El Ferrol for another vessel or go over the Pyrenees. Rashly, he chose the mountain route.

On shore there were Spanish courtesies for the minister plenipotentiary that gratified Adams' notion of proper respect, and there were pleasant political chats with convivial Irish grandees like those who charmed the Jays. Adams everywhere advanced his simple, emphatic argument: the independence of the United States would enormously benefit every European power but England, and it was therefore the most logical course for every king and emperor on the Continent to forthwith back the new republic with all their resources. There was no need for Spain to fear the spread of revolution in her own colonies. "The Spanish Constitution was such as could extinguish the first sparks of discontent, and quell the first risings of the People," declared this most pragmatic American whose interest in revolution stopped at the borders of the thirteen United States.

The Adams family, Dana, and Thaxter sampled the Spanish pork (which they found excellent), the cabbages (astonishing), the law courts (interesting but incomprehensible, save for the dramatic Latin gestures). Dana chronicled the female fashions, marveling that, contrary to previous reports, the ladies made "no difficulty in showing the foot" and wore veils that were not meant to conceal. They went into all the cathedrals they could find, and Adams proudly declined to bend his knee when the bishop walked past during mass. "I contented myself with a bow," he later noted. "The eagle eye of the bishop did not fail to observe an upright figure amidst the crowd of prostrate adorers: but . . . he concluded I was some traveling heretick and did not think it worth while to exert his authority to bend my stiff knees." Adams fancied he saw in the bishop's reproving eyes a message: "You are not only a Heretick but you are not a Gentleman, for a Gentleman would have respected the religion of the country and its usages so far as to have conformed externally to a ceremony that cost so little."

No matter, a nod was as far as an Adams could go in compromise. The title of minister plenipotentiary seemed to stiffen all of Adams' joints and did not promise much flexibility in the arduous diplomacy that lay ahead.

Once they began climbing into the Pyrenees in their mule-drawn carriages, the going was grim. Though Adams admired a fandango in a village plaza, he found the "people ragged and dirty, and the houses universally nothing but mire, smoke, fleas and lice." In Spain, he noted, there is "nobody fat but the clergy." Most of the inns were appalling. The ground level was divided between the stable and the kitchen, where slept the innkeeper and his large family, the servants, muleteers, and a fattening hog or two. An upstairs chamber housed the Americans, with two straw beds for the lot on a floor that "had never been washed or swept for an hundred years."

After Burgos the spirits of the travelers reached an abysmal point. "Every individual person in company has a great cold," Adams noted in his diary. "We go along barking and sneezing and coughing as if we were fitter for an hospital than for travelers on the road. My servants and all the other servants in company, behave worse than I ever knew servants behave. They are dull, inactive, unskillful. The children are sick, and in short my patience was never so near being exhausted as at present."

Thaxter, whose talents were well known to Adams (and these decidedly did not include a facility at foreign languages), suddenly seemed to be a monstrous liability as they went over the mountain passes. The thin air frazzled the Adams composure. "Mr. Thaxter is as shiftless as a child," Adams exploded. "He understands no language, neither French, nor Spanish, and he don't seem to think himself obliged to do anything, but get along and write in his journal." It is not clear from Adams' meticulous diary what he himself did other than write in it. In any case, Adams was in a bad way: "In short, I am in a deplorable situation, indeed—I know not what to do—I know not where to go."

Dana, also scribbling away in his journal, was not only whooping and sneezing but had come down with a debilitating mountain sickness, complete with dizzy spells.

After Bilbao they abandoned the carriages and took to muleback. When they had crossed the French border and descended to Bayonne, they discharged their muleteers, their mules, and all things Spanish. They bought one post chaise and rented two others for the dash to Paris. But at Coué they were caught in a storm of snow and ice that glazed the roads. Dana was still suffering from headaches and a case of nerves, but Adams' despair seemed to have vanished, and as they rattled along through the vineyards of France his spirits rose. He was again the confident minister plenipotentiary with full powers to gather his country's fruits of victory at the conference table and his own share of glory. The only hitch was that as yet there was no conference and victory seemed far-distant, even problematical. The English had taken Charleston, Benedict Arnold had defected, and American soldiers were going hungry. In some places, they were rising in mutiny. The hope that some good might come of Spanish efforts at mediation (which was the actual impetus for the Adams mission) had faded.

It might seem in retrospect to have been a ludicrous moment to dispatch a commissioner to negotiate peace. Still, it was reasoned, if the prospect brightened it would be better to have a man on the scene than an ocean away. And the appointment had suited the tactical needs of the moment in the factional battles of Philadelphia. The peace commissioner would simply have to wait in Paris for a better season. For such idle waiting Adams was unprepared by temperament or talent.

The Adams-Dana party reached Paris at nine in the evening of February 9, and checked in at the Hôtel de Valois on the rue Richelieu. Early the next morning they rode out to Passy to meet with Franklin, who was less than overjoyed to see them. Congress had failed to inform Franklin officially of Adams' mission, though word of it had reached Passy. It was strange that Franklin, the most widely respected American diplomat, the one who had handled virtually all of the nation's affairs in Europe and who had enticed or wheedled a seemingly inexhaustible flow of French money into American hands, should be excluded from the final negotiations. He took the affront philosophically and, in a letter to David Hartley just a week before Adams' arrival, suggested mildly that if Congress had so decided, "it is perhaps because they may have heard of a very singular opinion of mine, that there hardly ever existed such a thing as a bad peace or a good war; and that I might therefore easily be induced to make improper concessions."

Actually, even if Franklin had been only half as astute as he was, he would have guessed that the selection of Adams over himself had less to do with such philosophical considerations than with the factional horse trading among the Gallicans and Anti-Gallicans, the pro-Lees and the pro-Deanes. Whatever his feelings, he was cordial when Adams and Dana arrived. He took them on a day of diplomatic rounds: a half hour's chat with Vergennes, bows and smiles of greeting from the Secretary of State for the Marine and from the Count de Maurepas. They returned in time for dinner at Passy with Chaumont and a walk to see the Count d'Estaing, still recovering from wounds suffered in a sea fight in the Caribbean.

But there was no invitation to Adams or Dana to take up their residence at Passy. Benjamin Franklin, no doubt, thought it a bit much to be expected to have his work habits and his household routine subjected again to the withering eye of Adams or perhaps even worse of Arthur Lee, who, though officially recalled after the Embassy was turned over to Franklin's exclusive management, lingered on in Paris. There was, certainly, a technical justification in withholding the invitation. After all,

Adams was no longer to be involved in Franco-American affairs and there was no official reason for collaboration. Prior experience surely offered no personal reasons for it.

Adams and Dana therefore returned to their hotel, to find that Arthur Lee had left his card. They quickly hurried over to see that embittered politico and made arrangements to confer with him the next day.

The conversation with Lee emphasized the continued presence and growing importance of the Franklinet, as Franklin's grandson Temple was now generally known in Paris. The Lees and Adams deplored the fact that this bastard son of a bastard father—an ardent English loyalist—was representing at the Court of France the most self-consciously moral republic ever created. At the time, the Franklinet was appearing at the Tuesday Court levees only when his grandfather's gout made the carriage ride too painful. These were purely ceremonial appearances involving not the slightest reflection of policy, and young Temple had little to do but make the requisite gracious gestures, at which he had grown quite adept. Even such ceremonial dances, when performed by a young man of doubtful origins and dubious morality, seemed to Lee and Adams to taint the virginal purity of the Cause.

Complaints concerning the Franklinet reached Passy but did not seem to bother Franklin so long as the complainers stayed on the rue Richelieu.

The boys were packed off to M. Pechigny's Academy at Passy and John Adams proceeded to the most strenuous idleness ever practiced by an unemployed diplomat. He toured Paris systematically (it was the Adams way), having his servant drive him to every celebrated site. He shopped for cambric, handkerchiefs, ribbons, and tablecloths to please Abigail. These expeditions, however, only exacerbated his homesickness and his dislike for the "dissipation, vanity and knavery" of Europe. He wrote to Abigail that he was growing "every day more and more wearied and disgusted with Europe, and more and more impatient to return forever to that country where alone I was or shall be happy."

The continuing popularity of Franklin irked him exceedingly, though he protested, perhaps too much, that he dreaded the infection of envy more than the pox "contracted here by an acquaintance with the elegant nymphs of the boulevards." His iron discipline could keep him safe from the nymphs but not, unfortunately, from the other malady.

He chafed at the galling pace of events and in the midst of Paris thought of himself abandoned in a backwater. "I wish I were at home," he wrote James Warren, "that I might do something worthy of history; here I can do nothing. The beauteous olive branch will never decorate my brows. I must spend my life in the pride, pomp and circumstance of glorious war, without sharing any of its laurels."

His despair of olive branches and laurels was transitory, like his wail of anguish atop the Pyrenees. When uncertain of direction John Adams drove on with increasing frenzy. He tracked down every rumor that floated through the town and dispatched his conclusions to Philadelphia along with copies of long articles in the press and a stream of letters, reports, and memoranda. These consumed not only his own time and energy but Dana's and Thaxter's as well. Some of this massive outpouring of correspondence was helpful and most of it was interesting, but when he chose to instruct Vergennes on diplomacy, it became plain that there is nothing so dangerous as pride perched powerless on a shelf.

Without any consultation with Franklin, Adams dispatched a letter to Vergennes informing him of his mission and requesting advice as to whether he should at once make contact with the English Prime Minister.

The notion of announcing a peace mission at a time when England had no reason to meet American terms was so absurd that it seemed to confirm Vergennes's worst fears about the wisdom of leaving any responsible negotiations to John Adams. It undoubtedly spurred French efforts to persuade the Congress to do something to curb this American patriot who was as subtle as a cavalry charge.

Vergennes's answer succeeded only in infuriating Adams. The note conveyed the customary flowery sentiments and urged him strongly to conceal his mission, particularly from the English. This was unpleasant news, but the goad that drove Adams to fury was Vergennes's suggestion that "it is convenient to wait for the arrival of Mr. Gérard [then making his way through Spain] because he is probably the bearer of your instructions and he will certainly have it in his power to give me explanations, concerning the nature and extent of your commission."

Adams flew into a rage on receiving Vergennes's letter because it seemed to violate the privacy of an envoy's instructions and proved that the French emissary was seeking to step between him and Congress to ascertain those instructions. Now although Vergennes's letter was less than tactful, Adams seemed to ignore the realities of the situation. "The Count de Vergennes," he noted naïvely, "had been so long in the habit of intrigues to obtain the instructions from foreign courts to their ambassadors, and probably paying for them very dear, that he had forgotten that the practice was unlawful."

The fact of the matter, well known to Adams, was that Gérard had been intimately involved in drafting those instructions. He had outlined the French position repeatedly to Congress, and members of the Gallican party consulted with him at every stage of the debate. He was shown the final draft of the instructions before it was presented to Congress and had dispatched a summary of it to Vergennes.

Adams detested the blunt reminder of that reality more than the reality itself. And he wanted to preserve at least the fiction of independent American action because he hoped to modify his instructions in practice, winning more fishing rights for New Englanders and better boundary lines than the Congress had suggested.

Pressed by Adams, Vergennes agreed that there was no obstacle to making known the general purposes of his mission but emphatically warned against communicating officially with the English or revealing any notion of a commercial treaty with England. Vergennes likened this rush to discuss postwar business relations to a preoccupation "with the ornament of a house before the foundation is laid."

Adams read the most sinister motives of commercial competition in that warning and obeyed it only grudgingly. From that low point, the relationship between Adams and Vergennes went swiftly downhill. Vergennes was incensed at the action taken by Congress to depreciate American currency by forty to one. It may have helped the desperate financial straits of the new country, which were almost as dismal as the military. But quite apart from outright governmental gifts to America, private French creditors who had extended loans of some $200 million now suddenly found that they held paper worth no more than $5 million.

Vergennes was more tactful this time but ice-cold: "I do not presume, sir," he wrote Adams, "to criticize . . . because I have no right to examine or comment upon the internal arrangements which Congress may consider just and profitable." But he pointed out how French merchants who had trusted Congress might now consider themselves "plundered."

Adams countered with a sermon on the advantages which French trade had gained from the Americans' rupture with England. "The obligations are mutual," he asserted, suggesting that the generosity of King Louis was copiously adulterated with self-interest. There was a kernel of truth in Adams' contention, of course, but it had the ungrateful ring of a patient telling the surgeon who had saved his life that he did it only for the fee and his medical reputation.

Vergennes sought to break off the exchange: "The details into which you have thought proper to enter have not changed my sentiments; but I think that all further discussion between us on this subject will be needless."

Needless to Vergennes, but not to Adams. He wrote again, repeating his sermon. When that brought no reply he fired another volley criticizing the lack of French naval activity in behalf of America. He was not asking for help but demanding it, pointing out yet again the debt that France owed America for declaring its own independence and asserting that "the United States of America are a great and powerful people, whatever European statesmen may think of them." Vergennes, ignoring the bumptious protestations of American grandeur, soberly informed Adams of the naval operations then under way, meshed with the strategies of General Washington on land.

Delighted to hear it, said Adams in effect, but you do us no favors that we do not reciprocate. Then he went back to his earlier point, demanding the right to inform the English at once of his political and commercial mission. Vergennes again went over all the arguments against such premature contact with the English, urging him to pass his letter on to Congress.

From the Hôtel de Valois (where Arthur Lee helped stoke the fires) there issued a continuing stream of belligerent letters, until in one such communiqué Adams proposed to continue indefinitely his self-appointed role as political mentor to the King's minister, in the process sideswiping Benjamin Franklin. "I am determined," Adams wrote, "to omit no opportunity of communicating my sentiments to Your Excellency upon everything that appears to me of importance to the common cause . . . without the intervention of any third person. And I shall be very happy and think myself honored, to give my poor advice to His Majesty's Ministers upon anything that relates to the United States or the common cause whenever they shall be asked." The prospect was too painful for Vergennes to contemplate.

Historians have not come up with any explanation for Adams' headlong rush to diplomatic disaster. One can only ascribe it to Lee's needling, the boredom of a Puritan in Paris with nothing to do, and the workings of Adams' noble but somewhat obtuse spirit.

In any case, Vergennes cut him off: "To avoid further discussion . . . I think it my duty to inform you that Mr. Franklin being the sole person who has letters of credence to the King from the United States, it is with him only that I ought and can treat of matters which concern them."

The minister then turned over the entire Adams correspondence to Franklin, suggesting that he send the file to Congress to let them know "the line of conduct which Mr. Adams pursues with regard to us, and that they may judge whether he is endowed, as Congress no doubt desires, with that conciliating spirit which is necessary for the important and delicate business with which he is entrusted."

At the same time Vergennes wrote to Luzerne in Philadelphia: "As to Dr. Franklin, his conduct leaves nothing for Congress to desire . . . the method he pursues is much more efficacious than it would be if he were to assume a tone of importunity in multiplying his demands, and above all in supporting them with threats, to which we should give neither credence nor value, and which would only tend to render him personally disagreeable."

Franklin, throughout the Adams-Vergennes duel, had played with his customary soft and beguiling touch on the taut strings of the French Court. In the matter of the abrupt American devaluation, he confessed to an ignorance of economics, assured Vergennes that he would take up the matter with Congress, and hoped to ease the blow to French creditors. (Actually Congress never altered its harsh fiscal policy.) Franklin saw the necessity of tact because it was he, not Adams, who had to find French money to stanch the flood of congressional drafts and to handle the multitude of problems involved in a steady funneling of French military and economic aid across the ocean.

Franklin sent off the Adams-Vergennes correspondence to Congress with a covering note outlining the conflict and reporting that Vergennes would have nothing more to do with Adams. His own criticism, mildly phrased as it was, was devastating. He said that due perhaps to a lack of a proper outlet for his energies Adams "seems to have endeavored supplying what he may suppose my negotiations defective in." Franklin reported Adams' oft-repeated contention that France was as much or more indebted to the United States than the United States was to France. "I apprehend," wrote Franklin, "that he mistakes his ground, and that this court is to be treated with decency and delicacy." An expression of gratitude, Franklin went on, "is not only our duty but our interest." He offered Adams a chance to amend the record but Adams refused.

Adams saw in his humiliation only a conspiracy by Vergennes and Franklin, but if that was the case, never had a victim dug himself a grave with such stubborn zeal. It seems more likely that he was the victim of another conspiracy, first hatched on Artillery Row in London when the anti-Franklin cabal was formed. As usual in the story of that snipers' warfare, the marksmanship was pathetic. In this instance Adams suffered far more than Franklin.

In any case Adams' position in Paris had become untenable. He was at odds with Franklin and Vergennes not only on matters of philosophy, tactics, and life style but on the attitude to be taken toward that most dashing of heroes, John Paul Jones. Adams had had a brush with the "admiral" during his first stay in Paris. They disliked each other on sight.

Jones referred to Adams behind his back as "Mr. Roundface" and "the upstart." Adams thought Jones "an intriguer." He was put off by Jones's exuberant showmanship: the dress uniforms he designed for himself and his officers had golden buttonholes and magnificent glittering epaulets. Jones had discarded Congress's regulation green uniforms and dressed his Marines in spanking red and white. Adams thought this revealed the man's character. He saw—and loudly deplored—such "eccentricities and irregularities." He detected a dangerous tendency in Jones's eyes, which had "keenness and wildness and softness," and in his voice, "soft and still and small." And he loathed Jones's widely proclaimed exploits of the bedroom. Jones seemed to him quite Franklinesque.

In 1780 John Paul Jones was more of a hero than ever. He had been carrying the American flag to the enemy with a vengeance. His flagship, the *Bonhomme Richard* (named after Franklin's Poor Richard), was taking prizes in the English Channel and the Baltic. It was only the previous September that Jones had fluttered the hearts of all Europe in the celebrated capture of the *Serapis.* Jones's little flotilla had been engaged in a battle that was not going altogether well. A broadside fired by an American ship had, by some mysterious fluke, struck the *Bonhomme Richard.* As his ship was going down Jones leaped to the deck of the *Serapis* with his men behind him. They overpowered the crew and took the vessel into a Dutch port as a prize of war. The fastidiously neutral Dutch were embarrassed, but Jones turned the captured vessel over to a French commander and went on to Paris to wear his laurels. He became the adored social lion of the capital. Louis ceremonially presented him with a sword of honor, and when Franklin brought the hero around to the Queen's levee, she gave him a chain and seal. "Sweet girl," Jones said when he was asked later to comment on Marie Antoinette.

Jones was given the command of another American vessel, the *Alliance*, due to sail on March 3, 1780, for the United States with two most distinguished passengers, Arthur Lee and Ralph Izard, bound home at last to tell the full story of the Franklin betrayal.

The sailing of the *Alliance* was delayed, ostensibly for repairs. The pathetically suspicious Lee was convinced that it was because Jones could not be dragged away from the wicked women of Paris and the adulation that marked his progress from party to levee to grand ball to soiree to bedroom. Aboard the *Alliance* was an eccentric officer named Pierre Landais, who had gone around the world with the French explorer Louis Antoine de Bougainville and had served with distinction in the French and American navies. Although he had an abiding hostility toward John Paul Jones, it was considered no more than coincidental that Landais had been in command of the ship whose misdirected broadside sank the *Bonhomme Richard.* There was no doubt of Landais's raging jealousy, but Jones was certainly not its only or major target. Jealousy seemed to radiate from the man. He had commanded the *Alliance* on Adams' return from his first voyage, and Adams noted at the time: "Landais is jealous of every thing. Jealous of every body, of all his officers, all his passengers nor any body else."

Clearly the combination of Lee, Izard, and Landais was dangerous. At Lee's instigation Landais dumped Jones's baggage on the dock, took over the *Alliance,* and set sail. (Jones insisted that Landais had gotten rid of his baggage to make room for a post chaise that he had taken aboard as part of his personal belongings.) It seemed an open-and-shut case of mutiny, and the French were willing to overtake the *Alliance* at sea and return her to France if Franklin so requested. But Franklin could not bear to bring back Lee and Izard after waiting so long to see them gone. On the voyage Landais was reported to have become so unmanageable that he had to be confined, but the ship made port safely, and Lee and Izard were in a position to resume their campaign in Philadelphia.

Franklin was then relieved of the remaining thorn in his side. Regarding the shambles in Paris as temporarily beyond his control, Adams turned toward Holland, where he thought he might complete Henry Laurens' aborted mission, digging for guilders in the bulging pockets of the burghers.

Both Vergennes and Franklin had grave doubts about the venture. Dutch neutrality—valuable to the French and Americans because it made trade possible in Dutch ships—was a delicate reed. They feared it might not stand up under the heavy tread of honest John Adams' forthright diplomacy. They gave their reluctant blessings, however, added cautions which they knew Adams would not take, and put no obstacle in his way.

Adams would travel as a private citizen because as yet he had not heard of Congress's action, taken a month earlier, to appoint him commissioner to The Hague so long as Laurens remained in the Tower of London. He approved of all that he saw on his trip through the Low Countries; the roads, the vineyards, the grain fields, the sheep. He even brought himself to a mild religious tolerance. After "cursing the knavery of the Priesthood and the brutal ignorance of the people," he added in his diary, "yet, perhaps I was rash and unreasonable, and that it is as much virtue and wisdom in them to adore, as in me to detest and despise."

At Brussels he enjoyed a comforting tea with what he termed "an agreeable circle of Americans." These included William Lee and Mrs.

Izard and her children. Adams traveled on, made Rotterdam on August 7, and went by canal boat to The Hague, where, incognito, the American minister plenipotentiary set about making contacts. He conferred briefly with Charles William Frederic Dumas, Franklin's friend and correspondent, who for more than a decade had loyally (and generally without recompense) worked as the American representative in Holland. There was also Alexander Gillon, who called himself "the Commodore of the South Carolina Navy." (He had bought a Dutch frigate and named it for his native state.) And there were the merchants who were to steer Adams to the guarded coffers of the Dutch republic.

Away from the dissipations of Paris and what he had come to consider the Vergennes-Franklin conspiracy to frustrate him, Adams' spirits revived. Actually they soared. In no time he was dreaming of winning not only Dutch money but Dutch recognition (unmindful as ever of the political realities which made Dutch neutrality far more valuable than co-belligerence). And to mark his euphoria he prophesied that the French language would soon go the way of Latin and that in the coming century "English would be the general language . . . and that America would make it so."

He formally suggested that Congress form an Academy for "refining improving and ascertaining" the new universal language. But Congress, when not tearing itself to shreds, was struggling to maintain the barest semblance of nation in a war that was going badly. And European diplomats, paying no mind to the cocky claims of the representative of a band of poverty-stricken, alms-seeking, utterly dependent band of rebels, fixed their attention on the East, where the Tsarina of Russia and the Holy Roman Emperor were about to take a hand in this war that had begun in Boston, Massachusetts, and was involving all of the Old World.

I X

IN WHICH ONE PURITAN CAJOLES THEIR HIGH MIGHTINESSES IN HOLLAND AND ANOTHER WAITS UPON THE SCARLET EMPRESS OF RUSSIA

WHEN EUROPEAN STATESMEN contemplated the war that began in Boston and was now lapping at their shores, they tended to see it as a mishap, but perhaps a providential one. Ranging into exotic parts, England had been stung by a swarm of mosquitoes and was being distracted by the attendant itch. The result was that a realignment of power became possible, with all of its inviting and/or terrifying prospects.

The intellectuals of France and Britain might see in the American experiment a certain philosophical significance and welcome it. The Court of Spain might see the same and dread it. Businessmen might begin to reckon the profits of a transatlantic trade. But for the most part European ministers of state looked upon the future of those rambunctious American mosquitoes as incidental to the issues of the European power balance.

Maria Theresa, the Hapsburg Queen of Hungary and Bohemia, mother of Marie Antoinette and of Joseph II, the Holy Roman Emperor, trembled in her customary tearful way lest England and France consume each other and leave Europe to Frederick II of Prussia, her private bugaboo. Maria Theresa was old now and had seen her triumphs fade. There was a time when she had negotiated the most unlikely alliance in Europe —Hapsburg Austria, Bourbon France, and that unpredictable colossus, Russia—against Prussia. But in the end her allies had "mediated" her out of a piece of Bavaria which her troops had already seized. She and her minister and mentor, the aging Prince Wenzel Anton von Kaunitz-Rietberg, had gone on trying to pull the strings of Marie Antoinette as if the Queen of France were an Austrian puppet. Maria Theresa reinforced her maternal advice with the blandishments of the Count Mercy d'Argenteau, a naturalized Frenchman who, with his mistress, ran a glittering salon in Paris where he did Vienna's work.

To end the present inconvenient war, Maria Theresa resolved to step in where Spain had failed, and try to mediate the hostilities. Her ministers suggested the possibility of a truce which would allow the British to sit tight wherever they presently sat in America—New York, Georgia, the Carolinas—and give freedom or something like it to the remaining colonies. For Vergennes this particular peace dove suffered from bad timing and a suspect origin. It came too early and it carried Hapsburg ambitions along with its olive branch. England, too, was unreceptive. The trial balloon evoked only passing interest in the Courts of Europe.

The next dove to go aloft came from St. Petersburg. It would be difficult to imagine a more incongruous source of possible salvation for the Puritanical republican rebels than the bizarre Court of Catherine II, Empress of Russia and queen of paradoxes. She was a rationalist who subsidized Diderot and Voltaire, but she walked from Moscow to Kiev to exhibit her piety to her clergy and her peasants. She was a German, but she was at least an accessory to the murder of her Romanov husband because he was too much in love with all things Prussian. She was the most feminine and flirtatious of women, but she seized power in a bloodless coup, riding in a broken-down carriage at the head of a handful of guardsmen. She would touch no liquor and was inclined to reprove a mildly saucy story, but she took a succession of lovers as a king takes mistresses, thereby reversing the sex roles of her Court, so that young nobles fussed over their toilet and wore the most revealing codpieces to catch their ruler's appraising eye. "I love uncivilized countries," she wrote. "As I have said a thousand times, I belong to Russia."

She belonged to a country in which the overwhelming majority were serfs to be bought, sold, mated, or decimated at the will of their owners; serfs who could be traded for an ox or a dog, or given away as a present. She belonged to a country where nobles rode to and from their palaces in sleds that were in fact sumptuous mobile living rooms, gilded, furred, and satined for the comfort of their usually overfed passengers. Catherine talked and wrote learnedly, wittily, and probably sincerely of freedom. The Little Mother of Russia had attempted active reforms on occasion, even to the freeing of the serfs in the copper mines. But, unprepared for the sudden sun of emancipation, the liberated slaves had stumbled about blindly, walked off their jobs, stopped the mines, reeled around the countryside, and had taken to looting. Sadly the disciple of Voltaire had written: "It is easy for the Philosophes who write on paper but I must write on stubborn flesh."

Popular freedom was an idea she would teach her grandchildren or discuss in polished correspondence. She practiced it only behind the closed doors of her private quarters, where any servant who stood up when the Empress entered was fined a ruble for such a lapse from classless democracy. (The fines were given to the poor.) If a servant was busy playing cards when the Empress wanted an errand run, she would take over his hand rather than break up the game. That was the private Catherine, playing at democracy as a child plays house.

True, the Imperial Catherine had secularized some of the Church lands and browbeat the clergy who protested. But she never moved against the sanctity and power of the state hierarchy. She was careful to observe all the rites of the Orthodox Church, which in fact she headed, though she had been raised as a Lutheran. In this, she followed Voltaire, who, when asked to explain how he could bring himself to take Holy Communion, said that he "breakfasted according to the custom of the country."

She banned capital punishment except in cases of high treason, and even in the case of such threats to the Crown she consistently overruled her judges when they ordered spectacular lingering deaths or macabre drawings and quarterings, ordaining instead a merciful swift execution. In practice, however, many lesser felons, spared the death penalty, died under the knout—which was administered brutally—or else perished in chains on the way to Siberia. And it is doubtful whether all or many of the governors and serf owners in remote areas paid scrupulous attention to the injunctions against torture contained in the humane "Instructions" that Catherine issued in the early days of her reign.

Certainly her orders to be merciful were countermanded by the officers who put down the devastating revolt led by Pugachev, that preposterous impostor who pretended to be Catherine's hapless murdered husband, Tsar Peter III. Thousands were tortured and hanged, and whole villages went up in smoke at the hands of both rebels and soldiers. After Pugachev was executed Catherine put Diderot and Voltaire firmly back on the shelf.

Though she yielded up her dreams of the Rights of Man when confronted by the facts of the country which she had adopted, Catherine could at least teach her lovers to gather the art works of the Western world and her largely illiterate courtiers to strike French or English poses. (It was said that an ingenious Finn made a living teaching his native language to the children of nobles by convincing them it was French.)

Above all, she continued the work of Peter the Great not only by opening the windows of Russia to the West but by stretching its walls. These came to encompass not only parts of Poland and the Baltic states but also the Crimea and Greece. (Since this southern expansion was at the expense of the infidel Turk, conquest could be paraded as crusade.) Significantly, Catherine had her grandsons christened Alexander and Constantine to remind the world of her Eastern pretensions. She envisioned the Russian banners flying to the borders of China and perhaps beyond, commanding all the trade routes of the East. The Empress had an enormous political appetite and knew how to furnish her table. She could withstand the scorn of the sanctimonious Maria Theresa, who envied her success on the battlefield and in the conference chamber but deplored her equally spectacular, energetic, and celebrated conquests in bed. (Maria Theresa generally referred to Catherine as *"cette femme."*) Catherine took her revenge in regal generosity. She tossed Austria a piece of Poland, and Maria Theresa was reported to have wept yet again at the sad partition of that victimized kingdom while digesting her allotted portion of it.

Catherine's diplomacy was guided in part by her one-time lover and lifelong friend, that curious combination of brilliance and sloth, of Western shrewdness and the gaudiness of a sultan, Gregory Potemkin. His— and her—objective was to keep Russia so powerful that it must always be wooed but need never yield. She sought peace with the West not in any alliance of friendship but in the bonds of fear. Catherine summed up her diplomatic hopes in a letter to her ambassador in Poland: "I wish to remain on friendly terms with all the powers, even to be on the defensive, so that I may always take the part of the most oppressed side and thus become Europe's arbiter."

It was, therefore, not altogether surprising that this ruler of a country, which a couple of generations earlier had been regarded as a primitive medieval hinterland beyond the pale of civilization, should now presume to settle the bickerings of Europe and the troubles of America.

She was prodded to the step because her ships had been seized by privateers, and the traditional ports for Russia's commerce had been blocked by warring navies. In February 1780, the Spanish fleet had taken a number of neutral vessels, including several Russian ships.

To Sir James Harris, the British ambassador in St. Petersburg, this Spanish naval action seemed an act of Providence, rescuing Britain diplomatically as it had been saved militarily by the heaven-sent gale and smallpox that had frustrated the invasion effort of the French and Spanish fleets. English diplomacy had not only lost its thirteen colonies but antagonized every power in Europe save Russia. Even there the English were in trouble. While France had proved eminently helpful to Catherine in various "mediations," whether in Bavaria or Turkey, England had remained aloof, counting on the sympathies which Catherine professed for the world's most democratic monarchy. (She regretted the fact that her beloved barbaric Russia could not in her time be brought to emulate the English system.)

This divided monarch in her middle age was described as having the head of a general on the body of an attractive buxom matron. Her mind itself was subdivided into that of a general and that of a philosopher. Her attitude toward the American rebels varied depending on the role she might choose for herself at any given time. The philosophical Catherine could lecture the British ambassador on the wicked behavior of his government, but when he asked her what she would do if Russia's captive nations demanded independence, General Catherine would reply: "I would rather lose my head."

Philosopher Catherine might welcome the birth of freedom in correspondence with her French intellectual protégés, but even after Louis XVI officially received Franklin, General Catherine instructed her ambassador in Paris on no account to pay the American an official visit as prescribed by the courtesies of the diplomatic corps.

The Court and Parliament of George III refused to understand that Catherine, however flighty her loves and caprices, however ardent her admiration for English ways, took her job more seriously than her personal predilections. And her job was to work for the security and aggrandizement of Russia.

George's minister Harris was left to play a difficult game with no trump in his hand. He was cut off from communications with the Foreign Office. At best a letter might take a month and a half or more to reach London. And when the ice clogged the harbors there was nothing to do but wait for the thaw. Even in good seasons instructions rarely came; when they did they were absurdly foggy. He was on his own in this most un-British Court, where all business came to a standstill whenever Catherine changed lovers; where an ambassador had to appear at every dance and levee or risk the displeasure of Her Majesty; where business had to be done in bedrooms or anterooms or with ministers who accepted bribes as the necessary lubricant of diplomacy. It was not the element which an English gentleman finds congenial. And Harris was the starchiest of English diplomats. He could not bring himself to accomplish the coup of his predecessor, who had endeared himself to the Empress by finding her a handsome Polish lover. Harris abandoned hope of winning Catherine to an outright military alliance, but he thought he might, with luck, persuade her to denounce the war against England and to arm her ships as a warning to France.

In the summer of 1779, when Spain's entry into the war left Britain isolated and fighting against odds on both sides of the ocean, Sir James decided that he must put his plan before Catherine in private. There were two routes to such an encounter, one through the current lover—the Empress's adjutant general of the bedchamber—and the other through Prince Potemkin. The Prince, one-eyed (from an encounter with one of Catherine's athletic favorites), grown paunchier and more slothful, still held the best key to Catherine because although he no longer shared her bed, he totally possessed her affections and her respect—which was more than most of her lovers possessed.

Harris chose the Potemkin path, a difficult step for him because until then he had played with the Prince's arch-rival, Count Nikita Ivanovich Panin, the Foreign Minister. Potemkin proved unexpectedly amenable, however, at a quiet meeting off in the country. Harris returned to St. Petersburg to wait for a sign. Each day he would take up his post at the summer palace and study the Empress's moods. These were unfailingly affable. As was her way with favorite diplomats, Catherine would often invite Harris to a game of cards or a light unceremonial snack around a card table with the Grand Duke or some other chosen intimate. No servants intruded; no guards stood at attendance. But also no business was to be transacted.

One evening late in July he was playing cards with the Empress during a masked ball, and the talk was flowing in its accustomed trivial channels. After Catherine had retired for the evening and the English minister was making his way through the glittering ballroom, the Tsarina's lover of the moment, an officer of the Guards, caught up with him. The Empress would see him at once. He was led through a labyrinth of dimly lit corridors, reserved for visitors who were not to be seen on their way to the Tsarina's private apartments. The interview went well. The Empress expressed her concern for the fate of England, though she underscored her reluctance to plunge her country into a war. Perhaps Harris' suggestion of a gesture might be practical. Would he spell out the proposal in writing? she asked.

He did so promptly and then waited all through the autumn and winter of 1779 and 1780 until at last news reached St. Petersburg of the Spanish seizure of the Russian ship. By rare good luck it had been the same vessel that was stopped only a little while earlier by a British cruiser, whose commander, with a great show of gallantry, courtesy, and profuse apologies, had sent it on its way unharmed.

The British ambassador pressed his case, sure that its time had come. And so it had. Potemkin summoned Harris and beamingly announced that henceforth the Russian merchant fleet would sail fully armed and would defend the rights of neutral shipping against all belligerents. Moreover, a Declaration of Neutral Rights would go out to all nations still out of the war. The Empress would thus advance the high principle of the freedom of the seas, a principle that set England's teeth on edge.

Harris was dumfounded. He had wanted a gesture that would frighten England's enemies and raise the specter of an Anglo-Russian alliance. Instead he got a virtual alliance of neutrals that might challenge England on the high seas, his country's lifeline, the one element in which it could match all of its enemies. No matter that Potemkin explained that the Declaration was aimed against Spain; it would hurt England far more. The victory for which Harris wheedled, danced, courted, and played cards to all hours had been transformed into a diplomatic fiasco.

Catherine's Declaration of Armed Neutrality, issued in March 1780, proved singularly ineffective, however. Though most of the neutrals joined it at the Tsarina's invitation, they evaded or defected in short order and after a while Catherine herself laughed it off as her declaration of "armed nullity." She could afford to do so because she was then entranced with a new prospect: she would mediate the war and make herself and Russia the arbiter of the Western world, balancing its powers to suit herself.

There was another aspiring arbitrator, Joseph II, the Holy Roman Emperor, who wished to pick up the mantle of mediation dropped by his mother, Maria Theresa. He was a man of large fancy, as befits the titular head of a prestigious but largely fictitious empire, the secular head of the Roman Catholic Church, ostensibly the coequal partner of the Pope. It was a picturesque but meaningless title in the Age of Reason and the politics of nations.

Joseph was a handsome, witty man and a realistic politician who yearned to make his rank more than a nicety of protocol entitling him to precedence at courtly functions. He thought he could do business with a woman like Catherine. He suggested a neat division of the world. Let the freethinking libertine Catherine of Russia become the head of the Eastern Church while he retained the Western half and thus they would defend Christendom. With that glorious responsibility Catherine could have the Crimea, Greece, the islands of the eastern Mediterranean, and Constantinople without objection from the West. For himself, Joseph would like some choice slices of the Balkans. He journeyed to Mogilev in White Russia to solemnize the compact, traveling incognito but in a disguise so transparent that all Europe followed him intently.

Joseph was dashing and Catherine was flirtatious. The two played out a frothy, amatory-political duet in the palace set aside for the meeting. They carved the world with a wink and a joke.

The deal was festively consummated and a treaty was drawn up incorporating all the provisions reached in the Mogilev idyll. It could not actually be signed, however, because these two loving monarchs and all their diplomats could not agree as to which should be the first to append the royal signature.

Though the Americans were considered almost irrelevant at Mogilev, both Catherine and Joseph had made clear their positions on the war. Just as Catherine had sought to persuade England that it would have to yield on some points to the Americans, Joseph had tried to convince France that it could not count on Spain, or hope for total victory. Harris had been unmoved by Catherine's advice, and the French ambassador, after one such lecture from Joseph, had told him: "Each to his own lorgnette."

Mediation was clearly in the air in the spring and summer of 1780. And to the French and Americans, Catherine seemed a splendid agent of peace. Her championship of the freedom of the seas, the very principle cherished by American traders, had been enshrined in the Franco-American treaty. In Philadelphia, Catherine was being hailed as a heroine of liberty, notwithstanding serfdom, medievalism, and scarlet scandal.

The British, disappointed by the Armed Neutrality and unappeased by the smiles that Catherine continued to shower on the mystified Harris, preferred to have Austria as an arbiter. That prospect became even more attractive to the English when in the autumn of 1780 the old Empress Maria Theresa died and Joseph acquired an influence more substantial than the venerable but rickety throne he held as Holy Roman Emperor. The English Foreign Office thereupon translated Catherine's offer of mediation into "co-mediation," paving the way for Joseph, who with great alacrity offered Vienna as the site of the peace conference.

Fearing skulduggery in Spain—for the doings of the British agents

Cumberland and Hussey were followed intently in Paris—and realizing the imminence of bankruptcy, Vergennes was in a mood for peace. And he rested high hopes in Catherine. "The interest of this princess," he wrote to Montmorin, "would please us the more because we believe her and her ministers to be well disposed to us, and because we believe American independence would be stipulated." Vergennes was also in a mood for compromising American boundaries, if Congress were willing. He tried to bring Congress around to considering the possibility of a truce. By October 1780, the French minister in Philadelphia, the Chevalier de la Luzerne, had prevailed upon the obstreperous delegates of that body to accept the idea, provided that the British troops and naval forces were evacuated. Congress said it still preferred a long truce to a short one, feeling that this would be tantamount to an acknowledgment of independence. However, Congress was dead set against any concessions that might leave the English in possession of any part of the former colonies.

Congress also resolved to take a hand in the Russian game. The foreign policy of the United States was nominally the province of a committee of Congress, but in fact few committee members were even in Philadelphia. The committee's secretary, Tom Paine, had resigned, and only James Lovell was paying any attention at all to the signals from abroad. He had been bombarded with letters from Adams urging an aggressive participation by Americans in the diplomacy that was shaping their fate. Accordingly, in December 1780, he persuaded Congress to send the upright, sedate American diplomat Francis Dana into the most intrigue-ridden, complicated, Byzantine Court of the libidinous Catherine.

Before his appointment, Dana had been shuttling between Paris and Amsterdam, distressingly underemployed. He had been toying with the idea of going to Spain to help Jay surmount *his* frustrations when unofficial word of his new appointment reached him. Vergennes and Franklin were decidedly lukewarm to the idea. American matters in St. Petersburg had been handled by the French ministers, who knew their way up the backstairs blindfolded. A neophyte would be lost in that bizarre Court. More important, the arrival of an American minister would present Catherine with a ticklish problem. To receive him would force an unwanted rupture with Britain. The only alternative was to snub the American. Catherine would scarcely be grateful for being handed a thorny dilemma at a moment when she saw herself as an angel of peace.

Vergennes and Franklin bestowed their limp blessings on Dana's mission provided that he travel to St. Petersburg in a private capacity and there bide the day when he could reveal himself as a minister without the danger of a rebuff. To Dana, schooled in Adams' suspicions, this smacked of sabotage, but he accepted the limitation. When Congress's instructions arrived they were touched with that absurdity which generally marked Philadelphia's view of Europe. At the right moment Dana was to propose that the United States be accepted into the League of Neutrals, though no country on earth could be less entitled to the credentials of a neutral. Dana was assured that this move to join in Catherine's crusade for freedom of the seas "from which she has derived so much glory . . . will open the way for your favorable reception." He was also instructed to ask for a treaty of friendship and commerce with Russia, which, if granted, would have negated any possibility of Catherine's serving as a mediatrix with a claim to impartiality. In short, he was asked to offer Catherine a choice of frustrations.

Thus armed with what seemed like a passport to catastrophe, the unfortunate Dana was sent on his way with no provision for travel money, expenses in St. Petersburg, or any staff. He would have to pay his own way. He had, however, a hearty pat on the back from Adams in Amsterdam: "America, my dear Sir, has been too long silent in Europe. Her cause is that of all nations and all men; and it needs nothing but to be explained to be approved." He had similar encouragement from Arthur Lee along with the customary warnings of deviltry at Passy.

For a secretary, Dana had chosen one of the free-lance Americans in the little court that had gathered around Adams at Amsterdam. But after a month or two of contemplation concerning life in the Russian autocracy and the possibility, however faint, of a diplomatic mishap that could send him to Siberia, the chosen candidate declined the honor. John Adams rallied in the crisis and gallantly offered his son. John Quincy had passed his French courses at Passy; he had learned diplomacy at his father's knee; and moreover he was bored by his Dutch schoolmasters. Following John Adams' instructions, those tutors were grimly hammering away at mathematics, naval architecture, agriculture, and natural history. They were expressly directed to avoid any mention of painting, poetry, music, tapestry, porcelain, and other frivolities. John Quincy, tired of school, was ready for a diplomatic career.

Thus staffed, the prim, tight-lipped lawyer in homespun set out to woo the glittering "scarlet woman" of Europe. If one could think of Dana as a Don Quixote, it would be impossible to imagine a less likely Sancho Panza than the well-bred and straitlaced fourteen-year-old boy who went along as his aide. With a single American servant they rode by coach across Germany, through Cologne, Frankfurt, Berlin ("the prettiest city I have anywhere seen"), and Leipzig. Dana in his diary noted the general and freely discussed discontent under Frederick the Great, and he cited the Prussian monarch's dictum: "Let my subjects say what they will, while they do what I will." They rode through Danzig, across the Russian border without incident, to Riga, Narva, and finally St. Petersburg. The seven-week ride ended on August 27, 1781, at the modest Hotel de Paris, where they checked in as private travelers. Few even knew of their arrival.

Dana's presence was not altogether unnoticed, however. The British minister Harris filed a routine protest in advance against any inclination to accord recognition to the American he mistakenly called "Deane." He was assured by the Ministry of Foreign Affairs that "Silas Deane could not employ his time more uselessly than by remaining in her [Majesty's] dominions." Dana's coming had also been heralded by a note from Vergennes to his minister in St. Petersburg, Charles Olivier de Saint-Georges, Marquis de Verac. "M. d'Aena [*sic*], American, proposes to visit Russia incognito," Vergennes had written. (Anonymity seemed to become this diplomat whose simple four-letter name was to be consistently misspelled or misremembered.)

Perhaps mindful of Dana's lack of employment in Paris and of the likelihood that he would be similarly frustrated in St. Petersburg, Vergennes suggested to the Marquis de Verac that he do his best to find "such pleasurable relations as might be available" for the American. "D'Aena is of a gentle and unassuming character and likely to behave modestly at St. Petersburg," Vergennes added, noting that he might even be useful in any serious mediation inasmuch as "the participation of the Americans must be a sine qua non of our policy."

If, however, Dana unexpectedly showed signs of forcing the issue of American recognition on a resistant Russian Court, Verac was ordered to stay out of the affair and leave the American to his fate. The instructions in no way varied with what Vergennes had told Dana to his face and reaffirmed the French determination to abide by the letter of the pact with the United States.

When Dana approached Verac, that diplomat was cordial and might have been helpful had they understood each other. The difficulty was that Verac spoke no English, Dana spoke no French, and "Master Johnny" Adams quickly demonstrated that though his schoolwork had much impressed his father, his French was totally inadequate for ordinary conversation, much less for a discussion on the intricacies of backstairs diplomacy.

The result was that the most affable diplomatic niceties of the French minister were frequently garbled by inept translation into what seemed to be brusque snubs. Primed by long association with Adams to look for treachery in the French, the American minister incognito found it in the mistranslations by his schoolboy aide.

Verac ventured to suggest that Dana had come too soon, that the Russian Empress, her heart set on mediation, was determined to give no offense either to the French or to the British. This was certainly an accurate appraisal, but to Dana it confirmed the existence of a French plot. He wrote to Adams: "I was about to ask you what this Gentry can mean; but I believe that we are at no loss to answer this question. . . . Such frivolous reasons appeared to me to have been assigned to show the time is not yet come, that I have presumed to question them. This, I imagine, may give offense, when I would not wish to do it. But must an implicit faith be put in all things which may come from a certain quarter?"

The French minister, going well beyond Vergennes's instructions, endeavored to fill in Dana on the prospects of mediation. He told him that Catherine and Joseph envisioned two separate treaties, one wrapping up a European peace, to be negotiated and signed by Europeans; and another concluded between the English and the Americans without the intervention of even the mediators unless they should be asked for their help. In that way Catherine would not be called upon to recognize the United States until after George III had done so. "Have the goodness, Sir, to observe," he added, "that I do not say that I approve this scheme. I merely say the august mediators have adopted it."

Petulantly Dana dashed off a report to Philadelphia asking for authority to go at once before Catherine and explain the advantages to her and to all the world of American independence. Of Verac, he wrote: "Nor can it be my duty nor the expectations of Congress that I should blindly fall into the expectation of any man. . . . My present opinion is that the Mediators do in fact consider the United States as an independent power." He dismissed Verac's explanations, cautions, protestations as "a specimen of that finesse from which the politics of Europe can never be free."

Beyond arguing with Verac and writing angry memoranda in all directions, there was little for Dana to do, holed up in his hotel. The Empress was away from St. Petersburg and would have been unapproachable in any case inasmuch as she was between lovers. Count Nikita Panin, the Foreign Minister, whom Dana had been advised to cultivate as a man predisposed to American interests, was difficult to pin down. The methodical Dana could scarcely be expected to fit into his eccentric schedule.

The count's valets would lift him out of his bed (something of an engineering enterprise, since the count, now in his fifties, had become heavily larded) at two in the afternoon. By six-thirty in the evening he was in a mood to discuss public business. But negotiations would never be swift with a man whose precarious state of health would always provide a rationale for postponing a decision. By seven o'clock such interviews had to be cut short in order to prepare for dinner, usually a gargantuan spread. Then there was time for a bit of gambling, a bit of lovemaking, and perhaps some sleep until three in the morning, when he would summon his secretaries and work on the business of the Empire until five or six. During those early-morning hours he worked with consummate skill, however.

Aside from the difficulties of catching such a man in a mood for discussion, the count was an unlikely American ally. True, he was able, educated, relatively honest, and thoroughly experienced. He had entered political life when he was twenty-nine and handsome enough to catch the eye of Catherine's predecessor, Elizabeth. It was said that Panin had been summoned to the Queen's bed but fell asleep in the royal bathroom while awaiting his entrance cue. He therefore lost the opportunity to serve at the heart of the Empire but was instead dispatched as ambassador to Denmark, then to Sweden, and so on to a career of service in which an untimely snooze was not likely to humiliate his sovereign.

Throughout his political life Panin had been known to favor England, which he much admired, and Austria, which he thought a natural ally. He had always been mistrustful of France. The only explanation for the advice given by Adams and others to concentrate on Panin lies in the fact that the count was generally credited with having devised the Declaration of Armed Neutrality, misread in Philadelphia as a reaffirmation of an American concept of freedom. To make matters even less propitious, the count was at that moment lapsing into political eclipse.

The only American Dana met in St. Petersburg was that adventurous free-lance "diplomat" Stephen Sayre, whom Dana had last encountered on his first trip to London before the war. Sayre was an old partisan of the Lees. He had joined them at the house of Dennys de Berdt when their anti-Franklin cabal fired the first volleys. He and Lee had shared a nom de plume (combining their initials as A.S.) in their diatribes against the American agents when they were actively looking for such posts for themselves. He and Arthur Lee both became sheriffs of London as a reward for riding on Wilkes's bandwagon. Since that time he had been spotted in the wings or onstage in a number of diplomatic scenes, his role never clear, his meaning, if any, uncertain.

Sayre turned up in Berlin as secretary to Lee in the heyday of "militia diplomacy," but there the friendship ended. A member of the British minister's staff had stolen Lee's papers from his hotel room. The British minister was duly reprimanded for the impropriety and the papers were restored—after they were read. But the embarrassed Lee had sought to put the blame for the breach of security on Sayre, a burden that proved too great for friendship. Sayre thereafter became militantly anti-Lee.

He was observed as a shadowy figure of uncertain credentials at an early international meeting on neutral rights in Copenhagen and later claimed a major share in negotiations with kings, lords, and ministers. The only evidence of authority in these dealings was that Sayre seemed to keep a constant supply of money on hand. Precisely what Sayre was doing in St. Petersburg in the winter of 1781 seems to have baffled Dana. Sayre had persuaded the rebel Duchess of Kingston to back him in a scheme to outfit Russian privateers to prey on English shipping in the Baltic. The British minister had complained of this American "spy," and Sayre had answered by floating a rumor that the British minister was plotting to set fire to the Russian Navy.

Franklin had vehemently warned against Sayre, which ordinarily might have endeared him to Dana, but the free-lance's flamboyant style alienated the austere minister incognito.

Moreover, still living on his own shoestring, Dana could scarcely afford Sayre's imaginative and highly speculative propositions.

He did, however, trust Sayre enough to let him carry letters to Adams in Amsterdam and recommended his reliability as a reporter. "The account he will be able to give you touching the principal characters on the political stage here will be, I believe, nearly the true one," he wrote.

Watching the crowds surging through the gates of the Hermitage, Dana could have joined them, making his way to the Queen, for a flourishing disorder in the palace was Catherine's way of being close to the people she ruled. But he thought that beneath the dignity of an American diplomat, even an unofficial one. If he could have afforded a sword to hang at his side, he might have been admitted to the throne room. Since he could not, he watched the lumbering coaches of the diplomats go by with their gleaming retinues and stayed closeted in his hotel room.

When he was smilingly received by the Vice-Chancellor of the Empire, Count Ostermann, Dana misled himself into thinking he was getting somewhere. His reports to Philadelphia glowed with a kind of triumph. He did not realize that Count Ostermann was a front man, chosen for his impressive bearing and his ability to treat trivia with decorum and so keep the bearers of irrelevancies from bothering the Great. The temperature in St. Petersburg in that first winter of Dana's discontent dropped to thirty below and the smoky stove in his rooms gave him headaches. He succumbed to flu and frustration.

The letters that came from Adams in Amsterdam were jarring, like the noise of a cheerleader in a sickroom: "Pray what is the reason," Adams wrote, "that the whole armed neutrality cannot agree to declare America independent and admit you in behalf of the U.S. to accede to that Confederation? It is so simple, so natural, so easy, so obvious a measure and at the same time so sublime and so glorious. . . . Let there be light and there is light."

John Adams was himself having a bit of trouble turning on the light in the United Provinces, as the Dutch republic then called itself. If there was any part of Europe that Adams would find congenial, one would have supposed it to be this orderly, clean, industrious nation that had won a revolution of its own and established a confederation along republican lines with just a fillip of aristocracy to keep it safe from mob rule. Moreover, it had risen to imperial grandeur, demonstrating the potential of republics that resist the weight of foreign empires.

That imperial glory had passed its prime, however. Mere vestiges lingered on like the souvenirs a traveler keeps to remind him of grander days, when he cut a figure in the world. Now the United Provinces was kept inviolate by its neighbors only because it served as a buffer state and trading post.

It was a curious republic, rather a collection of city-states, each ruled by an oligarchy of pompous periwigged merchants. These sent representatives to a body known as the States General, which was collectively addressed as "Their High Mightinesses." Sitting on top of this odd amalgam of democratic and aristocratic pretensions was the Stadtholder, who was not elected but who inherited his post like a king. He was the head of the House of Orange. In 1780 the Stadtholder was William V, poised on the summit of the state like a lump of lead.

His eyes bulged ludicrously, his flabby cheeks puffed out. He ate prodigiously and showed it. He occasionally passed out at the dinner table but he was not actually an alcoholic. Frederick the Great, who had given his niece in marriage to William, generally referred to the Stadtholder as "my booby of a nephew." When the French wished to be kind, they called William a mediocrity, though some at Versailles insisted he was imbecilic. Actually he was not unintelligent (he had a genuine grasp of European history), and he was not personally unpleasant. His major difficulty was that his mind tended to move like a weathervane, so that he would point wherever the conversation of the moment blew him. Exhibiting a fine appreciation of his own weakness, he once told the Prussian ambassador, "You are going to make me do something foolish." It was a safe prediction. William seemed to suffer from a conviction that he was no match for anyone who happened to be around him. Though he was much absorbed in military matters, he would cheerfully confess that if he were not the head of the House of Orange he could never rise higher than a corporal in his own army.

He resisted only one person in the ruling circle and that was perhaps the most intelligent of the lot—his wife. Princess Frederika Sophia Wilhelmina was astute, charming, attractive, and witty, but it was said that William would refuse to go to Paradise if she advised it. She was thought to be overly attached to Prussia because of her overbearing uncle, but in fact her rarely taken advice was generally sound and always aimed at keeping the United Provinces on the tightrope of peace and neutrality.

Instead of his charming princess, William leaned his ponderous weight on the Duke of Brunswick, whom the acerbic Frederick dubbed "Fat Louis." The Prince and Stadtholder perpetuated his own childhood by formally signing over to "Fat Louis" much of his power when in 1766 he reached his majority and was faced with the terrifying prospect of acting on his own. Thereafter he would merely go through the motions of a reigning monarch. These were arduous enough: up at six, and dutifully to his prayers; then audiences with discontented leftover nobles, with discontented merchants, with discontented secretaries. To relieve the contentious routine, there was only a military review of the palace guard or a horseback ride. The evenings of this weary prince were spent at the opera, a card game, dinner, drink, and bed.

It was a bland regimen unseasoned by scandal and rendered digestible by a scrupulous abstention from weighty questions. The leftover nobility of early days troubled the country like unhappy ghosts. The middle class of traders and bankers who ruled the cities detested the aristocracy and the Prince, their wives openly snubbing the long-suffering, loyal wife of William, the Princess Frederika. They likewise detested "Fat Louis," who, in addition to other obvious faults, was not even Dutch.

And pushing up from below that ruling class of prosperous oligarchs were the restless professionals of the cities who called themselves the Patriots and filled the coffeehouses with talk of the Enlightenment and of Freedom. They were led mainly by lawyers who weighted down the revolutionary spirit with soggy pedantry. Moreover, as much as they might dislike Their High Mightinesses, the Patriots disliked William and the whole House of Orange even more. So in the end they formed a grudging alliance with the burghers.

Below the Patriots were the restless mechanics, sailors, porters, workmen of the cities who in times past had been known to take their politics noisily and sometimes violently to the streets. For them the House of

Orange was a counterweight to the regents of the cities, a reminder of past grandeurs and a rallying point. Lastly there were the conservative Dutch peasants, for whom the preposterous William was the symbol of stability, of peace, and of the continuation of a commercially prosperous satellite relationship with England.

In general, then, William had the loyalty only of the people. Though the country was on the whole pro-English, the powerful and many-faceted opposition was receptive to the ideas that washed over the border from the south. France had endeared itself, to some sections at least, by its persistent refusal to recognize the legitimacy of the House of Orange. (The French Court insisted on referring to the Stadtholder by one of his lesser titles as the Prince of Nassau-Dietz.)

Into this slowly simmering heavy Dutch soup rode John Adams. He came with his two sons, happy to get them away from France and into an environment of simple, industrious sobriety. Systematically he went about finding his bearings. He sought out Dumas, whom he somewhat mistrusted as a friend of Franklin's, though he found him eminently useful as translator, contact man, and guide to prospective sources of money and political leverage. Dumas helped Adams to catalogue the personalities on the Dutch scene systematically, by their political views, by their attitudes toward America, by their financial resources and connections.

When Adams reached Amsterdam, Henry Laurens, designated as the American minister to the Dutch, was still listed as among the missing. Not wishing to poach on a colleague's territory, Adams suggested that Amsterdam was a superb listening post and sounding board, and that he would willingly man it until Laurens showed up. However, even more could and should be done. He wrote to Congress: "We are still in daily hope and expectation that Mr. Laurens will arrive; but should he decline to come, or in case any accident has befallen him, I most earnestly recommend to Congress the appointment of some other gentleman, with a proper commission, with full powers and especially to borrow money and to sign proper promissory notes for the payment of it."

He did not wait for such credentials to arrive, however. He cultivated the editors of the most prominent journals, planting pro-American articles and excerpting from others to document his copious reports. He brought Thaxter over from Paris to set in motion the wheels of that same industry that had threatened to overpower Vergennes. *"Nulla dies sine linea"*—never a day without a line—was his watchword. Consistently he overfulfilled his quota. At the same time he dispatched Dumas to bankers and coffeehouses to begin the process of prying the guilders out of the pockets of those Dutch who were so solid and who talked so well of freedom. Dumas kept busy translating their excuses.

While his expectations of good republican money were wilting, Congress, suffering from the communications gap of transoceanic mail, and still living in Adams' early optimism, was writing the usual drafts on him as they did on all diplomats abroad. These he could only pass on to Franklin in the hope, generally fulfilled, that he would inveigle French funds to meet them. The absurdity was neatly capped when Commodore Gillon of the South Carolina Navy asked the impoverished Adams for a loan on the credit of his state.

In a temper Adams wrote the commodore: "In this situation I should be criminal to comply with the request in your letter." Even if Adams had money enough to meet the bills of the United States and some to spare, he added, he would not lend it to an individual state. "There are commissioners now in Europe from Virginia, Pennsylvania and Massachusetts who would have similar reasons for requesting my aid."

In October 1780, a ghost came out of the sea: that worthless treaty draft which Arthur Lee had negotiated with one of the regents of Amsterdam, which Henry Laurens had carried with him and which obstinately bobbed to the surface of the ocean off Newfoundland to be fished up by British seamen. The British now waved it angrily at the United Provinces that were ostensibly neutral with a friendly tilt to England.

Actually England's dissatisfaction with the Dutch stemmed from the fact that Dutch ports had come to serve as a vital link in a French supply line. By threatening war, England hoped to sever that line and demonstrate the perils of neutrality when it leaned away from England. The Lee treaty draft was a convenient pretext.

Though the regents of Amsterdam who had signed the document along with Lee now acknowledged the authenticity of the draft and tried to justify it, John Adams "could not remember to have found one person who pretended to see the wisdom of it."

In the general consternation that followed the British disclosure of the Lee document, Adams found that all his most promising contacts were shrinking at his touch. The Baron van der Capellen, for example, who had formerly expressed such admiration for the valiant Americans, now begged Adams to leave his name out of his negotiations for money. "I am convinced that my name would contribute nothing," he wrote, and went on to detail the reasons why "American credit has never been so low as it is at this hour." His reasons did not include the panic that was gripping the United Provinces at the British threat. Instead he noted "the capture of Charleston, the invasion of Georgia and South Carolina, the defeat of

General Gates . . . the decided superiority of the English in the West Indies and New York, the defection of Arnold—all copiously reported, edited and embellished by English journalists."

The Dutch were obviously too well informed; American stock was in fact at its nadir, as was the mood of John Adams. Christmas came on a Monday in 1780 and the stock exchange, that pressure point of the Dutch pulse, had been closed for two days. Stockjobbing and politicking had to be shifted to the coffeehouses, and Adams tried to pick up what news he could there. The British ambassador was recalled, said the rumors. Some thought the British did not intend immediate warfare but would settle for an apology, a public consumption of humble pie, and a return to a submissively pro-British policy. Others thought that the dread "mobility" would be roused to mayhem in the streets. "And not a few expected that the American ambassador would not escape," Adams later recalled.

At the year's end Adams tried whistling in the dark. His report to Congress, dated December 31, speculated that if the English declared war on the United Provinces, perhaps all of the League of Armed Neutrality would rally to the victim's side, and England would have to face an alliance of France, Spain, the United States, the United Provinces, Russia, Denmark, Sweden, and Prussia. It was a forlorn hope because by then "armed neutrality" had in fact become Catherine's joking "armed nullity." At the end of his report Adams confessed that the year 1780 "has been to me the most anxious and mortifying year of my whole life."

However, from the low point of New Year's Day 1781, Adams' mood soared quickly into near euphoria. The British had indeed declared war on the United Provinces over the Christmas holidays but with no great enthusiasm and unaccompanied by any military action. Horace Walpole noted the event: "We lose provinces and islands, and are comforted by barrels of pickled herring."

Sentiment in the Dutch cities began to swing to America, though many still hoped and clamored for peace. "They are furious for peace," Adams wrote to Dana. "Multitudes are for peace with England at any rate, even at the expense of joining them in a war against France, Spain, America and all the rest. They are in a torpor, a stupor such as I never saw any people in before. . . ."

Beyond some feverish activity in the shipyards there was little evidence of actual war in the United Provinces. "I have been in the most curious country, among the most incomprehensible people," Adams wrote to Jay, ". . . I was not able to discover, nor did I ever find one man in the country who would pretend to say what course the republic would take . . . although there cannot be a peace between them and England, yet I do not see a probability of their being in earnest in the war for some time. . . ."

Still, sensing that the wind was in general favorable for America, and armed at last with credentials from Congress giving him full negotiating powers in the absence of Laurens, Adams resolved to apply his own brand of diplomacy: a frontal assault, open, straightforward, undiluted by finesse or grand stratagems. In March he prepared a memorial to Their High Mightinesses asking that the United States be admitted to the League of Armed Neutrals to join in the fight for Freedom of the Seas. The Marquis de Vauguyon, whom he consulted, advised against it, though he said he would raise no obstacles and, as a friend, if not as a diplomat, he would do anything he could to help. (The friendly tone endeared him as an individual, though Adams saw in his opinions the familiar Franklin-Vergennes conspiracy.) Congress had advised Adams pointedly to be guided closely by the French, but he plunged on. Dumas scurried about with translations under his arm, for submission not only to the States General but to the Russian, Danish, and Swedish ambassadors as well as to William. Then in due course Dumas had to pick up the replies and translate those, all of which were polite rejections.

A month later Adams composed a much longer memorial, this time asking for American recognition and describing at length the blessings that would flow in upon the United Provinces from American trade. Again and at length the Marquis de Vauguyon argued against it, always taking care not to ruffle the delicate sensibilities of this unmanageable American. Again Dumas was pressed into service translating, making appointments, rushing to and from the inn where Adams now made his headquarters. (Ironically, the inn was called At the Sign of the Parliament of England.)

Again there were the rejections. The Stadtholder's personal messenger returned Adams' letter to him at the inn with regrets. But now there was a difference, reflecting the changing tide of opinion in the *drôle de guerre* to which the Dutch had grown accustomed. Permission was given to publish Adams' memorial. It was now up for debate in the coffeehouses and in the councils of all the cities. Adams and America had emerged from obscurity into a kind of limelight.

Initial response from the provinces was promising, but while Adams waited impatiently for some definitive sign from the burghers, a summons came from Vergennes. It was July 1781, and the talk of mediation by Russia and Austria was growing louder and more meaningful. Adams had dismissed all such proposals and peace feelers that floated throughout

Europe in the spring and summer of that year as so many tricks hatched by the wily English, bait for the weak and the traitorous.

As much as he loathed the idea of inviting Adams to return to Paris, Vergennes was quite determined to play the game correctly. If he wanted to confer with an American on the mediation proposals, it would have to be their designated spokesman on peace, John Adams.

Adams made his reluctance known to Vergennes. He thought the Dutch situation more important than imperial mediations, but if Vergennes insisted, he would come to Paris. He stayed at his old hotel, the Valois, and examined the trial balloons from St. Petersburg and Vienna, propositions which would have imposed a truce with the lines drawn according to the military position at the moment of signing. Adams forcefully rejected that notion, then followed up with second, third, and fourth thoughts on the matter, piling on additional reasons for his rejection, insisting that the imperial mediators recognize the United States of America before any negotiations, offering to go to Vienna personally to present his case. But while he plowed that furrow to the end, no doubt to Vergennes's annoyance, he advised Congress: "The English are obliged to keep up the talk of peace to lull their enemies and sustain their credit. But I hope the people of America will not be deceived. Nothing will obtain them real peace, but skillful and successful war."

No sooner had Adams returned to Amsterdam than he was engulfed in troubles that swept over him as if the dikes had burst. To begin with, he came down with a debilitating fever. On top of that he was obliged to admit that the Dutch with all their virtues were nothing like as generous as the French with all their vices. It was hard for Adams to accept that anomaly, but the facts were indisputable. With all his efforts he had raised a bare £200 and he still had to refer Congress's bills to Franklin for payment by the French. Previously the Dutch bankers had said they could not deal with Adams until he had full credentials. Now that he had them there were other excuses, for the Dutch weighed their actions on commercial, not political, scales. And America was still a bad risk. Adams, who once had so admired the solid republican Dutch, now anathematized them as "a nation of idolators at the shrine of Mammon."

Finally, bitterest blow of all, came word that as a result of his ill-considered contretemps with Vergennes, Congress had relieved him of the sole responsibility to negotiate peace. He would be only one of a commission that would include Franklin, Laurens (if he should be let out of the Tower of London), and Jefferson. (There had been a terrible wrangle at Philadelphia and the step had been taken after intensive French lobbying, over the protest of the Anti-Gallican faction and passionate outbursts from Abigail, who threatened to go to Philadelphia to protest the humiliation of her husband.)

Adams' bitterness was scarcely concealed beneath a tone of pious resignation. He wrote: "I am a sheep and I have been fleeced but it gives me some pleasure to reflect that my wool makes others warm. . . . I am a bird, that my feathers have been plucked and worn as ornaments by others. Let them have the plumage if they will, it is but a gewgaw." To Dana he wrote that the new commission "removed the cause of envy, I had like to have said; but I fear I must retract that, since J.A. still stands before B.F." in the order of members inscribed by the commission.

To Franklin he wrote a denunciation of all diplomacy: "I am very apprehensive that our new commission will be as useless as my old one. Congress might, very safely, I believe, permit us all to go home, if we had no other business, and stay there some years; at least, until every British soldier in the United States is killed or captivated. . . . I believe I had better go home and wake up our countrymen out of their reveries about peace. . . . My talent, if I have one, lies in making war."

X

WHEREIN ARE SET FORTH THE PLOTS, STRATAGEMS, BLUNDERS, CONTENTIONS, AND COZENINGS ATTENDANT UPON THE BIRTH OF THE UNITED STATES OF AMERICA IN A PARIS HOTEL ROOM

On a September morning in 1781, the marmoreal dignity of General George Washington seemed about to crack. He stood on the pier at Chester, Pennsylvania, waving his cocked hat in one hand and a white handkerchief in the other. Remarking this unusual animation in the Commander in Chief, an observer said that he looked "like a little boy who had just been given everything he's always wanted."

What he was being given—or at least, promised—was General Cornwallis and his entire British-German army wrapped up in French ribbon. Washington had come down from Philadelphia to meet the Count de Rochambeau, commander of the French expeditionary forces in America, for an urgent conference. The general's lapse from solemnity was occasioned by the news that Admiral François Joseph Paul, Count de Grasse, had sailed his fleet of twenty-five ships of the line and four frigates from the Caribbean to Chesapeake Bay and had just landed some 3,000 Marines to link up with Lafayette's Army of Virginia.

Washington had hoped that the French naval force would sail farther north and take New York. He was won over to the Rochambeau-Lafayette strategy of besieging Yorktown after his own call for fresh

American troops from nearby states to join in the assault on New York drew an embarrassingly tepid response. Washington's order to switch strategies had been intercepted. However, the message had been couched in a cipher unfamiliar to British headquarters in New York. It was sent off to the code breakers in London, a purely academic exercise inasmuch as the situation was unlikely to stand still for the ten weeks it took to bounce a message to London and back. A British squadron, expecting de Grasse in New York, sailed out to intercept him off the Delaware capes but was driven back. The genial sixty-year-old de Grasse, in great good spirits, was all for springing the trap on Yorktown at once. He was restrained by the twenty-four-year-old Lafayette, who always exhibited a nice regard for American sensibilities. The marquis admitted that the job could be done with the forces on hand—mainly French—but it seemed unsporting not to invite the Americans to share in the glory of the war's climactic moment. And in any case American reinforcements might help hold down the casualties.

De Grasse agreed, but set himself a deadline for the end of October. He was impatient to return to the Caribbean, where he hoped to clear the British away from the Sugar Islands. The elements of the trap were all in place by October 1. Mad Anthony Wayne was barring Cornwallis' escape into North Carolina. Washington and his friend Benjamin Lincoln had brought their ragged men down from the north. And the siege of Yorktown was on.

The odds were decidedly against Cornwallis, holed up with some 5,300 English and 2,000 Hessian soldiers. Moving in on him was Rochambeau's expeditionary force of 8,000 plus some 5,600 Americans under Lafayette, von Steuben, and Lincoln; and de Grasse's formidable fleet was strung out along the York River. There were also 3,200 local militiamen flocking in from around the countryside. On the seventeenth Cornwallis sent up a white flag and ordered a drummer to sound the surrender.

On October 19, the allied forces drew up in two columns about a mile long; on the right the Americans in a grab bag of miscellaneous uniforms, many of them in tatters; on the left the French in elegant regalia. Cornwallis had broken open the English quartermaster stores so that his soldiers could put on spanking new scarlet uniforms for the occasion. They trooped between the lines with drums beating and flags furled to lay down their arms. Efforts had been made to keep civilians away from the ceremony so as to avoid undue humiliation of the vanquished. It was reported that English officers took pains to salute their French counterparts with appropriate punctilio while ignoring the American soldiers except for Washington, to whom Cornwallis offered his sword.

The ritual was performed with eighteenth-century grace, and Cornwallis was sent back to England on parole, pledged on his honor to refrain from all anti-American military or political activity.

The Marquis de Lafayette wrote home: "The play is over. . . ."

It was late November before the word of Yorktown reached Europe. In London the news demanded a propitiatory sacrifice. Lord George Germain, the man ostensibly responsible for American affairs, was a likely goat but inadequate either to assuage the appetite of the opposition in Parliament or to relieve the war-weariness that was spreading throughout England.

In February 1782, General Henry Conway, no firebrand but a sober, honest, elderly former Secretary of State, offered a resolution in the Commons calling for an end to the war in America. It lost by one vote and moved the King to wail that "the House of Commons seems so wild at present, and to be running on to ruin that no man can answer for the event of any question." A week after that closest possible shave, General Conway offered another resolution denouncing as enemies of King and country all those who would seek to continue "offensive war" in America. It would, in effect, end all campaigns against the Americans and pave the way for an act empowering the government to make peace with the revolted colonies. It carried 234 to 215.

"The turn and temper of the House was so strong that nothing could resist it," Lord North explained to his bewildered monarch. Then North once again pleaded to be allowed to resign. The King's first reaction was to go into the ritual dance which he and his First Minister had so often performed and which in the end always left Lord North in place. But now the time for such performances was past, and waiting in the wings were the Whig politicians George feared and loathed. The King toyed with the idea that if Lord North had to go into oblivion, his sovereign might as well go, too, though he preferred his ancestral domains in Hanover to total obscurity. He drafted an abdication message:

"His Majesty is convinced that the sudden change of sentiments of one branch of the Legislature has totally incapacitated Him from either conducting the war with effect, or from obtaining any peace but on conditions which would prove destructive to the commerce as well as essential rights of the British Nation. His Majesty therefore, with much sorrow, finds he can be of no further utility to his native country which drives him to the painful step of quitting it forever."

A final paragraph of the message would formally turn the country over to his "dearly beloved son and lawful successor, George, Prince of Wales."

That last consideration was perhaps the bitter pill on which the King gagged, for he nourished a well-known and often expressed dislike of his "dearly beloved son and lawful successor." And the Prince reciprocated those feelings fully, choosing his gaming companions, his mistresses, and his politics in a manner designed to upset his father. (George III had had a similar feud with his grandfather George II, and the attitude of his son might seem a kind of retribution, except that George III quite rightly regarded himself as a moral George caught between two reprobate Georges.) In any case, George put aside his abdication draft and accepted North's resignation in a closed-door conference.

Lord North spent some time privately negotiating his retirement. In the end the King granted him lifetime rights to a sinecure at a salary of £4,000 a year. The opposition, unable to believe that the long stewardship of North was finally coming to an end, mustered their forces for a late session on a snowy March night. The Members ordered their coaches for close to midnight—all except Lord North. Very early in the evening he cheerily announced his resignation, then strode to his carriage, which was standing by. "Good night, gentlemen," said Lord North to his thunderstruck and thoroughly chilled colleagues, huddled outside Parliament. "You see what it is to be in on the secret."

The government that was pieced together in the wake of North's departure was a multiheaded monster. The First Minister, Lord Rockingham, had aged since he presided over repeal of the Stamp Act and was hailed as a hero. He was now as scintillating as a "wet blanket," an epithet favored by his critics. Beneath him were two Secretaries of State who were temperamentally inclined to devour each other. One of them—in charge of foreign affairs—was Charles James Fox, who delighted in being called Fox Populi. He was a particular bête noire of the King. When George congratulated himself on his refusal to become "a tool in the destruction of the honor of the country," Fox nailed him: "There was one grand domestic evil, from which all other evils, foreign and domestic, had sprung: the influence of the Crown."

Fox regarded himself as a popular leader expressing the hope that the English would one day follow their Irish and American cousins into rebellion. On the other hand, he created scandals more easily than revolutions. His losses were spectacular at the faro table, and his victories notorious in the bedroom. In both pursuits he was often joined or preceded by the Prince of Wales.

Fox's unlikely teammate in this cabinet of contradictions was the Earl of Shelburne, whose area of responsibility was colonial affairs, including America. He was an introverted politician who, it was said, had escaped from a loveless childhood and a dominating mother into a military career and thence into politics. He had acquired a reputation for secretiveness and the title of "the Jesuit of Berkeley Square," where he had a town house.

Though Shelburne had been in the opposition throughout the war and though he thought the Americans had been mishandled, he clung to hopes that they might yet be reminded of their heritage and brought into a kind of sentimental-commercial union with Mother England. Shelburne also had a certain lingering respect for the royal prerogative, and when faced with a firebrand like Fox, he tended to play the role of the King's man in the government.

This was part of the King's strategy. He had deliberately put together an administration of domestic opponents designed to splinter. Similarly, the prime mission of the new administration was to make peace by sowing divisions among the enemy. If the peace for which Parliament and public were clamoring was to be made tolerable, the Americans and French would have to be brought into a mood of mutual distrust. The Earl of Shelburne was cast as Iago.

Ever since Yorktown, British agents had been scurrying about Europe probing for diplomatic openings that might disrupt the Franco-American infatuation. For the most part these agents came with feeble credentials and unwholesome reputations. They peddled suspicion and promises in an atmosphere of melodrama.

There was, for example, Thomas Digges. Benjamin Franklin described him as "a very great villain." Digges had allegedly taken three or four hundred pounds from Franklin to aid American prisoners of war, and not a penny of it reached the captives. "If Digges was not damned, the devil would be useless," Franklin declared. Digges used his Maryland origins as bait for the Americans while he worked for the British Secret Service. He had engaged Adams in seemingly clandestine correspondence, though there can be little doubt that the Secret Service was in on it. He fed Adams' insatiable appetite for pamphlets and press clippings from London spiced with occasional bits of decoy military intelligence provided by his superiors. Digges could have drawn scant comfort from Adams, who, back in 1780, told him that any scheme calling for a separate peace with America was "visionary and delusive, disingenuous, corrupt and wicked."

Undeterred, Digges turned up in Amsterdam incognito and left word that Adams was to contact a certain gentleman "in room number ten at the First Bible Hotel." Adams saw him, confirmed that he and his fellow commissioners were empowered to make peace—a matter of public knowledge—but told him little more. In his report Digges said he detected a hint in Adams' manner that he might be willing to deal with Britain behind France's back. There is no evidence that Adams gave Digges any basis for such a report, but, on the other hand, Adams always found it hard to conceal his mistrust of the French and impossible not to proclaim to all who would listen that the United States was master of its own diplomacy. This might have fed Digges's hopes.

Paul Wentworth, the New Hampshire aristocrat who dreamed of a British baronetcy, also popped up in Amsterdam early in 1782, abetted by Russian agents eager to promote a "mediated" end of the American war. And one Nathaniel Forth, a French specialist of the Secret Service, was dispatched to test Vergennes's loyalty to the Americans with a proposition by which France would get Canada and expand her small holdings in India. America would regain only those areas not in British military control. Vergennes sent Forth reeling backward to England, taking great pains to inform the Americans and Spaniards of the British moves to disrupt the alliance. The British playwright Cumberland and the Irish monk Hussey were still at work, and the most successful double agent (or perhaps even triple agent) Edward Bancroft still shuttled between London and Passy retailing state secrets. However, none of these unlikely doves was to carry the olive branch.

The first suggestion that Britain was seriously seeking peace came in a disarming billet-doux to Benjamin Franklin from Mme Brillon, that charming neighbor of his who had so often perched on his lap and twined his gray locks between her fingers. On the face of it the note seemed less than momentous. Mme Brillon, passing the winter of 1782 at Nice, had met some pleasant English folk. (Though England and France were at war, eighteenth-century manners forbade a vulgar hostility that would preclude social amenities between the gentlefolk of both belligerents.) Among these new friends was a certain Lord Cholmondeley, who would no doubt be a charming addition to the tea table at Passy, she told Franklin. The letter, which might have seemed no more than chitchat, was followed in short order by Lord Cholmondeley himself, who came to Paris ahead of Mme Brillon and sent a note craving a mere five minutes of the doctor's time. After an exchange of amenities and news of Mme Brillon, Lord Cholmondeley remarked that Lord Shelburne, whom he knew well, had spoken highly of Franklin and would no doubt appreciate some friendly word. Lord Cholmondeley was about to leave for England and would be delighted to take such a letter.

Franklin, unaware that Shelburne was then entering the new administration in England, dashed off a quick note full of graceful courtesies, in which politics was interlaced with personal trivia: Mme Helvetius (one of the more serious loves of Franklin's robust old age) was made "very happy by your present of gooseberry bushes," Franklin told the Earl of Shelburne. (A British lord could offer a French lady gooseberry bushes and deliver them without charges of treason in that quaint war.) Franklin expressed his personal esteem for the earl, congratulated him on the "returning good disposition of your country" as shown by the vote in the House of Commons, and voiced his hope for a "general peace."

Lord Cholmondeley delightedly took the letter to the Earl of Shelburne. He saw it as an opening. He now needed a man to take back an answer to Franklin that might begin to woo that most powerful American diplomat away from French blandishments and French money. At that moment Henry Laurens, the unfortunate diplomat who had presented the British with the means of forcing the Dutch into war, had been ailing in the Tower of London and no doubt had grown weary of copying out *The History of the Decline and Fall of the Roman Empire*. Congress had authorized Franklin to propose the exchange of Laurens for Burgoyne, who had been put on parole after his capture at Saratoga, but Burgoyne had been freed in another deal. Meanwhile Cornwallis, chafing under the terms of his parole, had suggested to Laurens that he might be a reasonable counterpart in a trade. Laurens' freedom might be exchanged for his own liberation from the constraints on his honor to abstain from all activity in the war. Laurens eagerly agreed, but only Congress could properly authorize such an exchange, and what with the slow pace of transatlantic communication and the habitual dilatoriness of Congress, Laurens might languish in the Tower for months. Shelburne needed a gesture to demonstrate his goodwill to the Americans, and Laurens could prove likely material out of which to spin an image of generosity.

Laurens had a friend and long-time business associate, a Scotsman named Richard Oswald. He was an affable man who had made a considerable fortune in the slave trade, but this circumstance did not seem to inhibit his professions of admiration for the American ideal of human freedom. He had retired from the business world and could afford to cultivate a libertarian philosophy which would very likely sit well with Benjamin Franklin. Moreover, he had property and family in America and had spent considerable time there, which gave some substance to his pro-American sentiments. True, he had come up with a preposterous proposal that did little to enhance his reputation. He had suggested that Catherine the Great be persuaded to swoop down from Siberia and attack Spanish strongholds in Central and South America. If such an alliance could be made with that capricious queen, he argued, Russian troops might garrison New York, releasing British troops for the war against France and Spain. Catherine would be lured by the promise of California, a foothold in Mexico, perhaps the whole west coast of South America. In short, bribe Russia to knock Spain out of the war. The scheme got nowhere with the British war planners. But if Oswald could not take Spain out of the war, it was thought that he might take the Americans out not by military means but by offering them the independence which they and the French had all but won already on the battlefield.

Oswald had conversed freely with his friend Laurens and had persuaded the prisoner to agree that if he were paroled he would do nothing against the interests of England.

(This was a strange commitment from a man who still held credentials as a member of the American commission to negotiate the peace. When Congress later heard of it there was an immediate move to cancel his appointment and recall him at once. That move failed to win approval because of peripheral factional considerations having little to do with a defense of Laurens. Actually, the hapless, aging, and ill Laurens had never yielded to British efforts to use him effectively. He consistently maintained that the United States would settle for nothing less than independence and a viable territory.)

Shelburne took Laurens out of the Tower without the exchange of any high-placed British prisoner, and with Oswald putting up the bail. The minister then invited Laurens to a series of intimate chats. Though he found the captive American "touchy and conceited, vulgarly so," he thought he might nevertheless be useful. In these conversations Shelburne described himself as one who regretfully had come to accept the inevitability of American independence. Then, basing himself on Digges's report, he suggested that John Adams, at least, was prepared to negotiate behind the backs of the allies. Laurens found that impossible to believe. Whereupon the "Jesuit from Berkeley Square" proposed that Laurens go to see Adams himself.

Laurens was thus dispatched to Holland and Oswald to France, bearing Shelburne's answer to Franklin. They traveled together, posing as two gentlemen on a holiday. And Laurens obligingly gave Oswald a letter to Franklin recommending his old friend as a man of "candor and integrity." They parted when they had crossed the Channel, Oswald heading for Paris, Laurens for Haarlem.

John Adams was then luxuriating in the glow of a diplomatic coup for which he could—and most emphatically did—take full and exclusive credit. He had disregarded the gentle warnings of the French and of Franklin; he had followed his policy of no-nonsense diplomacy and beat upon the doors of Dutch stadthouses to demand recognition of the independent United States of America. And at last the doors had opened to him in province after province. No matter that Dutch bankers were still clutching their purse strings, no matter that it was the fortunes of war more than diplomatic persuasion that had forced Dutch hands; to Adams would belong the honor of placing himself in a position to take the best advantage of the changing wind. That, indeed, it might be argued, is the essence of diplomacy.

On March 28, that factotum of American diplomacy, Charles W. F. Dumas, reported to Adams: "The great work is now accomplished." Their High Mightinesses, the States General, would formally receive John Adams to present his credentials as the representative of the United States of America. America's friends among the Dutch politicos were out celebrating the occasion "with glass in hand" and could not be reached for comment, Dumas added.

Adams had already purchased a house "on a noble spot of ground" in The Hague, as he described it in a letter to Francis Dana. That lonely American, huddled in his hotel room in freezing St. Petersburg, read with mingled emotions, no doubt, of Adams' plans for the new embassy, a mansion "fit for the Hôtel des Etats Unis or if you will, l'Hôtel du Nouveau Monde." Mme Dumas was assigned to shop for the Embassy, according to carefully chosen color schemes: green and gray for Ambassador Adams' chambers; gray and turquoise for the dining and living rooms; red and yellow for John Thaxter's room; red, white, and blue for Master John Quincy Adams, who was then on his way back from Russia (and incidentally taking so long a time about it that his father had alerted a variety of agencies to be on the lookout for him). Young Charles Adams, grown homesick, had been dispatched to Braintree, so Mme Dumas did not have to concoct still another color combination.

In the heady excitement of victory preparations, it was understandable that Adams might feel a twinge of anxiety when on April 16 he learned that his old friend Henry Laurens was waiting to greet him at the inn of the Golden Lion in Haarlem. Laurens, after all, had been originally charged with the mission to the Dutch, and Adams had been functioning only as his stand-in. Throughout his diplomatic career Adams had felt that others, mainly Franklin, had reaped what Adams had sown. Was it to happen yet again? However, a two-hour chat at the Golden Lion reassured him. Laurens was in poor health, totally uninterested in diplomatic glory, and, in any case, incapacitated by his status as a British prisoner on parole. Indeed, Adams pointed out to him that in view of his position he could scarcely expect to be briefed on confidential aspects of the situation. Adams did disabuse him of any notion that Digges might have given, of a disposition to deal with the British for a separate peace. And Laurens, in turn, offered his own jaundiced view of Lord Shelburne, which confirmed Adams' suspicion that the peace overtures from London were part of a royal flimflam. "Artifices to raise the stocks," Adams called them.

Laurens then went back to London, and Adams joyfully proceeded to the final ceremonies of diplomatic recognition and the task of digging for guilders. Oswald meanwhile had reached Passy armed with a personal letter from Shelburne nicely calculated to appeal to Franklin's intellectual turn of mind. Here was no stiff ministerial request for negotiations, no formal communiqué from one belligerent to another. Shelburne recalled nostalgically the philosophical conversations he had had with Franklin nineteen years previously and said how glad he would be to resume those talks "upon the means of promoting the happiness of mankind." He said he had chosen Oswald as his personal envoy to Franklin because "he is a pacifical man, and conversant in those negotiations which are most interesting to mankind."

Franklin indeed found Oswald "a wise and honest man," and in short order came to be quite fond of him. Shelburne's envoy suggested delicately that inasmuch as American independence had been the only principal war aim and its realization now a foregone conclusion, peacemaking would be a simple matter if only France did not press other humiliating conditions. In that case Britain would go on fighting, of course, and it would be a pity to see America embroiled in war for objectives that were irrelevant. Franklin fended off that opening maneuver. He brought Oswald around to see Vergennes, who probed British positions in a delicate diplomatic skirmish. The peace was not quite so simple, Vergennes suggested. There might be other demands made upon the English, but these could be formulated only in consultation with all four of the allied nations then at war with England. An English negotiator had a simpler task, he reminded Oswald. "Your court being without allies and alone, knowing its own mind, can express it immediately. It is therefore more natural to expect the first propositions from you."

Confidentially Franklin suggested to Oswald that if Britain desired not only peace but a reconciliation, it might well consider ceding all of Canada to the United States. This would compensate for the losses suffered by Americans in the war and at the same time forestall future border quarrels. Oswald nodded approvingly. Canada, indeed, had always been a prime territorial objective of Franklin's. (The more captious historians have suggested that perhaps he was motivated in part by his own real-estate holdings in Nova Scotia.)

Franklin had written out a brief for the cession of Canada and referred to it frequently during one conversation in Oswald's hotel room in Paris. With seeming reluctance, Franklin allowed Oswald to read it and even let him take a copy of it back to Shelburne. Franklin did not think it necessary to inform Vergennes of this informal demand. Such small duplicity was enough to encourage the hopes of an Iago. Oswald returned to London with his trophy and so ended the first round. "We parted exceeding good friends," Franklin noted.

Oswald returned to Passy with assurances that the matter of Canada might very well be settled in Franklin's way. But now Shelburne's rival in the Cabinet, the fiery Fox, took a hand. If relations with America were Shelburne's province, a peace with France was Fox's. He sent his own peace envoy, who turned out to be Thomas Grenville, son of the man who had devised the original stamp tax that had launched the Revolution and the worldwide war that followed. In introducing him to Franklin, Fox wrote: "I know your liberality of mind too well to be afraid lest any prejudices against Mr. Grenville's *name* may prevent you from esteeming those excellent qualities of heart and head which belong to him, or from giving the fullest credit to the sincerity of his wishes for peace, in which no man in either country goes beyond him."

Although the scheme of having Oswald work Passy while Grenville worked Versailles seems an extraordinarily cunning device to divide the allies, it was not a well-coordinated strategy. In British diplomacy, muddle consistently triumphed over Machiavelli. Grenville and Oswald were soon at such cross-purposes that at times it seemed that Franklin, representing their enemy, would have to mediate between them.

One would have supposed that an accredited British diplomat would find his own way to Versailles without depending on an American rebel to take him there, but Grenville did in fact wait for Franklin to introduce him to Vergennes as he had Oswald. That first session with the French minister proved less bland and more serious than the earlier exchanges with Oswald.

Ever since Parliament had resolved to end the war, the British view had been that American independence was the sole issue and that once that objection was granted the British Empire would be left intact in India and the Caribbean, as it was at the end of the Seven Years' War in 1763. Accordingly, Grenville suggested that if England freed America and gave

France back the islands she had lost during the war, France should relinquish her conquests.

Vergennes smiled. America's independence, he said, was not a matter for bargaining; it was an accomplished fact. "America does not ask it of you. There is Mr. Franklin, he will answer you as to that point."

"To be sure," Franklin told Grenville, "we do not consider ourselves as under any necessity of bargaining for a thing that is our own, which we have bought at the expense of much blood and treasure, and which we are in possession of."

Vergennes went on to point out that wars do not usually end with the simple attainment of the originally announced objectives. After all, that Seven Years' War, to which this was a sequel, had begun in a dispute over "some waste lands on the Ohio and the frontiers of Nova Scotia." When the war was over, England had picked up all of Canada, Louisiana, Florida, an assortment of islands in the West Indies, and selected territories in India and Africa.

The present war, however, said the British envoy, had only occurred because France had encouraged the Americans to rebel. That charge was wholly untrue, Vergennes answered with more heat than candor. The United States had declared its independence before France offered any support. "There sits Mr. Franklin," Vergennes said, "who knows the facts and can contradict me if I do not speak the truth."

Vergennes, having deftly removed American independence as a counter in the bargaining, retreated to the language of diplomatic obfuscation, referring to "justice" and "dignity" as the abiding principles of the French Court. With careful attention to the proprieties, he announced that he would have to keep his other allies, Spain and Holland, informed of each step in the conversations.

Franklin shared a coach with Grenville on the ride away from Versailles and noted that the English envoy seemed dejected. It was already plain to Grenville, and soon would be to Shelburne, that bargaining would be difficult and that it was all the more important to divide the Americans from the French.

Vergennes was sticking to the letter of the alliance with scrupulous exactitude. He had done his best to bind the Americans to a similar policy. Congress, under pressure from the Chevalier de la Luzerne, had instructed its commissioners to follow the French lead in all respects. But Vergennes knew that such a provision had set the commissioners' teeth on edge. Though Franklin, the most Francophile of the Americans, might abide by such instructions, would his colleagues? Were they not, even after all the bloodshed and the furious assertions of independence, after all the expressions of gratitude for French money, French troops, and French ships, still Englishmen? He was enough of a statesman to know how little gratitude weighed in the decisions of nations and how perishable it was. He hoped only that it would last throughout the negotiations of the coming months. If the Americans settled too quickly and released the British forces from their preoccupation with the rebels, would they not be in a position to continue the war?

Indeed, that spring Britain was showing that it was far from defeated. Admiral de Grasse had sailed from the scene of his glory in Chesapeake Bay to total disaster off the tiny Caribbean islands known as Les Saintes. He was headed for Cuba with a cargo of twenty-six chests filled with gold and silver (worth roughly $500,000). His objective was to pick up a Spanish flotilla and a small Spanish army which would make it possible to take Jamaica from the British. A British fleet under Sir George Rodney, however, caught up with him, and, in a bloody battle that took 3,000 French lives, scattered the fleet. The French flagship was captured and with it the hero of Yorktown, de Grasse, along with the treasure chests of half a million dollars.

Franklin tried to cheer his French friends with a story of a Turkish sea captain who told his Venetian captors: "Ships are like my master's beard. You may cut it but it will grow again."

There was no doubt, however, that the victory of Les Saintes plus the fact that the British garrison at Gibraltar was continuing to hold out despite all that the Spaniards could throw at the Rock, did much to palliate the British gloom. It did little, however, to pacify the feud within the British Cabinet.

Grenville's shuttle trips to Versailles had deepened Fox's conviction that Vergennes would certainly require some tokens of victory beyond American independence. In fact, Fox informed the King that he was operating on the "supposition that the present negotiation for Peace will fall" and that all diplomatic pretense at negotiation should be directed to "detaching from France her allies and of conciliating the Powers of Europe to this country." He would play with Catherine and her League of Neutrals and he would grant American independence at once, a step he felt sure would dampen American enthusiasm for the alliance, which would then be an acute embarrassment.

George thought Fox's ideas on Russia "wild" and American independence "a dreadful price" to pay for peace. He and Shelburne and Oswald favored a variation: Pay the "dreadful price" if necessary, but make it contingent upon a "general peace," thus using the Americans to restrain French and Spanish demands and so hasten the day of their own freedom.

Americans, whatever their gratitude or their commitments, would not willingly fight for Spanish claims to Gibraltar or French claims to India.

And in the talks that now went on at Passy and Versailles, among Oswald, Franklin, Vergennes, and Grenville, each with different objectives, there were solid indications that though Americans could take French money and shout *"Vive le roi!"* the United States was ready to master the first lesson of nationhood: to guard its self-interest above all other considerations. It would honor all commitments, yes, but interpret them flexibly, not quixotically, and reconcile by word play sentiments, however lofty, with practical ends, however contradictory.

It was a subtle game. From London, Franklin's friends such as David Hartley wrote to him not merely of peace but of "sweet reconciliation," and Franklin harmonized his responses to make a series of duets that suggested pliability while he stoutly maintained that, of course, the United States meant to go hand in hand with France toward peace. There were gestures to go with the singing of duets. A word from Franklin on prisoners of war brought swift action, and all seven hundred were released, put aboard ships, and dispatched home in relative comfort and "good spirits," with twenty shillings each as a gift of the Crown. Franklin read into the gesture an implied recognition that these were no longer considered rebels, fit for hanging, but honorable combatants of a foreign foe.

The mood at Passy in that spring of 1782 was exuberant. Franklin noted in self-satisfaction that though Adams' policy of clamoring for recognition from all the powers had been successful in Holland, even he was being rebuffed by the envoys of every other European country. In Paris, Franklin had never sought such courtesies and hence had never been rejected. Now the diplomats were coming around to him, which was as it should be, he congratulated himself. The Swedish ambassador had even talked of a commercial treaty with the United States and couched his offer in flowery tributes to Franklin. "Such compliments," Franklin noted in a cocky mood, "might make me a little proud if we Americans were not naturally as much so already as the porter, who, being told he had with his burden jostled the Great Czar, Peter, then in London walking the street: 'Poh,' says he. 'We are all Czars here.' "

The Marquis de Lafayette was also a regular at Passy. Congress had suggested that he involve himself in the negotiations for peace and under that directive he acted as an American. Vergennes needed to have trustworthy eyes and ears at the convivial breakfasts, lunches, and dinners at which Franklin entertained the British envoys; and in that capacity Lafayette served as a Frenchman.

Vergennes had, in fact, agreed that the Americans should negotiate separately with the British. "They want to treat with us for you," he told Franklin, but France would have no part of that. Let each power make its treaties separately with England, Vergennes suggested. "All that is necessary for our common security is that the treaties go hand in hand and are signed all the same day."

There was a clear distinction, however, between separate bargaining and a separate peace. Vergennes had solid contractual reasons to hope that the Americans would understand the distinction and allow him to coordinate the joint effort, but he had equally solid political reasons to fear that they would not.

Franklin fenced with Fox's Grenville and Shelburne's Oswald and watched with considerable satisfaction as they fenced with each other. Oswald, he noted, had a crotchet or two. (The British envoy had disclosed his scheme to invite Russia to come down the Pacific coast and demolish Spanish pretensions. Franklin thought the scheme "visionary" but made no comment.) Still, Oswald was too old to be ambitious, whereas Grenville was out to make a career for himself and so would prove more troublesome. Grenville had already argued a bit too stiffly with Franklin, and had pushed too hard and too bluntly in his efforts to drive a wedge between France and America. That matter, touching so closely on the cloudy area between honor and statecraft, called for a subtler approach. Oswald had a far more winning way. With "an air of great simplicity and honesty"—as Franklin noted—Oswald had confessed his country's military and financial difficulties and had added: "Our enemies may now do what they please with us; they have the ball at their feet."

Finding the metaphor apt, Franklin proceeded to some nimble footwork. He had the idea of bluntly asking Shelburne to give over all the negotiations to Oswald, but it would be presumptuous for a member of one side of the negotiations to name his own counterpart. Instead he said as much in a letter to Oswald which was obviously meant for transmittal to Shelburne. The letter precipitated a series of conferences between Oswald and Franklin. What is there left to negotiate after independence is granted? Oswald asked. Franklin had prepared a memorandum on that subject and was delighted to show it to Oswald. He had listed four points as absolutely vital to a settlement: independence full and complete; a settlement of boundaries between the new nation and whatever British colonies remained loyal on the Continent; a revision northward of the Canadian border to where it was before Parliament had passed the Quebec Act of 1774, which incorporated all of the Great Lakes; and freedom for Americans to fish and whale off the Newfoundland Banks. There were four other points which Franklin said he would recommend for a lasting reconciliation: reparations for the damage to American lives and property; "a few words" acknowledging Britain's mistakes; full trading privileges in British and Irish ports for American vessels; the cession of all Canada to the United States.

The first four the United States would insist upon. The others they would hope for. He suggested to Oswald that such terms could be concluded without the involvement of any other nation. In reporting to Shelburne, Oswald commented: "From this conversation I have some hopes, my Lord, that it is possible to put an end to the American quarrel in a short time, and when that is done, I have a notion that the treaty with the other powers will go more smoothly on."

Franklin had in that brief memorandum stated America's peace terms. The rest would be a matter for the cartographers and legal experts. And the lawyers were on their way.

Throughout these preliminary conversations Franklin had reported their general drift to his colleagues. He had written repeatedly to Adams in The Hague, Jay in Madrid, Laurens wherever he could find him, and Robert Livingston, who had been given the title of Secretary of State. Livingston forever complained that his ambassadors wrote too seldom and never fully enough. He yearned to play the role which Congress had allotted to him, but plainly he could not pull the strings across an ocean at a time when a diplomat's message would have to wait a minimum of ten weeks for an answer, plus another ten weeks for clarification of that answer, and when there was always the likelihood that messages would be intercepted en route. The peace would have to be left to those on the scene.

To John Jay the summons from Franklin to join him in Paris came like a deliverance from on high. He had followed the Spanish Court and Floridablanca as they made their rounds from palace to palace. He had wheedled and thundered, tried tact and tactlessness, sobbed out his frustrations to the sympathetic ear of France's Montmorin—and had gotten nowhere.

Franklin had seen little point in the Spanish mission. In January 1782 he had written that if he were in Congress he would suggest that Jay be instructed to say thank you and farewell to the Spanish government. In the middle of March he wrote: "Since Spain does not think our friendship worth cultivating, I wish you would inform me of the whole sum we owe her, that we may think of some means of paying it off speedily." In April he wrote more urgently "to press your coming hither to assist" in the negotiations with the English. He suggested leaving Carmichael behind to avoid seeming to abandon the Spanish Court in utter defeat. He pressed for some word so that he could find lodgings for the Jays and their second child, a girl born in Spain. And in May he sent a letter to Jay in care of a Spaniard who, he hoped and confidently expected, would open it and pass along the contents to the appropriate authorities. Referring to the Spanish Court, Franklin wrote: "They have taken four years to consider whether they should treat with us; give them forty more, and let us mind our own business."

Ironically, the news of Yorktown and of the British Parliament's moves toward recognition of American sovereignty had just begun to warm the Spanish chill. There were signs that Charles III and Floridablanca were beginning to consider the possibility that in due time they would have to follow London's lead in acknowledging the Americans as more than rebels, gadflies, or pawns. But the absolutist and bureaucratic Spanish Court, though it could not make the sun stand still, could slow the dawn by ceremony and red tape. Loans were discussed; loans were promised; loans were conditioned; loans were whittled down; projected bonanzas shrank to small potatoes. Jay grew waspish even with the patient Montmorin.

On one occasion that gentle French diplomat commiserated with Jay: "Why, monsieur, these various perplexities must keep you in a kind of purgatory." Jay snapped: "They do, monsieur le comte, but I am certain that if you say mass for me in good earnest I shall soon be relieved from it."

Jay left his purgatory regretfully, sad to acknowledge defeat, uneasy at leaving affairs in the hands of Carmichael, whose virtues and faults alike seemed odious to him. But when deliverance comes in the somber cloak of a higher duty, even a conscientious descendant of martyred Huguenots may yield to temptation. Deliverance from purgatory was not swift; it was accomplished in a slow carriage ride northward over the Pyrenees during which Sarah Jay came down with chills and fever. They arrived in Paris on June 23, 1782, just as Franklin was dispatching his four vital points of peace and his four recommended points for reconciliation.

Jay came to the peace talks with certain misgivings. Adams had written to him to say that he, for one, would never consent to talk to a British envoy who did not bear credentials empowering him to treat with the ambassadors of the sovereign and independent United States of America, that talks on any less formal level were a snare and a delusion. Jay himself had protested vigorously at the instructions by Congress putting the commissioners on a leash held by French diplomats. Gouverneur Morris had steamed him up to "revolt at the servility of the situation" and reject the assignment altogether. Jay did not go so far as that but told Congress that the terms of the commission "occasions sensations I never before experienced and induces me to wish that my name had been omitted." The painful paragraph not only would tie the hands of American negotiators but, in Jay's view, was "not quite republican."

Although Jay had himself been the target of Adams' friends, he shared Adams' somewhat legalistic view and some of his distrust of the French, though little of his dark suspicions of Franklin.

John Adams was more difficult to lure away from The Hague. Not only did he have the gravest misgivings about the sincerity of Britain's peace overtures, and a pronounced aversion to the atmosphere of Paris and Passy; he was then basking in the glow of victory and enthusiastic compliments. He had moved into the Hôtel des Etats Unis. He had wrung a loan of 500,000 guilders from the Dutch bankers. He had been received in audience by His Most Serene Highness the Prince of Orange, who cheerfully agreed to conduct the conversation in English at Adams' request but then mumbled so incoherently that the American ambassador could understand only a few words of royal small talk.

The Prince later told the French ambassador, the Marquis de Vauguyon, that he had been thankful that the American had not pressed him for an audience before, because, if he had been obliged to say anything offensive to the United States, as he might have been, he would now have to eat his words and, in any case, the opposition would have ammunition to throw at him.

Adams resisted Franklin's appeals to come to Paris throughout the summer of 1782 because he was bent on crowning his Dutch efforts with a treaty of commerce. Meanwhile he tried to enlist Laurens in an effort to get a staunch Adamsite named as secretary to the Peace Commission to offset the possibility that William Temple Franklin might slip into the job. To Edmund Jennings, whom he was grooming for the post, Adams wrote of how stoically one must bear the cross of Benjamin Franklin: "As far as cruel fate shall compel me to act with him in public affairs, I shall treat him with decency and perfect impartiality. Further than that I can feel for him no other sentiment than contempt or abhorrence."

Continuing to deepen and widen Adams' suspicions, Arthur Lee had warned that the new Secretary of State was a "devoted partisan of Vergennes and Dr. Franklin." (The two were coupled inseparably in the mind of the Lee-and-Adams faction.)

In his reports to Livingston, Adams kept up a running fire of aspersions. Without any evidence whatever, he suggested that France had influenced Spain to withhold recognition of the United States, though he offered no likely motive for such a policy. Adams pointed out how Franklin, an "index" of Vergennes's sentiments, had always tried to obstruct his own and Lee's efforts at militia diplomacy that might have won American recognition throughout Europe. In contrast, he, Adams, had pursued a different policy "with patience and perseverance against all dangers, reproaches, misrepresentations and oppositions, until, thank God, he has enabled me to plant the standard of the United States at the Hague, where it will wave forever."

Totally disbelieving in the peace talks, he again proposed his scheme for a mightier war alliance involving Holland, perhaps Russia. To Francis Dana in St. Petersburg, Adams was more exuberant than ever and more scornful of his timid colleagues. "I shall be plagued with piddling politicians as long as I live," he wrote. "There are at this moment so many politicians piddling about peace, general and separate, that I am sick to death of it." All that was needed, Adams said, was for Catherine and the other neutrals to declare: "America is one of us. . . . These words once pronounced, peace is made. . . . Without it all may nibble and piddle and dribble and fribble."

The piddling, dribbling, and fribbling capacities of the world, so incomprehensible to simple John Adams of Braintree, were being made abundantly plain to poor Dana, whose very name was being drowned in the puddle of Russian politics. A simple incident revealed the piddling complexities of an ambassador's life. Someone in Holland—perhaps Adams himself—had sent to Dana, by the Russian Embassy courier, a portrait of Washington. Catherine's ambassador at The Hague was promptly scolded by Her Majesty's Vice-Chancellor:

"With your despatch came a portrait of Washington to be delivered to one Dina [*sic*] an American agent here. But as this man is not known to her Imperial Majesty or her Ministers, you are commanded by Her Majesty to return it to the source from which it reached the courier." He was to deliver no such messages to the unknown Dina. ". . . it is not pleasant to deliver them to people with respect to whom Her Majesty's Ministers are ignorant who they are or why they are here." Plainly an American diplomat could encounter a grimmer purgatory in St. Petersburg than in Madrid, where at least the Court could get the ambassador's name right.

Dana was not cheered by the triumphant accounts of how Adams had seen the daughter of the bug-eyed Stadtholder William and how pretty it was "to present a beautiful young Virgin World to the acquaintance of a fine figure of a princess." Nor was he moved to compassion for Adams when he posed as the martyred victim of petty minds, such as those at Passy. "I am weary, my Friend," Adams had written, "of the dastardly meanness, of jealousy and envy. It is mortifying, it is humiliating to me to the last degree, to see such proofs of it, as degrade human nature."

Dana was left to wait for better days on the banks of the Neva and Adams stuck close to the Hôtel des Etats Unis at The Hague while Franklin and Jay continued to play with the British for the stakes of a nation.

The British team underwent swift changes in the spring and summer of 1782. The feud between Grenville and Oswald came to a boil. It is said that Franklin fanned the fire under that pot. Throughout the summer Oswald would occasionally steal a march on Grenville by showing up at Passy for breakfast. The tactic was unfair because Grenville had to sleep late or else start the day with a headache. Franklin kept the two shuttling back and forth to come up with a formula that would allow them to treat with Americans. Parliament was still struggling with an Enabling Act which would make possible a formal acknowledgment of American independence, but in the meantime Grenville was trying to make progress under a writ empowering him to negotiate with France and any of its allies, or "any other Prince or state" that might be concerned.

At length Grenville blew up, complaining to Fox that he could not battle against Oswald, Franklin, and Shelburne. The row carried over into Parliament, where Fox staked all on a vote to grant American independence with or without a treaty. He lost, having misgauged the temper of the House and of the public, who could not accept a headlong rush to surrender.

Rockingham meanwhile expeditiously died of the flu, providing the way up for Shelburne and the way out for Fox. "The Jesuit of Berkeley Square," in his opening address as First Minister, scattered a jumble of metaphors: "The sun of England was setting" but one must work to "improve the twilight" and prepare for the sunrise but in doing so "the sword was sheathed, never to be drawn again."

"A den of thieves," Fox called the new ministry, and walked out.

Shelburne, now in full command, proceeded to set the stage and distribute the cast. Grenville was replaced at Versailles by a diplomat trained in the niceties admired by Vergennes. Oswald would play the primary role in the American negotiations at Passy. And to assure Franklin still further, Shelburne searched for men whose minds were well tuned to the doctor's interests. A breadth of knowledge was one prime quality. At first Shelburne tried to enlist Richard Jackson, "the omniscient," who had helped beguile Franklin's days when both were American agents in London before the war. When Jackson failed to take the assignment, the choice fell on Benjamin Vaughan. He came from the West Indies, had published an edition of Franklin's writings, knew Paine and Priestley, and was related (dimly and by marriage) to Henry Laurens. Vaughan had studied medicine and law and could chat intelligently on most subjects that might interest Franklin.

He bore no official credentials but served to swell the scene for Shelburne's script. That script had been written in light of the common European illusion that Benjamin Franklin was in fact the only American statesman. The addition of Jay was welcome neither to the British nor to the French.

The Jays were happy to be out of Spain but otherwise in the doldrums: John's father had died; Sarah Jay was wracked intermittently by the fever she had picked up on the trip over the Pyrenees. Her little girl was not only teething but had come down with the whooping cough, and by mid-August John was stricken with the flu. The weather was uncommonly wet and cold that summer, so that fires had to be kept going; the fruit was rotting before it ripened, and 1782 had already been marked down by wine tasters as a bad year. At the end of summer peacemakers were not inclined to give it better marks.

Oswald had become accustomed to Franklin's urbane manners and to his thinking, which leaped to its objectives and scarcely bothered with obstructive details. Then he met Jay and his hopes collapsed. The flu had barely left Jay and he still complained of chest pains, but it is likely that what provoked him to a cantankerous interview was something he picked up in Spain—an outraged dignity. Jay had stood still while Spanish grandees lectured him, dangled him at the end of a line of promises, ignored him, played with him. And Paris offered him no surcease, for a diplomat may choke on gratitude as well as gall. Here, now, was the enemy, in the form of this kindly, intelligent liberal, this elderly ex-slave merchant. John Jay need feel no inhibitions in such a confrontation.

He read the mild-mannered Oswald a series of lectures. Americans had come to "detest the very name of an Englishman," Jay thundered, then read off a list of grievances as if the war were just beginning instead of ending. The least the King could do would be to declare the independence of the United States and withdraw all troops forthwith. Then he proceeded to intertwine the Americans' demands with those of France and Spain and Holland, to weigh down the peace with vaguely worded concepts and connections until Oswald was thoroughly discouraged and bewildered. He told Shelburne that now it seemed the Americans hoped to arbitrate all the problems of Europe and become the "dictators to

Great Britain," if one might judge by Jay. Oswald went on to read into Jay's words the prediction—even the affirmation then and there—that America held the balance of power in the Western world.

The King said that it all showed that "Dr. Franklin's hints were only to amuse," and that, speaking through Jay, he now revealed his true demands to Britain: "to give everything without any return and then receive Peace if America will grant it, besides an hint that America is to guarantee the General Peace."

Was Jay's opening gambit an astute diplomatic ploy to exact further concessions? Was it the repressed diplomat stretching his muscles? Or was it an aftereffect of the flu?

In any case, Jay followed it up with a series of maneuvers that proved as disconcerting to his allies as to his enemies. He found Aranda personally charming but his credentials so worded as to avoid any recognition of the United States. Without Carmichael on hand Jay lacked the Spanish vocabulary to engage in legal subtleties. Instead they carried on a dialogue of maps. Jay would draw one line, roughly through the middle of the Mississippi. The United States would claim that as a border. Aranda would answer with a line far to the east.

Jay and Franklin went off to Vergennes with the maps and an agenda of other major problems. First, there was the matter of Oswald's commission to negotiate. It empowered him to treat with the representatives of the colonies, though the first item in the treaty would confer total independence upon them. Vergennes waved aside these technicalities, pointing out that he himself had to deal with the British envoy whose credentials referred to the King of England as if he were also the King of France under an ancient claim. He tried to explain that such things are not to be taken so seriously. Oswald's acceptance of American credentials under the designation of the United States of America would constitute recognition, would it not? Franklin agreed. Jay did not.

After leaving Vergennes, the two American peace commissioners confronted each other before the fireplace at Passy. Legend has it that Jay dramatically shattered his churchwarden clay pipe on the hearth to underscore his own declaration of independence from England, from France, from all congressional instructions binding him to Vergennes, and from Franklin. His shattered pipe, says the Jay myth, symbolized his readiness to smash anything that stood in the way of his country's honor and dignity.

It is difficult, however, to see great substance in that allegedly passionate confrontation. Franklin had already showed himself to be quite willing and able to climb out of Vergennes's pocket in order to deal with

England. He had urged Jay to leave Spain rather than go on suffering indignities. He had indicated no readiness to yield a drop of the Mississippi or a cod from the Newfoundland Banks. Indeed his dreams of the United States included all of Canada.

The unreal quarrel had real consequences, however, for it modified, at least temporarily, Jay's genuine admiration for Franklin. In his reports to Livingston, Jay preached a lofty isolation from European intrigue and warned that Franklin was too trustful of the French. That was ironic because Livingston was far more Francophile than Franklin.

Franklin seems to have been the only person who was not greatly unsettled by Jay's diplomatic style. Oswald, a few days after his first exposure to Jay, hurried around to Passy, prepared to see some terrible reflection of the new American image. He was relieved to find the old sage "good-natured and friendly" as ever. Franklin avoided any suggestion of disagreement between himself and Jay, although he granted that "Mr. Jay was a lawyer and might think of things that did not occur to those who were not lawyers." Franklin then resumed his arguments for "sweet reconciliation" based on the surrender of Canada. It was comfortingly familiar to Oswald. Actually within a few days Jay himself came around to a far more agreeable stance.

The reason lay not in any mercurial quality of Jay's character, for that diplomat was known to be unrelentingly dogged on a point of principle or tactics. It was not so much a change of mood as a change of direction. Jay was like a skiff heading down the Channel and being hit by crosswinds. The farther they blew him from France, the closer they blew him to England. The end of summer 1782 was a time when Jay felt, imagined, or anticipated only ill winds from Versailles.

A number of circumstances combined to tempt Jay to rashness at the very moment when he was in a position of command. He had recovered from the flu and Franklin was down with one of his recurrent sieges of excruciating gout and gravel in the urinary tract. At the same time Admiral de Grasse, a prisoner, had been chatting with the Earl of Shelburne, at the First Minister's country home of Bowood, and receiving a preview of a peace package. The admiral was then sent home carrying propositions which called for a personal and direct answer from Vergennes. There had been only the barest mention of America in the British suggestion, and that was that it be granted immediate and unconditional independence, already a foregone conclusion. Thus, there was no need to inform the Americans, the French felt. And since the exchange was to be personal rather than formal, there were reasons for keeping the matter generally under wraps.

Accordingly, when Gérard de Rayneval, under Vergennes's orders, headed for England to sound out the Earl of Shelburne, he kept his departure an official secret. It was so designated by all the gossips, agents, and double agents who assiduously spread the story.

To Jay it seemed a mission of betrayal. He piled up the evidence: He and the Count de Aranda had gotten nowhere in drafting an acceptable western boundary for the United States; Rayneval, at Jay's request, had written a memo outlining his personal views on the subject, which fell far short of American demands concerning the Mississippi and the fisheries; now Aranda had gone in secret to Versailles, and Rayneval had gone in secret to England. It seemed painfully clear to Jay that Vergennes was moving to undercut all of America's territorial hopes, to bottle the new nation between the sea and the Alleghenies, to deprive New Englanders of the vital cod and the haddock.

Franklin found the evidence scarcely enough to convict France. Rayneval's personal memo might or might not represent Vergennes's thinking, though it was well known that France had always tried to limit the Americans' territorial ambitions. Vergennes, however, had never insisted on these limitations and hitherto kept hands off the Anglo-American negotiations with scrupulous correctness. Franklin saw no reason to panic, though he did send Lafayette to Versailles to bring back some inkling of Rayneval's purpose.

On the next day came the clincher. The British had apparently intercepted a letter from François Barbé-Marbois of the French legation in Philadelphia to Vergennes, urging a policy of curtailing American rights to fish the Grand Banks. Proof positive, said Jay. It would be, suggested Franklin, if the letter were proved to be authentic and if it had gone from Vergennes to Barbé-Marbois, instead of the other way around. As matters stood, it was merely the recommendation of an official—and one not holding primary responsibility. Vergennes could scarcely be convicted for another man's letter.

Such arguments were useless. Iago had handed Othello evidence of his bride's infidelity, and common sense was never a match for passionate suspicion. Actually it took no extraordinary cunning to persuade John Jay of the perishable quality of diplomatic chastity. Jay clutched at any rumor that showed French willingness to confine, carve, or dismember America. And such rumors were easily come by and impossible to confirm or disprove.

In any case, Jay, feeling that at that very moment the interests of his country were about to be sold out, confided in the representatives of the enemy, asking them to keep his secret from his colleague and his allies.

He talked frankly and fully with Oswald and with Vaughan and found them quite ready to sympathize. The success of their tactic of dividing the Americans from France now seemed radiantly assured. Jay asked Vaughan to undertake a mission to Shelburne in strictest confidence. Vaughan was to say that the British, if they handled things well, could hope not only for peace in America but for "cordiality, confidence and commerce." (Vergennes had thought that France might make a better claim to such commodities.) Britain, by an immediate grant of independence, could "cut the cords which tied us to France." There was the treaty, of course, Vaughan was to point out, "yet it was a different thing to be guided by their or our construction of it." He was to warn Shelburne against dividing the fisheries with France and leaving out the Americans. Better to share with the Americans and leave out the French. And as for the Mississippi, if that were in American hands, the inland trade could go northward through the Great Lakes and the British-controlled St. Lawrence. Thus the American trade could be reserved for a British monopoly.

Vaughan sent off a courier at once with a message to Shelburne asking him to take no action until he could speak with him. He himself left on the evening of September 11, carrying, or so it might have seemed, the ashes of the Franco-American alliance as a peace offering from the ex-rebels to their ex-sovereign.

Were all of Jay's fears unfounded? Or did Rayneval indeed go to Shelburne's idyllic country manor at Bowood in order to carve up America like a plucked turkey? Or was America not even on the agenda? Actually the talk turned mainly on the possibilities of an Anglo-French entente in Europe, of French requirements in the East and West Indies and in Africa. Inevitably, however, they did touch briefly on America. This is the way Shelburne reported that discussion to the King: "The point of Independence once settled, he [Rayneval] appears rather jealous than partial to America upon other points, as well as that of the Fishery." Although there is other evidence that Rayneval sought to dissociate himself and France from American claims, one does not have the impression that there was dire treason being hatched at Bowood that justified Jay's desperate measures to undercut the French alliance behind Franklin's back.

Shelburne undoubtedly received Jay's message from Vaughan with considerable pleasure because it was clear that the Americans were even more willing to play at backstairs intrigue than were the French. England could thus proceed confidently with its plans to detach America from France. Jay's message suffered somewhat by his choice of messenger. Vaughan had been chosen to meet the philosophical predilections of Franklin, but he was not taken very seriously by his superiors. As the King was later to comment, "Poor Mr. Vaughan, he seems so willing to be active and so void of judgment . . ."

As for Rayneval, Shelburne had described him as appearing to be a "well-instructed, inoffensive man of business." To which the King retorted: "I own the art of M. de Vergennes is so well known that I cannot think he would have sent him if he was an inoffensive man of business."

Nevertheless, the King preferred to play with France, England's most venerable, familiar enemy, rather than with the unpredictable American rebels. He conveyed this in a short note to Shelburne: "Lord Shelburne does not, I am clear, admire the style of Mr. Vaughan's letters more than I do; He seems to look alone to our placing implicit trust in the Americans, whilst Lord Shelburne's ideas coincide with mine in thinking it safer to confide in France, than either Spain or America."

Shelburne, riding a restive Parliament, had to play with both. He had to win a quick American peace, in order to strip France of any transatlantic support, then woo France to curb the demands of Spain and Holland. The urgency of the situation allowed no time for quibbles of protocol, and Oswald in short order received revised credentials to deal with the representatives of the "Thirteen United States of America," listed by name. He was instructed to accept the four vital points listed by Franklin and to get on with the specifics.

Shelburne accompanied the new instructions with an appeal to American honor: "We have put the greatest confidence, I believe, was ever placed in men, in the American Commissioners. It is now to be seen how far they or America are to be depended upon."

It was a curious context in which to speak so stirringly of trust. Shelburne was counting on Americans to circumvent the strict bonds of their commitment to France so that in turn France could be wooed at a lower price from its other allies. It was a difficult challenge, and the American peace commissioners, in the cause of national self-interest, proceeded to meet it.

With Franklin still down with the gout and gravel, Jay proceeded to draw up terms of boundaries and fishing rights. Jay was leaning more toward England than to France and ready to go in any direction as long as it was away from Spain. One day he suggested to Oswald that England might consider moving its troops down from New York and Charleston to West Florida, which it could easily take away from Spain. If the British did that, the United States would be prepared to write into the treaty a share in control of the Mississippi. Oswald was interested. And would the

United States be willing to move the boundary of Florida somewhat to the north in the event that it turned out to be British? Jay didn't think that the United States would argue about "a few acres."

Franklin saw nothing wrong with such a proposal and approved Jay's draft terms, as, indeed, did Oswald. To Shelburne, however, who had to convince his King and Parliament that he was not selling America at too low a price, Jay's territorial demands seemed exorbitant. Moreover, the heat was now taken off Shelburne by the heroic holding action of the garrison at Gibraltar. Shelburne therefore rejected the Jay formula, lectured Oswald for being much too pliable, and dispatched a tougher Undersecretary of State, Henry Strachey, to bolster the British presence at Passy.

The Vaughan mission, undertaken in Jay's panic, had not driven Franklin to any show of resentment and there seemed to be every possibility that the two might continue to work together in a reasonable harmony. But what worried Franklin and Vergennes was the inevitable arrival of John Adams. By the middle of October the matter of form seemed to Adams to have been resolved in a way appropriate to the dignity of the United States. It was therefore proper for him to take a hand. He left the Hôtel des Etats Unis in a glow of self-satisfaction. "When I go to heaven," he wrote to Dana, "I shall look down over the battlements with pleasure upon the Stripes and Stars wantoning in the wind at the Hague."

He expected to find conspiracies lying in wait for him in Paris and warned Abigail that "artifices of the devil" would be used against him. Perhaps for that reason he did not make the short trip from The Hague in a blaze of diplomatic speed but jogged along, pausing to savor cathedrals, countryside, and city markets like a tourist. He did manage to pick up a little political gossip on the way, particularly from William Lee, which did nothing to allay his dark fears of the struggle ahead.

He checked in at the Hôtel de Valois in the rue de Richelieu in Paris on the night of October 27, after ten days on the road. He relaxed in a bathhouse on the Seine, then sent for a tailor, a maker of wigs, and a shoemaker to deck him out as befits a Peacemaker in Paris. (While thus submitting to worldly blandishments, the Puritan Adams noted censoriously in his diary that the domination of fashion "is one of the ways in which France taxes all Europe and will tax America.")

He spent his first day trying to find Jay, who was out, and then settled for a long conference with Matthew Ridley, a man with extensive business interests in Maryland, who had served—along with Benjamin Vaughan—on a committee to assist American prisoners of war. Ridley had been appointed an agent for Maryland and Adams had helped him arrange a Dutch loan for that state.

Ridley was well liked and trusted by Adams because their views neatly coincided. Closely observing the negotiations in Paris, Ridley recorded his impressions in his diary. Franklin, he noted, "is an intriguing, unfeeling man," who one day would be exposed. Lafayette too, in Ridley's eyes, was a meddling, ambitious politician. All this Ridley poured into the willing ears of Adams. Ridley gave Jay good marks for firmness and a willingness to defy Franklin and even Congress for the honor of his country.

It was a briefing which Adams scarcely needed but relished mightily. Adams prepared for the struggle not with England but with his colleagues. "Between two as subtle spirits as any in this world, the one malicious, the other I think honest, I shall have a delicate, a nice, a critical part to act. F's cunning, will be to divide us. To this end he will provoke, he will insinuate, he will intrigue, he will maneuver."

Ridley was clearly of the opinion (shared, he said, by Laurens) that it was impossible to conciliate Adams and Franklin. He did not try very hard. Still, there was a certain concession to appearances which Ridley thought Adams should make. At dinner, after Adams had been in town for two days, Ridley suggested that he make the trip to Passy for the sake of form.

Adams said he saw no need for such a move, that personally he "could not bear to go near" Franklin, and that inasmuch as he, Adams, was the first named to the commission, why should not the doctor come to him? Ridley pointed out that Franklin had no way of knowing that Adams had even arrived in Paris. True, Adams admitted, and began to haul on his coat. Then he took it off and announced that he could not bring himself to do it. Ridley succeeded in bundling up the peppery Adams and shipping him off to Passy that night. The encounter drew no blood, for Franklin, stricken with the gout, listened unprotestingly while Adams offered a passionate support for Jay as if there had been some desperate quarrel between the two.

It took a powerful diplomatic offensive to persuade Adams to call on that other object of his loathing, the Count de Vergennes.

Vergennes had expressed his astonishment that Adams had been in Paris for almost two weeks without paying the usual courtesy call. He was amazed that the French government would have to be informed by its own police that a distinguished American diplomat had arrived. Lafayette went around to Adams' hotel to report the count's astonishment. Franklin, in the course of discussing still another French loan he was then negotiating, suggested that it would be "kindly taken" if Adams did the necessary. Adams, who still felt that Vergennes and Franklin had humiliated and undermined him, robbing him of his rank as sole peace commissioner, resisted. Then on Sunday morning, November 10, he yielded and went to see the count.

It seems to have surprised him that the count behaved as if he bore no enmity. They chatted amicably. Adams was invited to stay for dinner. He was chosen to take the countess's hand to escort her to the table, and to sit at her side. He was plied by both count and countess with cakes and wines and dainties.

Sweeter than cakes and wine, however, were the compliments of courtiers who crowded the count's antechambers. How marvelous, they exclaimed, that M. Adams had been able to win recognition, a treaty, and money from the Dutch. "You have knocked off balance the Stadtholder and the pro-English party. . . . You have shaken up everybody. . . . You are the Washington of negotiators."

Matthew Ridley noted on that November day that Adams had just been told that "Mr. Washington was the greatest General in the world and that he, Mr. A., was the General Washington in politics. All this makes no impression on him."

Modestly unimpressed as he may have been, Adams was careful to record the compliments in his diary with obvious and understandable relish and to add: "A few of these compliments would kill Franklin if they should come to his ears." (He also included them in his "Peace Journal," which he later sent to be read aloud to the Congress.)

If only Vergennes had thought of allowing the countess and the courtiers to handle John Adams on his earlier visit, the road to peace might have been less tumultuous. This is not to suggest that John Adams' principles, rectitude, and devotion to independence could have been modified by the flourish of a compliment or an excellent choice of wine, but conceivably such treatment, applied early and often, might have reduced the irritation.

Now, having arrived in Paris to confront a sea of enemies, Adams was beset by smiles. Even Benjamin Franklin declined to disagree. When Adams for the first time read the instructions from Congress obliging the commissioners to consult with the French at every step and always to follow their advice, he burst out in indignation. But he found that his colleagues had already agreed that they need not follow such instructions scrupulously.

Only one grievance rankled: Why should William Temple Franklin be made the commission's secretary? Unfortunately, Jay had agreed to the appointment before Adams arrived in Paris. Adams insisted that Franklin must have pressured him unfairly, but Jay denied that he had been either browbeaten or gulled. Adams was disturbed because he suspected a truly fanciful plot whereby the Franklinet would ultimately succeed his grandfather as minister to France, and the old man now, nearing seventy-eight, would then connive to become the first American ambassador to England, a post on which Adams had set his own heart.

The pace of negotiations picked up at that point, and there was little time for playing the old games. The commissioners met every day at eleven in the morning with the tough-minded Strachey and/or the amenable Oswald. Often the talks would continue over dinner and into the evening. Vergennes, Lafayette, the generous, agreeable Chaumont were all shut out. The negotiators would meet at Passy or at Oswald's inn in Paris. Bancroft still hovered about but now had little to do since the developments were kept secret only from France and Spain. It is not likely that, however adept an agent he may have been, Bancroft could have been on the payrolls of those powers as well. He served only to drop vials of anti-French gossip at suitable moments when it might infuriate Adams or Jay and speed them on their way to a settlement. Rayneval was in London again, Bancroft reported one day to Adams. Who knows what this portends? The Count de Vergennes is rumored to have told His Majesty that he "has the peace in his pocket that he is now Master of the Peace."

It was true that Rayneval was dining in Berkeley Square with Shelburne. The English earl had embarked on the second phase of his strategy. With the American negotiations winding up, was it not time for France to move quickly toward peace by limiting the extravagant appetites of its remaining allies, Spain and Holland? The two drafted a treaty and, in language reminiscent of an earlier appeal to the Americans, the earl told Rayneval over the dinner table: "I have put myself at the mercy of France, and it is for her to pronounce my fate." As for America, it was true that Rayneval casually admitted that the French Court now knew nothing of the negotiations under way, but he suggested that perhaps it would be best to put off such vexing questions as boundaries and the compensation to refugees to the time when the definitive treaty of general peace would be formally drawn. These, after all, were mere preliminaries, were they not?

In fact, the negotiations were approaching a definitive form, and Shelburne had no notion of throwing them open once again. France and Spain might toss into the pot great gobs of extraneous matter—anything from Gibraltar to Honduras to Pondicherry. It was better to deal with the Americans swiftly. And the talks were progressing on a far better footing than could have been hoped only a little while earlier, when Americans were rebels allied with the enemies of Britain. These sessions, from all accounts, were quite friendly.

Adams, in retrospect, called them agreeable, exciting, "a surfeit of feasting, fatigue and ceremony." Such harmony would have been inconceivable if Franklin had not consented from the start to shut out the French and disregard the congressional mandate of the commission. On the details of the terms for peace there had never been any major disagreement among the commissioners. Fundamentally it was a matter of fish, loyalists, boundaries, and debts owed by Americans to Englishmen. Franklin, Jay, and Adams were their country's tradesmen bargaining for all they could get.

Their positions were rarely coordinated, however. For example, very early in the negotiations Adams caved in on the question of debts, saying simply, "I have no notion of cheating anybody." Franklin had been prepared to argue that the commissioners had no authority to negotiate private debts, but now had to give up that tactic and theoretically acknowledge the propriety of such claims. On the question of loyalists, Adams was astonished to find that Franklin, whose son was the most Tory of Tories and president of the Associated Loyalists, was far less compassionate than either he or Jay. Had Adams understood Franklin he would not have been surprised. For all his philosophical mildness, Franklin could venture beyond the drawing-room rules of war to a ferocity that was ahead of his century. After all, it was he who had perpetrated the most blatant journalistic hoax of the war. He had faked an American newspaper, in which he listed the number of American scalps ordered by the British to be delivered to them by their Indian allies. He ran this forgery off on his own press at Passy and saw that it was circulated throughout Europe. Franklin could be a very tough man in a fight.

When the British negotiators pressed for some accommodation for the loyalist refugees then facing terrible reprisals, Franklin drew up a balance sheet. Against the confiscation of the loyalists' homes and lands, he weighed the war's destruction of patriot property, including the loss of thousands of slaves liberated and recruited by the English to fight against their former masters. (The fact that all three of the American commissioners were vehemently opposed to slavery as an institution did not prevent them from regarding premature emancipation as simple theft.)

While Franklin presented his bill for British depredations, and Jay drew maps of the wilderness borders, John Adams saved his legal arts for the question of fish. He recalled, no doubt, the farewell warnings of his

Massachusetts neighbors that freedom would be a hollow victory without the right to the cod and the haddock.

"When God Almighty made the banks of Newfoundland, at three hundred leagues distance from the people of America, and at six hundred leagues distance from those of France and England, did he not give as good a right to the former as to the latter? If Heaven in the creation give a right, it is ours at least as much as yours. If occupation, use and possession give a right, we have it as clearly as you. If war and blood, and treasure give a right, ours is as good as yours. . . . If then the right cannot be denied, why should it not be acknowledged, and put out of dispute? Why should we leave room for illiterate fishermen to wrangle and chicane?"

Adams had made the point that whatever was decided in Paris those "illiterate fishermen" would smuggle, would sneak ashore on the Magdalen Islands or on Nova Scotia to dry their cod, would fish wherever there was fish, because this was their livelihood.

When Strachey conceded the substance, Adams demanded the form. Not a "liberty" as the British lawyer would put it, but a right was what Adams required.

"The Americans are the greatest quibblers I ever saw," commented Strachey.

Actually, the Americans had more than fine legal points and impassioned oratory to fling at the British. They had the sure scent of victory and the knowledge that the British team dare not go back to London empty-handed to face a hostile Parliament. Even Bancroft's rumors no longer panicked the Americans. In an effort to speed the commissioners to some concessions, Bancroft whispered to Adams that Vergennes had hopes of being made a Spanish grandee and was about to make a peace for Spain that would sell out America. Adams probably believed it but nonetheless continued to argue about fish.

On Friday, November 29, as the negotiations neared a critical stage—with the Americans fearing that any delay would bring some form of French intervention, and the British itching for some *fait accompli* to forestall a vote of no-confidence—a melancholy figure appeared at the Jay rooms in the Hôtel d'Orléans. It was Henry Laurens, obeying the formal demand from Congress that all those originally assigned to the Peace Commission show up in Paris. (The fifth man, Jefferson, never started from Monticello.)

Ex-president of Congress, ex-partisan of the Lees, ex-prisoner of the Tower, Laurens was ailing with the gout and bitterly grieved by the loss of his son, killed in South Carolina during one of those inconsequential skirmishes that continued while the diplomats argued over the way to peace. Laurens had come too late to influence either the partisan clash within the commission or the verbal barrage against the British. He expressed a mild shock that all this was going on without the knowledge or the blessings of the French ally, which irritated Adams, but on the other hand Laurens took a gratifyingly uncompromising stand on cod and haddock.

By the end of that day the terms were settled. By and large the British had given in to most of the American demands. Rights to dry fish off the Grand Banks were granted with some obscure reservations. The British won a commitment that Congress would recommend to the separate states a general policy that might give loyalists the hope of property restitution and personal protection. (In actual fact the states ignored those recommendations and proceeded to horrifying reprisals.) The Mississippi would be American and the British would enjoy navigation rights. The northeastern boundary was drawn without much wrangling.

The future of the Floridas, however, was consigned to a separate and secret article, giving substance to Jay's impetuous, unilateral stab in the back of Spain. If England were to take Florida from the Spaniards, said the provision, the Americans would reward their conquest with some 35,000 square miles beyond what they would concede to a Spanish Florida.

Now that peace had been made with the enemy, it would have to be made with the allies. That evening at Passy, Franklin dispatched a note to Vergennes: "I have the honor to acquaint your Excellency that the commissioners of the United States have agreed with Mr. Oswald on the preliminary articles of the peace between those States and Great Britain. Tomorrow I hope we shall be able to communicate to your Excellency a copy of them."

John Adams had no such worries, for the task of conciliating, charming, and wheedling France was Franklin's problem. Adams dined that Friday evening in exuberant spirits with his friend Ridley. Ridley noted that Adams waved the fish course away with a laugh: "I've had a pretty good meal of them today."

On Saturday, November 30, 1782, the four American commissioners met at the Grand Hôtel Muscovite on the rue des Petits Augustins. With them was William Temple Franklin, who would sign as a witness. The English were waiting in Oswald's rooms. Strachey, Oswald, and their Scottish secretary, Caleb Whitefoord, were on hand with the terms drawn up ready for signing.

The Americans read the document through and pointed out one omission concerning the time limit of one year during which loyalist refugees might stay in the United States to press their claims. The clause was inserted. Then the Americans thought of one last proviso before nailing down the peace: a clause that would prevent the English troops during their evacuation from taking with them any "Negroes or other property belonging to Americans."

Oswald and Strachey made no objections and the final item was written into the document. Then Oswald signed as the representative of George III. The Americans followed in alphabetical order, which allowed for no personal resentments, particularly since Adams had an undisputed precedence. Whitefoord and William Temple Franklin signed as witnesses and the seals of state were affixed.

There in the Hôtel Grand Muscovite the United States of America was given for the first time its shape and dimensions.

It was true that the terms would have to be ratified by Parliament and Congress, that they would not take effect until peace had come to France and Spain and Holland. But to the men on both sides of the room in the Grand Hôtel Muscovite, it was perfectly clear that these were technicalities. The United States of America had become a state and had shown that it possessed the essential quality of a state: the ability to seek its own interest above all conflicting claims of doctrine or principle. On that November day in Paris, Adams, Franklin, Jay, and Laurens were the only Americans who knew what their state would look like, for they had shaped it.

They went back to Passy to celebrate over dinner. Franklin sent off a copy of the peace terms to Vergennes, omitting the secret article. Diplomatic secrets in the eighteenth century proliferated like fruit flies in the sun and lasted about as long. This one proved even more perishable. On December 5, just five days after the secret article was duly solemnized, the Marquis de Vauguyon dropped in on John Adams. The marquis expressed a certain puzzlement about a point at issue between Holland and England in the peace discussions under way. Adams obligingly offered to enlighten him by showing him a copy of the Anglo-American treaty. The secret article, of course, was attached to it.

Confessing the boner in his diary, Adams added that he "had some difficulty to prevent his [Vauguyon's] seeing the separate article, but I did prevent him from seeing anything of it but the words, 'Separate Article.'"

At best, then, the French knew that they did not know all. And what they did know did not reassure them. All the promises of the Americans to consult with the French had been broken. They had rushed to close a deal with the British, leaving not a strip of Ohio or a drop of the Mississippi or a rock on the coast of Maine for the French to toss into a bargain for Gibraltar or a sugar island or a beach on the Indian Ocean. Technically the Americans were still in the war, technically the definitive peace had yet to be made, but actually the Americans had taken their winnings—independence, cod, haddock, and the Mississippi—and prepared to sit unconcernedly by while Vergennes strove for French, Spanish, and Dutch objectives. Vergennes's position had unquestionably been weakened. Moreover, the hope that France might inherit the American trade as promised by Deane, Lee, Beaumarchais, and Franklin in the days when France was being wooed, now seemed to flicker feebly. America and England were in full agreement on the Newfoundland Banks, as if the French had no taste for fish at all.

"The English buy peace rather than make it," Vergennes remarked bitterly to Rayneval. "Their concessions exceed all that I could have thought possible."

Vergennes at that moment might reasonably have been considered the worst possible prospect for a massive loan to the American cause. On the other hand, he was the best because there was no other. And Congress was as ever pressing for more and more French money. On December 5, Franklin wrote to Livingston:

"It is in vain for me to repeat again what I have so often written, and what I find so little notice taken of, that there are bounds to every thing, and that the faculties of this nation [France] are limited like those of all other nations. Some of you seem to have established as maxims the suppositions that France has money enough for all her occasions and all ours besides, and that if she does not supply us it is owing to her want of will, or to my negligence."

Franklin and Laurens did go to see Vergennes and found him cool, though far from hostile. He suggested that perhaps the Americans might hold off informing Congress of the treaty so as to avoid precipitating a peace celebration that would be premature since France had not yet settled with England. Franklin's answer may have been a trifle ambiguous; in any case, Vergennes was left with the impression that the Americans had tacitly accepted his suggestion. He was therefore distinctly upset when, on December 15, he received a short note from Franklin informing him that the Anglo-American terms were in fact being sent by a vessel then waiting to lift anchor and armed with a British passport to speed its way unhindered to Philadelphia. As if that were not bad enough, Franklin noted the keen disappointment he felt in not being able to send along with his dispatches at least some of the money he had been hoping to get from Vergennes. "I fear the Congress will be reduced to despair when they find that nothing is yet obtained." The ship was to leave at ten o'clock the following morning, and if Vergennes cared to make up this deficiency, Franklin would be pleased to have the courier wait for him.

Vergennes promptly answered in the tones of a loving parent stung by the effrontery of a child: "I am at a loss, sir, to explain your conduct and that of your colleagues on this occasion. You have concluded your preliminary articles without any communication between us, although the instructions from Congress prescribe that nothing shall be done without the participation of the King. You are about to hold out a certain hope of peace to America, without even informing yourself of the state of the negotiation on our part.

"You are wise and discreet, sir; you perfectly understand what is due to propriety; you have all your life performed your duties. I pray you to consider how you fulfil those which are due to the King. I am not desirous of enlarging these reflections; I commit them to your own integrity. When you shall be pleased to relieve my uncertainty, I will entreat the King to enable me to answer your demands."

To which Franklin responded with beguiling artfulness, playing upon Vergennes as a skilled musician plucks music out of reluctant strings.

Franklin explained that he had thought Vergennes feared only that the English would include with the dispatches some note that might give a distorted picture of the peace terms to Americans. When he found no such communication from the British, but only a passport guaranteeing safe passage of the preliminary treaty, he thought there was no reason to hold up the sailing; ". . . and it was certainly incumbent on us to give Congress as early an account as possible of our proceedings, who will think it extremely strange to hear of them by other means, without a line from us."

Then came a simple confession: "Your observation is, however, apparently just, that in not consulting you before they [the peace terms] were signed, we have been guilty of neglecting a point of *bienséance.*" (A gentle word for the American offense which means no more than a lapse of manners, betokening not a dishonest heart but only faulty breeding.)

This, said Franklin, indicated no "want of respect for the King, whom we all love and honor." He expressed the hope of the commissioners "that the great work, which has hitherto been so happily conducted, is so nearly brought to perfection, and is so glorious to his reign, will not be ruined by a single indiscretion of ours."

Then the pitch: "And certainly the whole edifice sinks to the ground immediately if you refuse on that account to give us any further assistance. We have not yet dispatched the ship, and I beg leave to wait upon you on Friday for your answer."

There followed a few more protestations of love, gratitude, and respect for the King of France, followed by a heavily underscored suggestion that the French tone down their complaints. The suggestion carried an unmistakable threat: "The English, I just now learn, flatter themselves they have already divided us. I hope this little misunderstanding will therefore be kept a secret, and that they will find themselves totally mistaken."

Vergennes did not answer Franklin at once but wrote instead to the Chevalier de la Luzerne in Philadelphia. In his letter he poured out his grievances: how France had been shut out from the negotiations; how Adams had refused to present himself until pressured to do so; how the Americans had deceptively "clothed their speech in generalities, giving me to understand that it [the negotiation] did not go forward, and that they had no confidence in the sincerity of the British ministry"; how Franklin had misled him about sending the dispatches; how the King of France, "if he had shown as little delicacy in his proceedings as the American commissioner, might have signed articles with England long before them."

Vergennes concluded sadly: "If we may judge of the future from what has passed here, under our eyes, we shall be but poorly paid for all that we have done for the United States and for securing to them a national existence."

The letter was not a mere exercise in disillusionment for the benefit of the French ambassador in Philadelphia. Vergennes suggested to Luzerne "that the most influential members of Congress should be informed of the very irregular conduct of their commissioners in regard to us. . . . I will add nothing in respect to the demand for money, which has been made upon us. You may well judge if conduct like this encourages us to make demonstrations of our liberality."

France, the benefactor of the American nation, seemed ready to cut it off without a cent. But Franklin was unworried, confident that the realities of politics would be stronger than the indignation, however justifiable, of politicians. "A little misunderstanding" was the way he referred to the crisis in a letter to Robert Morris. And so it was, for when Franklin saw Vergennes, he came away with 600,000 livres as down payment on a firm commitment of six million for the year 1783. With the war technically still going on, America had to be held to the French side by a bond stronger than gratitude: money.

Vergennes also sent the Chevalier de la Luzerne a letter countermanding his previous one and suggesting that he let the matter drop. He had always admired Franklin—now perhaps more than ever—and doubtless regarded a spanking of that minister by so unpredictable a body as the American Congress as not only unbecoming but possibly dangerous.

His countermand, however, failed to catch up with the original order, and Luzerne dutifully brought Vergennes's complaints to a Congress already engaged in a furious brawl. All of their discussions were totally irrelevant, inasmuch as nobody an ocean away could possibly have kept pace with the shifting factions and strategies at Passy, Versailles, and London. The debaters nevertheless argued remorselessly and violently over situations that had been resolved months earlier. Arthur Lee was railing away at Jay under the illusion that he was a Francophilic tool of Franklin, calling for the reinstatement of Adams as sole commissioner and denouncing Franklin for selling out the west.

When the preliminary treaty arrived on March 12, 1783, and the delegates beheld the shape of their state, as designed by the commissioners, they found it good—in fact, far better than any had dared to hope.

There was, of course, the admission on the part of the commissioners that they had violated their instructions and had worked behind Vergennes's back; and also that awkward evidence of duplicity—the secret article on the Floridas. There had been no formal complaint from France, however. When asked about the matter of a diplomatic protest, Barbé-Marbois retreated into an expression of French pride: "Great powers," he pointed out, "never complained, but they felt and remembered."

Congress sought to rescue America's integrity, which, some thought, had been besmirched by the commissioners. A move, backed by James Madison and Alexander Hamilton and commanding strong committee support, would have required informing the French about the secret article. Such a step would have seriously embarrassed the commissioners and confronted Vergennes with a problem he did not want. It would have thrown negotiations into a turmoil at a critical moment. Still, it seemed to many in Congress to be the only thing to do to satisfy the nation's honor and redeem the value of its word.

Before the resolution could be passed, however, word came that France and Spain had formally agreed to the preliminaries of peace with England and that hostilities would cease on all fronts as of March 20, 1783. Since England had not taken Jay's advice to seize West Florida, the secret article was moot, invalid, a footnote to history that ought not to stain the birth record of the United States.

Livingston did get off an angry scolding letter to the commissioners, which they answered jointly, declaring that what they did had been done for the welfare and security of the nation. Later each wrote his own apologia.

"Your latest dispatches, sir, are not well adapted to give spirits to a melancholy man, or to cure one sick with a fever," wrote John Adams to Livingston after the official reprimand. He recited his suspicions of the French and their desire to delay the signing. "Yet we must have signed or lost the peace. The peace depended on a day. . . . If we had not signed the [British] ministry would have been changed, and the coalition come in and the whole world knows the coalition would not have made peace upon the present terms, and, consequently not at all this year. The iron was struck in the few critical moments when it was of a proper heat, and has been moulded into a handsome vessel."

Privately Adams expressed himself more operatically. He wrote in his diary: "I have been injured and my country has joined in the injury. It has basely prostituted its own honor by sacrificing mine. But the sacrifice of me for my virtues, was not so servile and intolerable as putting us all under guardianship. Congress surrendered their own sovereignty into the hands of a French minister. Blush, blush! Ye guilty record! Blush and perish! It is glory to have broken such infamous orders. Infamous, I say, for so they will be to all posterity. How can such a stain be washed out? Can we cast a veil over it, and forget it?"

He confided his resentment not only to his diary but to Benjamin Vaughan, asking him to communicate his feelings to "some English gentlemen who might put their government upon their guard." It was a strange performance by the patriot Adams, for technically England was still at war with the United States. Adams showed Vaughan his original commission from Congress and detailed the French "plot" to rob him of that power. The French, under Vergennes, "could not get me removed or recalled, and the next scheme was to get the power of the commission for peace into the hands of Dr. Franklin," he confided.

He attempted to convince Vaughan that one reason the French and Franklin sought to undermine him was that he, Adams, was determined "to hurt Great Britain no farther than should be necessary to secure our independence, alliance and other rights."

This eagerness to endear himself to the British at the expense of Franklin and the French made sense only in the light of Adams' fond desire to become the first American minister to England and his fears that Franklin and Vergennes were out to frustrate that ambition. He wrote to Abigail that "French and Franklinian politics" had so antagonized England as to make his possible stay there "a purgatory," but he lobbied energetically to win that punishment for himself.

Beholding the lavish encomiums heaped on Franklin by the French, John Adams wrote again to Abigail that if he had been supine like Franklin he might have been given "gold snuff boxes, clappings at the opera . . . millions of paragraphs in the newspapers in praise of me, visits from the great, dinners, wealth, power, splendor, picture busts, statues, and everything which a vain heart, and mine is much too vain, could desire."

Franklin, in his own defense against Livingston's reprimand, pointed out that France had not officially complained, and no great harm seemed to have been done. He made it clear, however, that he had stood all along for fairer dealings with the French. He had come up against Adams' deadly conviction that "gratitude to France is the greatest of follies" and that Vergennes is "one of the greatest enemies of our country." Franklin complained that Adams was airing his suspicions to all who would listen, including English representatives. He thought, nevertheless, that the French Court would not be influenced by Adams' tirades to withhold their financial aid but warned Livingston concerning "the insinuations of this gentleman against this court, and the instances he supposes of their ill-will to us, which I take to be as imaginary as I know his fancies to be, that Count de Vergennes and myself are continually plotting against him, and employing the news-writers of Europe to deprecate his character, etc."

Franklin then put John Adams in a capsule: "I am persuaded . . . that he means well for his country, is always an honest man, often a wise one, but sometimes, and in some things, absolutely out of his senses."

John Jay came off best in the rancor that followed the treaty. This was odd because the secret article on the Floridas, which caused so much scandal, had been his idea. And it was he who had sent Vaughan to England with a message suggesting America's willingness to ditch France. Jay took no part in the Adams-Franklin feud. He sought to squash the stories nourished by the supporters of Lee and Izard to the effect that Franklin had tried to sabotage the treaty in order to safeguard his real-estate investments along the Ohio. He also wrote a testimonial to answer Adams' accusations that Franklin had foisted his grandson upon the commission as its secretary.

Jay had his own troubles, however. His eldest brother, Sir James Jay, dropped in on him from London. Sir James had been involved in a scandalous dispute with King's College in New York, for which he had raised considerable funds. As a New York senator he had then taken a political revenge by steering to successful passage a bill confiscating the estates of a number of loyalists, including some of his enemies among the college's governors. After that he was involved in a scheme to counterfeit

American currency and reportedly had arranged his own "capture" by the British. As a "prisoner" he was remarkably free in Britain.

With such a past he was made less than welcome at the Jays' hotel rooms in Paris. After a stormy reunion Sir James dashed off to Versailles to try to persuade the French that John Jay still nourished his inherited Huguenot hatred of France and would betray her in order to unite America with England once again. The French Court yawned at this latest evidence of the facility with which Americans knifed each other.

Later in the year 1783, Lewis Littlepage, that rambunctious young man who had helped to exacerbate the Jays' agony in Spain, turned up. He was, as ever, outraged, this time because he felt that Jay had cheated him of the honor of carrying the definitive treaty to Philadelphia. (Adams' secretary, Thaxter, had been promised the honor.) Littlepage challenged Jay to a duel and was cooled down only when Adams intervened.

Aside from these crises the Jays relaxed in the glow of peace in Paris. Sarah Jay reveled in the salons, and the theater (which her straitlaced husband shunned). People occasionally mistook her for Marie Antoinette and on one occasion the audience rose from their seats as if in the presence of the Queen.

In the summer of 1783, while awaiting the final ceremonies attendant upon the signing of the definitive peace treaties, the Jays moved in with Franklin at Passy. And though John Jay objected to the levity and seeming atheism of some of Franklin's guests, they got on well enough.

The bit players in the drama played out their assigned roles. Francis Dana in St. Petersburg discovered in 1783 that bribery was the way into the Russian Court and pleaded for a slush fund, but Livingston would have no part of it. Catherine the Great and the Holy Roman Emperor, Joseph II, in the end were allowed to sign the final peace terms ending the war in Europe, as a gesture of goodwill, though all their high-flown plans to mediate or arbitrate had come to nothing. The Dutch picked up the few marbles that had been left to them and retired. Charles III, Floridablanca, and Aranda dickered for scraps of land, kept their foothold in the Floridas, and allowed the Rock to stand under the British flag, though George III would willingly have bartered it for Caribbean real estate. Vergennes won his principal war aim: the humiliating detachment of the North American colonies from Britain. Beyond that he picked up only the most negligible colonial scraps: return to France of the bleak islands of St. Pierre-et-Miquelon off Newfoundland, a slave trading base in west Africa, and a commercial post of no political importance at Pondicherry, India.

And Edward Bancroft went off to America in the summer of 1783, carrying an enthusiastic letter of recommendation to Livingston from Benjamin Franklin.

The definitive treaty of peace, its terms unchanged from the preliminary version, was signed at the Hôtel de York in Paris on September 3, 1783. An American state had been born, conceived in the quarrelsome passions of Europe, blessed with the impudence, arrogance, knavery, and innocent faith in mankind that characterized its century, betokening in its infant eyes the canniness of the marketplace and the depths of the wilderness.

A week before the signing Benjamin Franklin delightedly beheld the launching of a giant balloon from the Champ de Mars. It was a globe of oiled silk, twelve feet in diameter, capable of lifting a weight of thirty-nine pounds. "Some suppose flying to be now invented," Franklin noted.

When he was asked: "What's the good of a balloon?" Franklin answered: "What's the good of a new-born baby?"

EPILOGUE

ANY WORK OF HISTORY must come to an arbitrarily chosen end point. It cannot tie up all the loose strands like a properly constructed novel. Still, one ought not to abruptly dismiss those men who have figured so hugely in this story without noting what became of them. A snapshot in the family album loses interest if we cannot say that this one married so and so, or that one ended up in the gutter. Here, then, is what happened to the principals of the drama after the curtain fell in Paris:

Benjamin Franklin went home to Philadelphia in 1785. Plagued by his recurrent gout and kidney gravel, he talked wistfully of retirement but never made it. "They have eaten my flesh and seem resolved now to pick my bones," he said of those who drafted him for public service, but his complaint was playful. He never resisted the call, serving as president of the Executive Council of Pennsylvania and (when he was eighty-one) as delegate to the Constitutional Convention. When he died in 1790, at the age of eighty-four, the United States mourned, of course. But so did France, in a three-day official rite for the arch-diplomat who had so beguilingly outsmarted that nation's most adroit statesmen.

To John Adams' great surprise no plot materialized to keep him from the post he most desired—that of the first American ambassador to Great Britain. He got on famously with George III, whose sober tastes, temperament, and habits Adams found quite congenial. But, bumptious as ever, the ambassador did not go down well with the ministers and MPs. Still, Abigail Adams finally had her European fling and relished it. Adams came home in 1788, having been elected to Congress even before he reached shore. He went on to be Vice-President under Washington, and subsequently the second President of the United States. In 1800, with the odious Alien and Sedition Acts hanging about his neck, he was defeated in his bid for a second term. With him fell the fortunes of the Federalists. Adams dramatically predicted that he would not long survive his political eclipse, then went on to live another quarter of a century in tranquil retirement, dying at the age of ninety-one on the fiftieth anniversary of the Declaration of Independence—July 4, 1826.

John Jay came back to New York in the summer of 1784, while the other peace commissioners were still abroad. He was given a gala reception and promptly informed that he had been chosen to succeed Livingston as the Secretary for Foreign Affairs. His Spanish agony continued to haunt him. He made a deal with Spain which would have yielded those precious navigation rights on the Mississippi so insistently demanded by Floridablanca. Congress repudiated the agreement, however. Jay went on to be the nation's first Chief Justice but interrupted his judicial career for a final attempt at diplomacy. He traveled to England to settle the outstanding issues left over from the Treaty of Paris, but his conciliatory spirit brought down on his head the wrath of the Jeffersonians. He resigned from the Supreme Court in 1795 and was elected governor of New York. After a six-year term in that office he retired to lead the life of an elder statesman for twenty-eight years, living on into the tumultuous changes of the Jackson era.

Henry Laurens, that supernumerary of the peace negotiations, came home to South Carolina in 1784, tired and worn. He rejected all political offers, preferring to restore his burned-out plantations and his ruined houses in town and country. He died after eight years in retired obscurity and, in accord with the provisions of his extraordinary will, was cremated on a hilltop overlooking his manor.

Francis Dana in 1783 gave up his fruitless efforts to win even a nod from Catherine the Great. He was rewarded for his persistence, if nothing else, by being made a Justice of the Supreme Court of Massachusetts, ultimately becoming Chief Justice.

The Count de Vergennes continued in office until he died in 1787, convinced that America's perishable gratitude could not be counted on to pay political or economic dividends. He lived long enough to see his King driven to bankruptcy, in large part by the drain of the American war, but not long enough to see the cataclysmic end of that King.

The agile Beaumarchais welcomed the Revolution when it came to France. He ran afoul of revolutionary politics, however, and ended up in prison charged with treason at a time when execution customarily followed close upon accusation. It took the wiles of a former mistress to save him. He had to flee to England and then to Holland. He returned to Paris in 1799 and with customary resilience regained both respect and fortune. However, he died before he could persuade Congress to pay him the money the United States owed for the ships, guns, food, and blankets he had shipped in the days of Hortalez and Company. His heirs sued and won a settlement that was no more than a fraction of the original bill.

The Count de Floridablanca was far less lucky than his French counterpart. He survived his sovereign Charles III and served for three years under Charles IV. The outbreak of the French Revolution chilled his ardor for the Enlightenment. He very nearly died when a French fanatic plunged a knife into his back, and was thereafter forced out of office by a political faction close to the throne. A Court shake-up restored to power his old rival, the Count de Aranda, who at once tossed Floridablanca into the donjon of the Castle of Pamplona. He was on the point of starvation when his brother arrived to free him.

Aranda took a cheery view of the French Revolution until the guillotine struck off the heads of the King and Queen of France. That upset the Spanish monarchy, and Aranda fell from favor. His sentence seemed mild—perpetual exile from Madrid and the Court—but it must have been a hard fate for that sophisticated diplomat. Floridablanca came to the political surface once again, tossed up by the French invasion in 1808. He returned to Aranjuez briefly in that year and died shortly thereafter, while holding a minor political office.

Many of Britain's hired agents were bitterly disappointed. Paul Wentworth, the New Hampshireman who yearned for a baronetcy, never got more than a six-week term as an MP. He lingered on in London for seven years after the peace treaty was signed, then buried himself in a plantation in Surinam. John Vardill, who wanted a theology chair of academic eminence in New York, was given a modest parsonage in Lincolnshire.

The careers of most men who took part in the frenzied diplomacy that attended the birth of the United States were drastically changed. Some were exalted and some were destroyed, but Edward Bancroft went his serene way as a double agent, unscathed by history. In 1783 he landed in Philadelphia with an assortment of credentials that included a recommendation from Franklin to Jefferson and another from Lafayette to Washington. He was described in these letters as a proven friend of the American cause. His business missions were remarkably varied: to look after Deane's interests in bonds and mortgages; to instill some life in the moribund Vandalia scheme for Franklin; to pry some money from South Carolina to repay the Prince of Luxemburg for funds lent to Commodore Gillon's South Carolina Navy; to safeguard his own interests in Robert Morris' widespread enterprises. Bancroft also claimed the tribute due to a visiting scientist and member of the Royal Society. He drank and dined with Washington's staff in New York, was entertained by the governor of New Jersey, and met with Jefferson in Philadelphia.

Though his year in America netted him and his principals scant business returns, the British Secret Service had no cause to complain. Bancroft filed his customary copious and intelligent reports on the American political scene.

In 1789, Bancroft came to public notice when Silas Deane died from an overdose of laudanum aboard the ship that was to take him home. Bancroft strove energetically to convince the world that Deane had committed suicide. Then he lapsed into obscurity, living out the rest of his days on a modest but comfortable pension, always on tap for consultation on American affairs. The spy died peacefully in 1821. His career of double-agentry remained a secret for nearly seventy years, until the British archives were opened in 1890.

NOTES
AND INDEX

NOTES

A definitive bibliography documenting this narrative and pointing the reader's way down all of the by-roads that open up would constitute a formidable work in itself. I here wish only to acknowledge gratefully the principal sources I have used.

Although I have dipped into the great national repositories of documents and into academic archives, by and large I have contented myself with the fruits of distinguished scholars who have combed, collected, arranged, edited, and annotated those historic files.

I have leaned most heavily on these general works: *The Revolutionary Diplomatic Correspondence of the United States*, edited in six volumes by Francis Wharton (Washington, 1889); *Letters of Members of the Continental Congress*, edited by E. C. Burnett (Washington, 1921–36); *Facsimiles of Manuscripts in European Archives Relating to America, 1773–1783*, by B. F. Stevens (London, 1898); *The Correspondence of King George III*, edited by Sir John Fortescue (London, 1928); and the monumental *Histoire de la Participation de la France à l'Establissement des États-Unis d'Amérique: Correspondence Diplomatique et Documents*, by Henri Doniol (Paris, 1886).

Two diplomatic historians have provided invaluable guides: *The Diplomacy of the American Revolution*, by Samuel Flagg Bemis (New York and London, 1935); and

The Peacemakers: Great Powers and American Independence, by Richard B. Morris (New York, 1965).

Aside from these general works more particularized studies provided major sources for each chapter.

CHAPTER I

Michael G. Kammen has done a superb job of chronicling the pre-revolutionary American lobby in his *A Rope of Sand* (New York, 1974). Two books on the lively British newspapers of the time offer insights into the public debate over what was to be done with the Americans: *The Preliminaries of the American Revolution As Seen in the English Press,* by Fred Junkin Hinkhouse (New York, 1926); and *The English Press in Politics,* by Robert R. Rea (Lincoln, Neb.; 1963).

Sir Lewis Namier offers an enjoyable and useful overview of the period in *England in the Age of the American Revolution* (London, 1930; reprinted, 1966). The King himself is fully treated in *George the Third,* by Stanley Ayling (New York, 1972); and in *George III, Lord North and the People,* by Lyman H. Butterfield (London, 1949).

Benjamin Franklin, who makes his bow in this chapter, has copiously documented his own life: *The Complete Works of Benjamin Franklin,* edited by John Bigelow (New York, 1887–88); *The Writings of Benjamin Franklin,* edited by Albert H. Smyth (New York, 1905–07). In addition, Carl Van Doren has selected and edited Franklin's *Autobiographical Writings* (New York, 1945). Franklin's pre-revolutionary propaganda efforts have been collected by Verner W. Crane in *Benjamin Franklin's Letters to the Press 1758–75* (Chapel Hill, N.C.; 1950). There are a great many biographies of Franklin; outstanding among them are Van Doren's *Benjamin Franklin* (New York, 1938); and Thomas Fleming's *The Man Who Dared the Lightning* (New York, 1971). Another study of great interest is *Poor Richard's Politicks: Benjamin Franklin and His New American Order,* by Paul W. Conner (New York, 1965).

CHAPTER II

The Lee brothers, Arthur and William, present themselves quite clearly in their letters. Many of these appear in Richard Henry Lee's worshipful biography, *The Life of Arthur Lee* (Boston, 1829). William's career is documented in *Letters of William Lee, 1766–1783,* collected and edited by Worthington Chauncey Ford (Brooklyn, 1891; reprinted, New York, 1968). The Lee papers are available at the Alderman Library, University of Virginia.

John Wilkes is summed up in Peter Quennell's *The Profane Virtues: Four Studies of the Eighteenth Century* (New York, 1945); and in Louis Kronenberger's *The Extraordinary Mr. Wilkes* (New York, 1974).

Some of the background on the affair of the stolen Hutchinson letters may be found in *The Ordeal of Thomas Hutchinson,* by Bernard Bailyn (Cambridge, Mass.; 1974). Franklin describes his own ordeal in his autobiographical writings.

CHAPTER III

Although standard histories tend to give Beaumarchais scant attention, his career is chronicled in great detail by Louis de Lomenie in *Beaumarchais and His Times: Sketches of French Society in the Eighteenth Century* (New York, 1857). Other useful biographies include Georges Lemaitre's *Beaumarchais* (New York, 1939); and Elizabeth S. Kite's *Beaumarchais and the War of American Independence* (Boston, 1918). Lomenie also deals at length with the mysterious Chevalier d'Eon. He—or possibly she—is sensationally but controversially further described in *Memoires sur La Chevalière d'Eon,* by Frederic Gaillardet (Paris, 1837).

Silas Deane emerges from *The Deane Papers,* published by the New-York Historical Society (1886–1890), and from an article, by Thomas P. Abernethy, "Commercial Activities of Silas Deane in France," in the *American Historical Review* (April 1934), 447–85. For much of the information on the death of Deane and his relationship with Edward Bancroft the writer is indebted to Julian P. Boyd's *Death by a Kindly Teacher of Treason,* published in three issues of the *William and Mary Quarterly,* Vol. XVI, April, July, and October, 1959.

Deane, like the Lees and Bancroft, is frequently mentioned in the records of the Congress and in the letters exchanged by all parties concerned—British, American, and French.

CHAPTER IV

Aside from the general references in the voluminous files of Frankliniana there is a copious literature, some playful and some scholarly, on Franklin's career in France. Outstanding among these are: *Benjamin Franklin and His French Contemporaries,* by Alfred Owen Aldridge (New York, 1957); *Franklin in France,* by E. Hale and E. Hale, Jr. (Boston, 1888); and *Mon Cher Papa: Franklin and the Ladies of Paris,* by Claude-Anne Lopez (New Haven and London, 1966).

The Franco-American alliance is treated more fully in Edward S. Corwin's *French Policy and the American Alliance of 1778* (Princeton, 1916); William C. Stinchcombe's *The American Revolution and the French Alliance* (Syracuse, 1969); and Samuel Flagg Bemis' "British Secret Service and the French American Alliance," in the *American Historical Review,* 1923–24, Vol. XXIX, pp. 475–95.

Other works that have yielded material for this chapter are Bernard Fäy's *L'Esprit Revolutionnaire en France et États-Unis à la Fin du 18me Siècle* (Paris, 1925); Gerald Sourzh's *Franklin and American Foreign Policy* (Chicago, 1954); and Carl Van Doren's *The Secret History of the American Revolution* (New York, 1941).

The story of John the Painter's abortive plot is well told in Boyd's *Death by a Kindly Teacher of Treason,* cited above.

Much of the material used in the day-by-day chronicle of events leading up to the signing of the Franco-American alliance comes from Henri Doniol's *Histoire,* cited above, and from the writings of Franklin, Adams, and their biographers.

CHAPTER V

The British reaction to the French alliance can be read in the royal correspondence as collected by Fortescue, already cited, and in A. C. Valentine's *Lord North* (London, 1910).

The voyage of the Carlisle Commission is well told in Van Doren's *The Secret History of the American Revolution* and in Valentine's *Lord North.* The letters of the members of the Continental Congress are also useful in picturing the American reception of the peace mission.

CHAPTER VI

John Adams describes himself even when he discusses his times and his contemporaries. His collected works, notably his *Diary and Autobiography,* edited by L. H. Butterfield (Cambridge, Mass.; 1961), is rich in incident and comment. He is also well documented in the letters of his colleagues. He has had a number of biographers but I found particularly valuable Page Smith's two-volume work *John Adams* (New York, 1962).

CHAPTER VII

The Spanish backdrop for Jay's diplomacy is constructed from a variety of sources, notably *L'Espagne Éclairée de la Seconde Moitié du XVIIIme Siècle,* by Jean Sarrailh (Paris, 1964); *The Eighteenth-Century Revolution in Spain,* by Richard Herr (Princeton, 1958); *España Ante la Independencia de los Estados Unidos,* by Juan F. Yela Utrilla (Lerida, 1925); and *El Siglo XVIII: La Historia de España en sus Documentos,* collected and edited by Fernando Diaz-Plaza (Madrid, 1955).

For material on Jay, I leaned heavily on the *Correspondence and Public Papers of John Jay,* edited by H. P. Johnston (New York, 1890–93); and on the biography *John Jay: Defender of Liberty,* by Frank Monaghan (New York, 1935).

Some of the cloak-and-dagger work has been exhumed from the archives by Richard B. Morris and is to be found in his book *The Peacemakers* (cited above). Samuel F. Bemis also covers that aspect in *The Hussey-Cumberland Mission and American Independence* (Princeton, 1931) as well as in the first section of volume I of *American Secretaries of State and Their Diplomacy* (New York, 1963).

The story of Lord George Gordon and the background to the riots that bear his name may be found in *The Strange History of Lord George Gordon,* by Percy Colson (London, 1937); *King Mob,* by Christopher Hibbert (Cleveland and New York, 1958); and *The Gordon Riots: A Study of the Rioters and the Victims,* by George F. Rude (London, 1956).

C H A P T E R   V I I I

The voyage of Adams and Dana through Spain, France, and Holland is best told in Adams' diary and autobiography and in letters written by the two men. W. P. Cresson has also handled this topic in *Francis Dana: A Puritan Diplomat at the Court of Catherine the Great* (New York, 1930).

Some of the Dutch background is filled in by F. Edler in *The Dutch Republic and the American Revolution* (Baltimore, 1911).

C H A P T E R   I X

The Tsarina Catherine has had a great many biographies, notably Gina Kaus's *Catherine: The Portrait of an Empress* (New York, 1935); and Zoe Oldenbourg's *Catherine the Great* (New York, 1965). A variety of contemporary accounts of Catherine are given in *Seven Britons in Imperial Russia, 1698–1812,* edited by Peter Putnam (Princeton, 1952); and in the letters and notes of the British ambassador Sir James Harris. Catherine's maneuvers with the neutrals are described in *La Diplomatie Française et la Ligue des Neutres,* by P. Fauchille (Paris, 1893).

C H A P T E R   X

The military mechanics of the Franco-American victory at Yorktown are succinctly reported by James Brown Scott in *De Grasse at Yorktown* (Baltimore, 1931). Richard Oswald's scheme to bring Russia into the war is described by R. A. Humphreys in "Richard Oswald's Plan for an English and Russian Attack on Spanish America, 1781–1782," *Hispanic American Review,* 1938, Vol. XVIII.

The story of the climactic peace negotiations is pieced together from the works and letters of the principal statesmen involved. In addition, to be consulted are the biographers of Franklin, Adams, and Jay already cited; the diplomatic historians Bemis and Morris; and the invaluable Doniol.

INDEX

Cleveland, John, 6

Clive, Lord, 13

Congress: and accusations against peace commissioners, 242; and British reconciliation proposals, 110–11; broken secrecy rules of, 135; Deane's attack on, 133; foreign policy and, 191; Franco-American alliance ratified by, 108; meeting at York, Pa., 85

Conway, Henry, 18, 207

Cornwallis, Charles, 106, 205, 206, 207, 211

Coudray, Philippe Tronson du, 115, 116

Craven, William Lord, 12

Cumberland, Duke of, 13–14, 17

Cumberland, Richard, 159, 161, 162–3, 210

Defoe, Daniel, 12

de Grasse, François Joseph Paul, 205, 206, 217, 227

del Campo, Bernardo, 166

d'Eon, Chevalier, 45

Despencer, Lord (Sir Francis Dashwood), 10, 30

d'Estaing, Count, 130–1, 163

Dickinson, John, 52

Digges, Thomas, 209–10

Double-agentry, 58, 126, 140, 210, 228, 249–50; *see also* British Secret Service

du Barry, Mme, 44

Dubourg, Barbeu, 62

Dumas, Charles William Frederic, 58, 62, 101, 182, 199–200, 202, 213

Dutch. *See* Holland

D

Dalrymple, Sir John, 161

Dana, Francis, 111, 171, 172, 173, 174; as diplomat in Russia, 191–6, 213, 223–4, 245; as justice in Massachusetts, 248

d'Argenteau, Mercy, 184

Dartmouth, Lord, 6, 17, 29, 38, 40

Dashwood, Sir Francis, 10, 30

Deane, Jesse, 118, 120

Deane, Silas, 56–61, 64, 69, 73, 80, 81, 91, 92, 121, 127; "Address to the People" of, 133; and Aitken, 74; and Bancroft, 58, 59, 74, 140, 141, 250; and Franklin, 57, 69, 130, 140; and Lee, 56, 61, 128–30, 131–41; and Marie Antoinette, 84; as member of international syndicate, 70; mysterious death of, 140–1, 250; recalled by Congress, 116, 128; recruitment of foreigners by, 71, 72, 115, 116; Thomas Paine's answer to, 134–5

Deane, Simeon, 107, 108

de Berdt, Dennys, 6, 22

Declaration (League) of Armed Neutrality, 189, 192, 195, 201, 202

Declaration of Independence, 80

Declaratory Act, 18

E

East India Company, 30

Eden, Eleanor, 106, 111, 113

Eden, William, 60, 76, 91, 103, 104, 105, 106, 107, 113; in America, 109, 110, 111, 112

Elizabeth of Russia, 45, 195

England: at close of American Revolution, 207–12; continuing American affection for, 109; and the Dutch, 200–1; and France, 47–8, 49, 52, 64, 68, 73, 74–5, 79–82, 88, 89, 91, 93, 94, 97, 102, 106, 219; Franco-Spanish invasion of, 147, 148–9; and the Gibraltar issue, 145, 147, 159, 160, 161, 217, 231, 239, 245; in India, 13, 30; mercenaries hired by, 71–2; muddling diplomacy of, 187, 215; and peace commission to America, 97, 101, 102–7, 109–13, 210, 224; rejection of American independence by, 98, 111, 112; riots in, 13, 16, 48, 49, 161, 162; and Russia, 102, 187–9, 190, 194; threats of reconciliation with, 75, 81, 82, 88, 90

Enlightenment, the, 67, 68, 78, 125; in Spain, 143, 144–6, 155

Elmer Bendiner was born in Pittsburgh in 1916 and was educated at the City College of New York. After three years as a newspaper reporter he joined the U.S. Air Force at the onset of World War II, becoming a navigator; he received the Distinguished Flying Cross, the Air Medal, and a Purple Heart. An experienced journalist, he has contributed to many publications, including Esquire, The New York Times Magazine, *and* The Nation, *as well as a number of medical and scientific journals. His first book was* The Bowery Man, *published in 1962; his second,* A Time for Angels: The Tragicomic History of the League of Nations, *published in 1975. Mr. Bendiner is married, has two daughters, and lives in Woodstock, New York.*

A N O T E O N T H E T Y P E

This book was set via computer-driven cathode ray tube in Video Janson. Janson was long thought to have been made by the Dutchman Anton Janson, who was a practicing type founder in Leipzig during the years 1668–87. However, it has been conclusively demonstrated that these types are actually the work of Nicholas Kis (1650–1702), a Hungarian, who most probably learned his trade from the master Dutch type founder Dirk Voskens. The type is an excellent example of the influential and sturdy Dutch types that prevailed in England up to the time William Caslon developed his own incomparable designs from them.

Composed by The Haddon Craftsmen, Inc., Allentown, Pennsylvania. Printed and bound by American Book–Stratford Press, Saddle Brook, New Jersey. Design by Margaret McCutcheon Wagner.